20073.

Bishop Lyttelton
Library
Winchester

JOURNAL FOR THE STUDY OF THE OLD TESTAMENT
SUPPLEMENT SERIES

53

Editors
David J A Clines
Philip R Davies

The University of Sheffield
343 Fulwood Road
Sheffield S10 3BP
England

THE MAKING
OF THE
PENTATEUCH

A Methodological Study

R.N. Whybray

Journal for the Study of the Old Testament
Supplement Series 53

Published by JSOT Press
JSOT Press is an imprint of
Sheffield Academic Press
The University of Sheffield
343 Fulwood Road
Sheffield S10 3BP
England

Typeset by Sheffield Academic Press
and
printed in Great Britain
by Billings & Sons Ltd
Worcester

British Library Cataloguing in Publication Data

Whybray R.N.
    The Making of the Pentateuch : a
    methodological study.—(Journal for the
    study of the Old Testament supplement
    series, ISSN 0309-0787; 53)
    1. Bible. O.T. Pentateuch—Criticism,
    interpretation, etc.
    I. Title   II. Series
    222′.1066   BS1225.2

    ISBN 1-85075-064-5
    ISBN 1-85075-063-7Pbk

for
Peter, Catherine and Elizabeth
who help me to remember
that there are other arts
than Biblical Criticism

CONTENTS

PREFACE

It is easier to cast doubt on earlier theories than to offer a satisfactory alternative. Inability to do the latter, however, does not necessarily invalidate the attempt to do the former, especially when, as is the case with the subject dealt with in this book, the problem is how to make bricks without straw. It is doubtful whether it will ever be possible to establish with any degree of certainty how the Pentateuch was composed. The main argument of this book, therefore, is to be found in Parts I and II, which seek respectively to demonstrate the deficiencies of the two main solutions to the problem which have been proposed: the Documentary Hypothesis and the traditio-historical approach. Part III is no more than a tentative sketch of an alternative view which, by attributing both a high degree of imagination and great freedom in the treatment of sources to a single writer, would render attempts to penetrate below the surface of the text to identify and reconstruct those sources futile for much of the narrative material.

There is a growing tendency among biblical scholars to concentrate, for a variety of reasons, on what is often called 'the final form of the text', leaving on one side the question how that final form was achieved. In so far as this new emphasis is likely to lead to a greater appreciation of the literary and theological qualities of the Pentateuch, it is to be welcomed. However, the question of its composition, though no longer in the forefront of scholarly research, is still actively discussed. The notion that the Pentateuch is a kind of many-layered *tell* whose strata can be uncovered to reveal the history of Israel's religious beliefs from the earliest times up to the time of the Exile or later is still presupposed in one form or another by many scholars and widely taught to students. A critique of this notion such as is attempted here is therefore needed. In attempting this, however, it is not my purpose to bring this kind of exercise back into the forefront of Pentateuchal studies. On the contrary, if from this attempt to describe the false trails so confidently followed by the scholars of the past century and more some readers draw the conclusion that their time would be better spent in a study of other aspects of the Pentateuch, I shall not disagree with them.

The present work is concerned almost entirely with the *narrative* material in the Pentateuch. The very extensive *legal* material constitutes a quite separate field of study, and requires a quite different kind of approach. For there, in contrast to the narratives, a diachronic approach is possible, and indeed essential: the Book of the Covenant, the laws of Deuteronomy, and the so-called 'Priestly Code' do in fact provide the material for an historical study of Israelite law and of the religious ideas which lay behind it. But those codes of law constitute a particular kind of source which originally was quite unrelated to the other sources which the Pentateuchal historian incorporated into his work.

I am indebted to many earlier, as well as to contemporary, scholars, not least to Julius Wellhausen, Hermann Gunkel and Martin Noth. Although their solutions to the question of the composition of the Pentateuch are, I believe, ultimately unsatisfactory, it was these three great masters of Pentateuchal research who pointed to the very real problems posed by the text and provided the impetus to succeeding generations to continue to seek solutions to them.

The arguments set out in Part I have been presented in summary form in papers read to the Research Seminar of the Department of Biblical Studies in the University of Sheffield and to the Old Testament Seminar at Cambridge University, and I thank those who participated critically and helpfully in the ensuing discussions.

I also wish to record my thanks to Dr G. Khan of the Taylor-Schechter Genizah Unit of the Cambridge University Library for drawing my attention to variations in references to the deity in mediaeval Hebrew texts, to Dr P.P. Sims-Williams of the Department of Anglo-Saxon, Norse and Celtic at Cambridge University for information about the present state of scholarship with regard to the problem of distinguishing oral elements in the Norse sagas and other questions concerning oral literature and for bibliographical references, and to the publishers of the JSOT Press for their acceptance, once again, of a work of mine in their Supplement Series.

R.N. Whybray

ABBREVIATIONS

AB	Anchor Bible, Garden City, New York
ANVAO	Avhandlinger i norske videnskapsakademi i Oslo, Oslo
ATANT	Abhandlungen zur Theologie des Alten und Neuen Testaments, Zürich
ATD	Das Alte Testament Deutsch, Göttingen
BA	*Biblical Archaeologist*, New Haven
BASOR	*Bulletin of the American Schools of Oriental Research*, Jerusalem, Baghdad, New Haven
BBB	Bonner Biblische Beiträge, Bonn
BEvT	Beiträge zur Evangelischen Theologie, Munich
BKAT	Biblischer Kommentar, Altes Testament, Neukirchen
BTB	*Biblical Theology Bulletin*, St Bonaventure, New York
BVSAW	Berichte über die Verhandlungen der Sächsischen Akademie der Wissenschaften zu Leipzig, Leipzig
BWANT	Beiträge zur Wissenschaft vom Alten und Neuen Testament, Stuttgart
BZ	*Biblische Zeitschrift*, Paderborn
BZAW	Beihefte zur Zeitschrift für die Alttestamentliche Wissenschaft, Berlin
CAH	*Cambridge Ancient History*
CAT	Commentaire de l'Ancien Testament, Neuchâtel
CBC	Cambridge Bible Commentary, Cambridge
CBQ	*Catholic Biblical Quarterly*, Washington, D.C.
EB	Etudes Bibliques, Paris
ET	English Translation
ET	*Expository Times*, Edinburgh
EvT	*Evangelische Theologie*, Munich
EVV	English Versions
FRLANT	Forschungen zur Religion und Literatur des Alten und Neuen Testaments, Göttingen
HK	Handkommentar zum Alten Testament, Göttingen
HTR	*Harvard Theological Review*, Cambridge, Mass.

HUCA	*Hebrew Union College Annual*, Cincinnati
IB	*Interpreter's Bible*, New York
ICC	International Critical Commentary, Edinburgh and New York
IDB	*Interpreter's Dictionary of the Bible*
JBL	*Journal of Biblical Literature*, Philadelphia
JSOT	*Journal for the Study of the Old Testament*, Sheffield
KHC	Kurzer Hand-Commentar zum Alten Testament, Tübingen
LXX	Septuagint
MT	Masoretic Text
NCB	New Century Bible, London
NF	Neue Folge
NS	New Series, Neue Serie
OBO	Orbis Biblicus et Orientalis, Freiburg, Switzerland and Göttingen
OTL	Old Testament Library, London and Philadelphia
RB	*Revue Biblique*, Paris
SBL	Society of Biblical Literature
SBS	Stuttgarter Bibelstudien, Stuttgart
SBT	Studies in Biblical Theology, London
StTh	*Studia Theologica. Scandinavian Journal of Theology*, Lund
TBAT	Theologische Bücherei, Altes Testament, Munich
TLZ	*Theologische Literaturzeitung*, Leipzig
TR	*Theologische Rundschau*, Tübingen
TZ	*Theologische Zeitschrift*, Basel
UUÅ	*Uppsala universitets årsskrift*, Uppsala
VT	*Vetus Testamentum*, Leiden
VTS	Supplements to *Vetus Testamentum*
WC	Westminster Commentaries, London
WMANT	Wissenschaftliche Monographien zum Alten und Neuen Testament, Neukirchen
ZAW	*Zeitschrift für die Alttestamentliche Wissenschaft*, Berlin
ZDA	*Zeitschrift für Deutsches Altertum und Deutsche Literatur*, Wiesbaden
ZTK	*Zeitschrift für Theologie und Kirche*, Tübingen

INTRODUCTION

The form in which the Pentateuch presents itself to the reader is that of a history. The narrative thread which begins in Genesis 1 continues unbroken up to the notice of the death of Moses at the end of Deuteronomy. Other elements—laws, poems and songs—are also to be found within the work, but these are all presented as spoken or sung by persons who appear in the narrative, and so form an integral part of it. There is no break in the chronological sequence of the events.

But is the death of Moses really the conclusion of this history? The narrative thread does not end with Deuteronomy. The book of Joshua which immediately follows is clearly intended to be seen as its continuation, as its opening words make clear: 'After the death of Moses ... '. There is a similar link between Joshua and Judges. Indeed, it could be, and has been, argued that the whole of Genesis to Kings is one long history.

The view of Martin Noth is entirely opposed to this supposition: for him, the 'Pentateuch' is shorter than it was traditionally supposed to be: Deuteronomy was not originally part of it. In fact Noth's separation of Deuteronomy from Genesis to Numbers was not entirely without precedent: it had already been recognized by earlier scholars that it is a different kind of book from the others and constitutes a separate block of material within the whole.

It is primarily with the first four books, Genesis to Numbers, that this study will be concerned, since it is on the basis of their treatment of these four books that both the documentary and traditio-historical hypotheses which are to be discussed stand or fall. This is not to say that the question of Deuteronomy and its relationship to the other books is not an important one, or that it will be ignored: it will come under discussion in the final section of this book. Meanwhile we shall follow the example of Noth in his *History of Pentateuchal Traditions* and continue to use the term 'Pentateuch' in discussing these books even though it would be more accurate to speak of a 'Tetrateuch' or simply of 'Genesis to Numbers'.

Is the Pentateuch a Unity?

Two main problems confront the student of the Pentateuch. One concerns the nature of the finished product: Is there a sense in which the Pentateuch is a single literary work, and if so, what does it have to say? The other question concerns its origins: Is it possible to discover the process by which it reached its present form?

It is common ground to all students of the Pentateuch that it is not a unified literary work in the sense in which a modern novel or a modern work of history can be so described.

Its narrative thread gives it a kind of *thematic* unity: it is an account of God's dealings with the human race that he had created, and in particular with that part of it which claimed descent from Abraham, up to their occupation of Palestine. But unity of theme is not by itself sufficient to make a unified work. It is further necessary to enquire whether the Pentateuch possesses a coherent structure such as we should expect to find in an historical work. In terms of modern literary canons, this does not appear to be the case. It contains long digressions which do not advance the story and often appear to be irrelevant to it. While there is undoubtedly a continuous narrative thread, this is often extremely thin, and the various incidents described are frequently joined together only very loosely. The work clearly contains material gathered from many sources; and the author or compiler, while weaving these together into a continuous narrative, has frequently allowed them to speak for themselves, even when they express contradictory views or see things from quite different perspectives. It would seem that it was his intention to give some kind of coherence to a mass of traditions— themselves no doubt selected from a still larger stock—in a way which would have significance for his readers; but, although the extent to which he reworked, expanded or supplemented these traditions is an extremely difficult question to answer, he did not attempt to force his materials into a neat pattern in which there are no loose ends.

But to judge the Pentateuch by modern literary canons would obviously be mistaken. A comparison with historical works from the ancient world would be more to the point. As will be seen in Part III, the methods of composition which appear to have been used to gather this diverse material into a unity are not without parallels.

Can We Discover How it was Compiled?

This is more than simply a literary question. Any attempt to discover the process by which the Pentateuch reached its present form must explain not only how, but also why its compiler or compilers acted as they did: if no plausible motive can be discovered, any hypothesis which may be put forward, however ingenious it may be, ignores the realities of human psychology.

But to discover the motives of anonymous literary men who lived as long ago as did the authors of the Pentateuch is a task far more formidable than can be carried out through knowledge of human psychology alone. We must also take into account the difference between our modern western approach to literature and that of the ancient world. To assume that the Pentateuchal compilers had the same notions of authorship, editorship, style and other like matters as ourselves would be a grave error. Yet, although our knowledge of other ancient literatures provides us with some clues which may be useful for our purpose, it is an unfortunate fact that we have no external information about the specific case of ancient Israel at all. We can only make conjectures about Israelite literary conventions which are based on the internal evidence of the finished literature itself. There are no ancient Israelite treatises extant to tell us how such historians set about their task.

It is therefore difficult to avoid the conclusion that the likelihood of modern scholars' succeeding in discovering—except, perhaps, in very general terms—how the Pentateuch was compiled is small indeed. This does not necessarily mean that it is not worthwhile to make the attempt. But the self-assurance with which many scholars, especially during the past hundred years, have propounded their views on the subject should be regarded with suspicion. Every hypothesis which has been advanced needs to be carefully scrutinized with respect both to its method and to its hidden presuppositions and assumptions. It will be found that often conjecture has been piled upon conjecture.

In what follows the main theories about the composition of the Pentateuch which have been proposed during the past century or so will be described and examined.

PART I: LITERARY HYPOTHESES

From the time when doubts were first expressed about the unity of authorship of the Pentateuch (traditionally attributed to Moses) until the beginning of the twentieth century the question was understood as being a purely literary one: a problem concerning the compilation of *written sources*. Although it was generally accepted that the authors of these written records had derived their information in the first place from living, that is, oral tradition, no attempt was made to investigate this pre-literary stage, since it was believed that nothing could be known about it. Thus the question which preoccupies the modern tradition-historian, namely, the possibility that some at least of the process of compilation may have taken place before the material was committed to writing, was not raised.

Viewed, then, as a purely literary problem, the phenomenon of the lack of consistency and unity manifested in the Pentateuch appeared to be susceptible of three main types of solution. The work might have been compiled by a single editor who joined together into a single but somewhat jumbled whole a mass of quite independent short written pieces (the 'Fragment Hypothesis'). Or, secondly, there might originally have been a single, consistent, unified account composed by a single author, to which, for various reasons, later writers made additions, so distorting the original unity of the composition (the 'Supplement Hypothesis'). A third type of solution is more complicated: it is that the Pentateuch is the result of the combination not of a mass of 'fragments' by a single editor but of a much smaller number of more extensive works ('documents') written independently and at different periods and to a large extent covering the same ground. These were woven together in a series of stages by different editors or 'redactors'. This is the Documentary Hypothesis. In contrast with the Fragment Hypothesis this might be described as a theory of 'horizontal strata' as opposed to one of 'vertical faults' in the Pentateuchal massif.

It should be remarked that these three types of solution are not necessarily entirely mutually exclusive. For example, if the Documentary Hypothesis is taken to be a satisfactory solution to the composition of the Pentateuch in general, this does not exclude the possibility that in addition to the main sources or 'documents' the Pentateuch may contain some shorter pieces ('fragments') which never formed part of these, but were combined with one or other of them at some redactional stage; nor does it rule out the possibility of some additions ('supplements') having been made after the main redactional process was completed. Nevertheless the three solutions remain distinct as basically *alternative* explanations of the composition of the Pentateuch in its general lines.

The immediate impression made on those who are confronted by these three solutions for the first time may well be that the least plausible of them is the Documentary Hypothesis. For whereas the Fragment and Supplement Hypotheses envisage relatively simple, and, it would seem, logical processes and at the same time appear to account for the unevennesses of the completed Pentateuch, the Documentary Hypothesis is not only much more complicated but also very specific in its assumptions about the historical development of Israel's understanding of its origins. It is not difficult to accept the proposition (as made in the Fragment Hypothesis) that at some stage in Israel's history the need should have been felt to assemble and give a connected form to the various records of the nation's history which had hitherto existed only in fragmentary form, nor is it improbable (as the Supplement Hypothesis proposes) that an 'historical' work could once have existed which later generations saw fit to supplement with additional material.

But the proposal of the Documentary Hypothesis that several similar but not identical works should have been composed at different times, and that, further, the need should subsequently have been felt to weave these, by stages, into a single work calls for far more elaborate explanations. In particular, the *motives* for the composition of each succeeding 'document', and also the motives for each of the succeeding redactions, need to be convincingly explained. An even more fundamental requirement of the Documentary Hypothesis is proof that the 'documents' postulated by it ever existed. The only way in which this can be done is by demonstrating convincingly that the innumerable small fragments of narrative and law of which the Pentateuch mainly consists can be satisfactorily classified and assembled in such a way as to produce several distinct connected works, and—equally important—can *only* be classified and assembled in this way. If they could equally well be assembled in some other way to produce a different set of such connected works, the Documentary Hypothesis would entirely fail. In other words, whereas the other two hypotheses only have to account for the *diversity* of the material contained in the Pentateuch, the Documentary Hypothesis has to prove, up to the hilt, that its hypothetical documents—and *only* they—possess a sufficient degree of *unity* to compel belief in their existence. Its proponents must justify their thesis at every point if they are to show that it is an *indispensable* theory and that the other, simpler solutions to the problem are inadequate.

A further point of some importance in considering the Documentary Hypothesis, and one which has not received sufficient attention, concerns the work of the 'redactors'. If the documents postulated by the hypothesis possessed some kind of unity and consistency—and it is this which is held to give them plausibility—then the redactors were the persons who wantonly destroyed that unity and consistency— and again, the hypothesis depends on believing that they did. But this is merely to charge the redactors with faults of logic and sensitivity of which the proponents of the Documentary Hypothesis are at such pains to absolve the authors of the documents. If the *redactors* were unconcerned about these things, it is difficult to understand on what grounds the proponents of the hypothesis maintain that the *authors* of the documents were concerned about them. It seems more logical to conclude that ancient Israelite ideas of consistency were different from those of modern western man: that the Israelites were in fact to a large extent indifferent to what we should call inconsistencies. But if this is so, the grounds on which the Documentary Hypothesis reconstructs the individual documents need further examination.

In spite of these difficulties it is the Documentary Hypothesis which, having been first in the field, commended itself to the great majority of scholars and still commands the allegiance of many. It is therefore primarily with it that this section of this book will be concerned, although, as will be seen, the Fragment and Supplement Hypotheses have to some extent recently experienced a revival under somewhat new forms.

A. *The Documentary Hypothesis*

1. *Its Main Features*

What is known as the Documentary Hypothesis, though popularly associated mainly with the name of Julius Wellhausen, is not the product of a single individual but of many. The first serious attempts to develop a theory of continuous written sources were made in the first half of the eighteenth century—with regard to the book of Genesis only—by H.B. Witter and Jean Astruc; and from the beginning of the nineteenth a vigorous scholarly discussion took place among scholars who accepted the principle of continuous sources but put forward a variety of alternative schemes. Wellhausen's brilliant classic exposition, from 1876 onwards, which achieved widespread recognition, was constructed on the basis of these earlier discussions. Its success was due to his unrivalled skill in showing more clearly than his predecessors how completely the literary analysis of the sources could be related to the religious history of Israel as reconstructed from other parts of the Old Testament. But the hypothesis in its final, fully developed form also owed much to a succession of Wellhausen's followers who, in a series of commentaries and Introductions to the Old Testament, refined it still further by their analyses of the finer details of the source material.

The history of the undertaking from its origins to Wellhausen and beyond has been sketched many times and can be read in any modern Introduction to the Old Testament. There is no need to repeat it here. Rather an attempt will be made to present the main outlines of the Documentary Hypothesis as a whole and to make some assessment of it.

Stated briefly and in purely literary terms, the Documentary Hypothesis states that the Pentateuch took shape in a series of stages in which, during the space of several centuries, four originally distinct books ('documents'), each written at a different time, were dovetailed together by a series of 'redactors' to form a single work. This was achieved in the following way:

1. The earliest of these works was that of the 'Yahwist' (J). It began with what is now Gen. 2.4b, and its various parts are now found in Genesis, Exodus and Numbers, together with a few short passages in Deuteronomy. Whether it ended at this point or continued into the book of Joshua or beyond

was disputed. It is not represented in Leviticus.

2. The 'Elohist' work (E) began with the story of Abraham in Gen. 15 and then followed the same general course as J.

3. J and E were subsequently combined to form 'JE' by a redactor (R^{JE}). The process of redaction involved the omission of parts of J and E, especially of the latter.

4. The third 'document', Deuteronomy (D), consists mainly of the book of that name.

5. D was subsequently appended to JE by a second redactor (R^D), who also inserted a few passages into JE and incorporated a few passages from JE into D.

6. The final work, the Priestly 'document' (P), began with what is now Gen. 1.1 and followed the same chronological scheme as J. Material from P predominates in Exodus and Numbers, and is the sole source of Exod. 25-31; 35-40 and of Leviticus.

7. P was subsequently combined with JED by a third redactor (R^P) to form the present Pentateuch.

8. A few passages (e.g. Gen. 14) are not derived from any of the main four documents but must be regarded as independent fragments. It is not possible to determine at what point in the above scheme they were inserted, but a late date for this is probable. A few other passages were added after the bulk of the Pentateuch was completed. Both Fragment and Supplement Hypotheses, therefore, retained a minor place in the scheme of the Documentary Hypothesis.

It will be obvious from the above that D occupies a position in the scheme which is somewhat different from that of the other documents, in that while J, E and P run concurrently through the books from Genesis to Numbers and are thus, according to the Hypothesis, genuinely dovetailed the one into the others, D does not. It is concerned only with the final part of the history, the period of Moses, and occupies the position of an appendix to the threefold history which precedes it. In terms of purely literary source-analysis, therefore, the Documentary Hypothesis is mainly concerned with the three hypothetical documents in Genesis-Numbers. However, since the Documentary Hypothesis rests on the *sequence* of the entire process of composition and on the relative dates of the main documents and redactions in relation to the stages of the development of Israelite religious beliefs and practices, the position of D in the scheme is important.

2. *Its Basis*

The distinctiveness of the Documentary Hypothesis does not lie in the discovery of evidence of disunity and inconsistency in the text of the Pentateuch. Although the first systematic use which was made of this discovery did in fact take the form of an embryonic 'documentary hypothesis' (that of Astruc), the Fragment and Supplement Hypotheses had subsequently suggested that the phenomena in question might be accounted for in quite different ways. The distinctive contribution of the fully developed Documentary Hypothesis of Wellhausen and his school was that it was a systematic attempt to show that the negative evidence—that is, the evidence of disunity—could best be accounted for in a positive and constructive way: that the disjointedness of the Pentateuch was not due to haphazard growth or to random collection of disparate material, but that the material was susceptible of being sorted and classified in such a way as to show that there lay behind it a series of consistent works or 'documents' which had once existed independently but whose integrity had subsequently been destroyed by their being dovetailed together. In other words, the Documentary Hypothesis was concerned with something far more difficult to prove than was the case with the other hypotheses: not simply with destruction but with *con*struction—or rather, with the *re*construction of these supposed literary works.

a. *The nature of the material*

As has been suggested above, the evidence for the disunity of the Pentateuch was the very same as that which provided the Documentary Hypothesis with its basis for the reconstruction of the documents. The marks which showed that text A could not belong to the same document as text B were also the marks which were held to show that text A *did* belong to the same document as text C, which manifested the same marks as text A. The first concern of the proponents of the Documentary Hypothesis, therefore, was to develop to its fullest extent the study of these indications. The results of this study may be set out in the form of a table of criteria which may thus be expressed either negatively or positively. Since every Introduction to the Old Testament provides such a table, usually in some detail, it may be presented summarily here, and in the negative form which is that most generally favoured.

Different choice of words and variation of style
The first example of this criterion to be observed was the use of different names for the deity. In Genesis, apart from some passages in which other names are used, God is sometimes referred to by his name *yhwh* and sometimes by the word Elohim. It was supposed by the proponents of the Documentary Hypothesis (henceforward to be known as the documentary critics) that this variation does not reflect a deliberate choice by a single author between two designations in order to suit the context, but rather that two different authors, whose works were subsequently combined, each consistently used one name or the other. The phenomenon is, however, of limited application as it occurs only in the book of Genesis and the first few chapters of Exodus.

But it was also noted that there are other examples of the use of two words having the same meaning where a single author might be expected to have used only one. Some of these are proper names such as Sinai/Horeb and Canaanite/Amorite; but there are also examples of the alternation of common nouns. Lists of these were compiled and are to be found in the Introductions. This analysis was not confined to single words, but was extended to phrases and to other stylistic phenomena.

Double (or triple) versions of the same stories
A classical example of this phenomenon is the double version of the story of Abraham's pretence, when he went to live in a foreign country (Gen. 12.10-20; 20.1-18), that his wife Sarai/Sarah was in fact his sister, further duplicated in part by a similar story about Isaac (Gen. 26.6-16). These three stories are remarkably similar in detail. In other cases such as the two 'creation stories' (Gen. 1.1-2.4a; 2.4b-25) there is little similarity of detail, but the event itself is essentially the same. Again, it was supposed that the same author would not have included both accounts in his work.

Repetitions of details within the same passage
Some passages appear to be unnecessarily and improbably repetitious. For example, in the introduction to the account of the Flood, it is twice stated that God decided to destroy mankind on account of its wickedness (Gen. 6.5-7 and 11-12).

Insertions of extraneous material into an otherwise continuous account
An obvious example of this is the intrusion of a narrative about
Judah (Gen. 38) into an entirely unrelated story about the adventures
of Joseph (Gen. 37-50).

Contradictions concerning matters of fact
These occur both in widely separated passages and within the same
passage. Examples of the former phenomenon are the numerous
differences in legal requirements in different parts of the Pentateuch,
all of which are stated to have been promulgated by Moses. Thus in
Exod. 20.24 permission is given for the offering of sacrifice at
numerous altars, whereas Deut. 12.13-14 forbids this, restricting it to
a single place to be chosen by God. The story of the Flood is a
classical example of the latter phenomenon: for example, Gen. 7.17
states that the flood water remained on the earth for forty days,
whereas Gen. 7.24 mentions 150 days.

Differences of cultural and religious point of view
It was argued that different passages reflect quite different cultural
and historical backgrounds and religious notions and practices,
pointing to a variety of authorship and to widely different periods of
composition. Thus the collections of laws scattered through the
Pentateuch (especially Exod. 20.23-23.19; the book of Leviticus; and
Deut. 12-26) show considerable differences in the social and cultic
backgrounds which they reflect. The 'law of the king' in Deut. 17.14-
20 presupposes some experience of monarchy in Israel and a hope
that it may be susceptible of reform, while the great prominence
given to the priesthood in Leviticus and the absence of any reference
to the king there suggest that it was composed in the exilic or post-
exilic period, when the monarchy no longer existed. The anthropomorphic presentation of God in Gen. 2 was held to reflect an
earlier and less developed theology than the more abstract
presentation of him in Gen. 1. Differences of ethical principles were
also detected in different passages, for example in the two stories of
Abraham's periods of foreign residence narrated in Gen. 12.10-20
and 20.1-18.

The above are not isolated examples, but illustrations selected
more or less at random from a very large mass of material collected
by the documentary critics and by other critics of the unity of the
Pentateuch.

b. *The reconstruction of the documents*
It had already been concluded by the earliest Pentateuchal critics such as Astruc that the supposed discrepancies in the text—specifically, the alternation of the divine names in Genesis—were the result of the conflation of two distinct written documents. This was a plausible solution to the problem when the number of phenomena calling for explanation was small. The discovery of numerous other kinds of discrepancy and inconsistency changed the situation, and at the beginning of the nineteenth century a number of scholars (Geddes, Vater and de Wette) put forward the Fragment Hypothesis as the only explanation which could account for the facts. Later documentary critics, however, sought to account for the new set of problems by postulating the existence of an additional document. In the fully developed hypothesis of Wellhausen, who in this respect followed Hupfeld and Graf, the passages in which God is referred to as Elohim were divided into two documents, designated E and Q (the siglum for the latter being later changed to P). The criterion of divine names was applicable only to Genesis and the first chapters of Exodus; but on the basis of the other indications of multiple authorship it was argued that the three documents J, E and P continued throughout Genesis–Numbers, D (Deuteronomy) forming the fourth.

The hypothesis thus depended on the discovery in each passage assigned to a particular document of a sufficient number of characteristics common to all the passages assigned to that document. Clearly not all passages possessed all those characteristics: for example, none of the material in the chapters from Exod. 6 to the end of Numbers can be analysed on the basis of the use of the divine names, nor can E be distinguished from P on that basis even in Genesis. The same is true of the other criteria. Some passages, indeed, are 'neutral' in the sense that there are no indications in them sufficient by themselves to justify their assignment to one document rather than another.

In such cases, however, a further argument could be adduced. The three documents J, E and P must, by the nature of the hypothesis, be *continuous* and comprehensive. It was conceded that in the process of their combination by the redactors they had not always been preserved intact, especially in the case of E. Nevertheless it was argued that if a 'neutral' passage appeared plausibly to fill a gap in one of the documents and so to contribute to its continuity as a consistent work, this was sufficient to justify its assignment to that document.

In the further development of the Documentary Hypothesis after Wellhausen the question of the *degree* of inner consistency required to postulate the existence of a separate document became a crucial and controversial one. Some scholars, in the pursuit of consistency, claimed to have discovered an older document later embedded in J, others similarly divided E into two, while yet others fragmented P into a number of lesser documents. D was also thought to have undergone various revisions and expansions. It has been argued by some critics that such fragmentation of the classical four documents is in reality nothing less than a revival of the Fragment Hypothesis; but this is not really the case, since the methods employed to identify the newly proposed documents and the theory of the gradual growth of the Pentateuch by a process of conflation of independent literary works by a series of redactors remain the same as in the hypothesis in its 'classical' form.

c. *The dating of the documents*

However ingenious its reconstruction of the documents might be, the Documentary Hypothesis would lack plausibility unless a convincing account could be given of the motives which led to the composition of more than one version of the same history and their conflation, in a series of stages, to form ultimately a single work. It was therefore important for the documentary critics to be able to relate the various stages of the composition of the Pentateuch to events or circumstances in the history of Israel which might account for these specific forms of literary activity: in other words, to make convincing proposals about the dates, both relative and absolute, of the documents and the redactions. This task was carried out mainly by the use of the last of the criteria listed above, that of differences between the viewpoints reflected by the various documents. This method can be seen at its best in Wellhausen's *Prolegomena*, in which he argued that the legislation of P concerning the cult reflected a stage in cultic history which was much later than that reflected in J and E and in the early stories of Judges, Samuel and Kings, and that these laws could not have been put into effect before the Exile.

Earlier scholars had already connected Deuteronomy with the lawbook discovered in the temple at Jerusalem by Hilkiah in the reign of Josiah (2 Kings 22), and had dated J and E to earlier periods under the monarchy, with J preceding E, on the basis of theological differences due to a progressive development of religious and ethical notions in the pre-exilic age. In this way the chronological order J, E, D, P was established, and approximate absolute dates fixed for the four documents. These results were accepted by the followers of Wellhausen, although differences of opinion were expressed about the precise dating of the documents, especially J and E.

It was one of Wellhausen's main achievements that he was able to achieve a correlation, more complete than had been achieved by his predecessors, between the history of the composition of the Pentateuch and the history of the religion of Israel. In particular, his impressive demonstration that P is not an early source and cannot be pre-exilic may be said to have permanently changed the course of Pentateuchal criticism.

Although there was not complete agreement between the documentary critics about the motives of those who composed or combined the various documents, it was generally accepted that they were all motivated by the desire to preserve the received traditions as far as possible while at the same time reinterpreting them in accordance with the theologies of their times. It was this desire to preserve which was held by the documentary critics to account for the large amount of repetition in the Pentateuch in its final form:

1. J and E are both selections, made in the southern and northern kingdoms respectively, from a stock of common traditions. E, which is shown by its more advanced theology and ethics to have been written later than J, may to some extent have been dependent on it (there was no agreement on this point). But in both cases the motive was to preserve, arrange in chronological sequence, and—to some degree— give a theological interpretation of the national traditions.

2. The motive of R^{JE} was to preserve the northern traditions recorded in E, which were in danger of being lost after the destruction of the northern kingdom, by incorporating them into J.

3. D, which is not primarily a narrative source, expresses, mainly in the form of laws, theological ideas which came to the fore at the time of Josiah's reformation. It was thus not intended to be an alternative to JE, with which its author was, however, familiar.

4. R^{D} was an exilic redactor whose purpose was to provide a

'canonical' account which combined the already familiar JE
with a theological interpretation consonant with that of D.
He therefore appended the book of Deuteronomy to JE and
also made a few 'Deuteronomic' insertions into it.

5. P's motive in composing yet another work running parallel
    with JE was to express, partly through narrative, but
    predominantly through a new corpus of legislation, the
    theology of the post-exilic priesthood.

6. R^P, like the earlier redactors, wished to preserve the older
    material—in this case the 'official' account in JE (and D)—
    but to bring it into line with the priestly theology of P, using
    P as its basic framework.

d. *Limitations and unanswered questions*

It would be a mistake to suppose that the documentary critics
claimed that the hypothesis solved all the problems regarding the
composition of the Pentateuch. It has already been noted that they
regarded some passages as unattributable to any of the four
documents. Further, they were not concerned with the pre-literary
stage of the material, which was in any case regarded as of no great
antiquity and as having arisen much later than the periods which it
describes (e.g. Wellhausen, 1883, p. 316; ET pp. 318-19).

It is also important to note that the original proponents of the
hypothesis and some—though not all—of its later adherents (e.g.
S.R. Driver) expressed reservations about the sufficiency of the
criteria to solve all problems of source analysis. This was particularly
true of the document 'E'. Wellhausen himself admitted—though he
was in no doubt about the existence of E—that it is not always
possible to distinguish it from J, and used the term 'Jehovist', by
which he meant the composite JE, in distinguishing the earlier
material from P.

It was also generally admitted that E had been preserved only in a
fragmentary state: in other words, that the important criterion of
continuity in a given document was not wholly applicable in the case
of E. Driver in his *Introduction*—to take a single example—treated
the question of the identification of the documents J and E in
particular instances with great caution, and was hesitant to make use
of the principle applied extensively by some other critics that what
does not appear to belong to one document must belong to the other,
even if there is no positive indication that it possesses the

characteristics of the latter. Indeed, he more than once stressed the uncertainty of the criteria themselves, speaking of 'degrees of probability' and of 'conclusions which, from the nature of the case, are uncertain' (1909, pp. IV, V). The reliability of the criteria was also unwittingly put in doubt by those critics who used them to postulate, by an even more minute analysis, the existence of yet more documents, so demonstrating that the same methods could produce quite different results.

Other important questions remained unanswered or disputed by the documentary critics:

The relationship between the documents

There was no agreement on the question whether the author of E was familiar with J. This was to become an important issue later because of its implications for an assessment of the extent to which the Israelite traditions had already acquired a fixed form before they were committed to writing. That P was familiar with JE was generally assumed.

Were the writers of the documents primarily authors or collectors?

On this question also there was divergence of opinion. The criteria of vocabulary and style and of difference of point of view had, it was believed, proved that each document clearly reflected the age in which it had been written: in other words, the traditional material which it utilized had been remodelled by one who was fundamentally an historian, interpreting it according to his own lights and restating it in the language of his own day. If this were not so, the analysis of the documents would be illusory. Yet it was at the same time recognized that there was evidence—in particular, the individual flavour which still clung to many of the stories of Genesis, and the remarkable similarity in many cases between two versions of the same story in different documents—that these authors had in fact been remarkably faithful to their traditional sources. Gunkel, in the Introduction to his commentary on Genesis, tried to combine these two facts by picturing the narratives as 'an old richly-coloured painting that has been darkened and heavily re-touched' (1901a, 3rd edn, p. LXXXVI; cf. 1901 b, p. 133); but this attempt to solve the problem is hardly convincing, and it must be admitted that it remains unsolved in terms of the hypothesis.

Were they individuals or 'schools of narrators'?
Wellhausen regarded the documents as the work of individuals.
Other supporters of the hypothesis, on the other hand (e.g. Budde
and Gunkel) considered that they had been compiled within
particular circles or 'schools of narrators' over a more or less
extended period, and were not to be attributed to any one individual.
The implications of this disagreement are far-reaching, but were not
fully admitted by the critics.

The work of the redactors
There was general agreement that conservatism was the reason why
the documents as they succeeded one another did not simply
supersede and consign to oblivion the earlier versions, but were
combined with them to form new works. It was held that the earlier
documents had acquired such an authoritative standing as 'standard'
accounts of the national tradition that, even though they might be
judged inadequate and in need of supplementation in a later age,
there could be no question of their suppression. A considerable
degree of unanimity was reached by the critics about the way in
which the conflation was carried out; but in comparison with the
authors of the individual documents the redactors remained somewhat
shadowy figures, and the extent to which they themselves had
contributed to the material by additions of their own remained
obscure.

The extent of the documents
Although the traditional division of the books of the Hebrew Bible
separates Joshua and the books which follow from the five books of
the Torah (Pentateuch), placing Joshua, Judges, Samuel and Kings in
a separate section known as the Former Prophets, it was an agreed
tenet of the Documentary Hypothesis that originally Joshua had
belonged together with the earlier books (forming the 'Hexateuch'),
of which it was the concluding section. The Pentateuchal documents
continued through Joshua, and were there combined in a similar
way. Some supporters of the hypothesis went further, maintaining
that they continued into Judges, Samuel and even Kings (so, for
example, Budde and Benzinger). Others vigorously disputed this
view. The question is an important one because it seriously affects
the view to be taken about the structure and purpose of the
Pentateuchal sources, and of the Pentateuch as a whole. A work

which ends with the death of Moses is a different kind of work from one which carries the story of Israel across the Jordan and describes the fulfilment of the promises to the Patriarchs in the conquest of Palestine, or from one which ends with the foundation of the monarchy, or the triumph of David, or some other point in the history of the monarchy.

B. *Pentateuchal Criticism Since Wellhausen*

1. *Further Development of the Hypothesis*

A line of Pentateuchal investigation which began even before the time of Wellhausen and has continued up to the present time has been the attempt to show that the four documents of the classical hypothesis are not the earliest written Pentateuchal sources, but are themselves the result of the conflation of even earlier written documents. For example, Procksch distinguished between an E^1 and an E^2. Smend (1912) similarly identified a J^1 and a J^2, a theory which continued to be maintained in slightly different forms, with different sigla in place of J^1, by Pfeiffer ('S'), Eissfeldt ('L'), Morgenstern ('K') and Fohrer ('N'). Different strata had been distinguished in P even before Graf (1866) and Wellhausen identified the so-called 'Holiness Code' in Lev. 17-26. These theories, however, were not regarded by their proponents as challenges to the Documentary Hypothesis. It is true that from a later standpoint they may well be thought to raise fundamental questions about the adequacy of its methods; but inasmuch as they are based entirely on the use of those methods, they should be seen as further developments and refinements of it.

Despite the criticisms which have been made, especially in recent years, of the hypothesis, there is some evidence that the majority of scholars continue to accept it, even though in various modified forms; though it is hard to find considered defences of it in its classical form in recent literature. R.H. Pfeiffer (1930, 1941) assumed its truth without adequate discussion, merely adding his additional document 'S' to the others. Hölscher (1952) and Eissfeldt (e.g in his *Introduction*, from 1934 onwards) continued to defend to the end of their careers the hypothesis which they had accepted in their youth. One of the very latest Introductions to the Old Testament, that of Kaiser in its English edition in 1975, asserts that 'it still fulfils, much better than all the hypotheses which are alternatives to it, the task of explaining the facts in the most comprehensive way possible' (p. 44).

Other modern scholars have found a place for the hypothesis in a modified form, often in combination with newer, traditio-historical approaches. Of these perhaps the most influential was Martin Noth (1948). Although his primary interest was in the pre-literary history of the composition of the Pentateuch, he declared his adherence to the hypothesis of the four documents (1948, pp. 1, 4-7, 247-67; ET pp. 1, 4-7, 228-47). However, he differed from Wellhausen in his view of their function and mutual relationship. He believed that the shape and most of the contents of J and E had already been fixed in a pre-existent common tradition ('G') which had perhaps already acquired written form. Consequently 'The work of J and E consisted to a large extent only in the formulation of the narratives handed down' in that common tradition (p. 248; ET p. 229).

With regard to the relationship between J and E, Noth regarded the extant remains of E, which is preserved only in very fragmentary form, as merely an 'enrichment' of the basic narrative J (pp. 25, 40, 255-56; ET pp. 24, 37, 236). He also maintained that, in the final version of the Pentateuch, JE itself functions only as an 'enrichment' of P, which now provides the basic framework for the whole (p. 11; ET p. 12). He was also severely critical of the criteria for the separation of E material from that of J. He rejected the criteria of vocabulary and style and of differences of religious ideas, regarding as valid only the criterion of duplicate versions of narratives and—to a lesser extent—of the alternation of divine names. Even these criteria, he maintained, must be applied with restraint: he did not accept—apart from very rare instances, such as the story of the Flood—the fragmentation of individual stories to establish the presence of two sources (p. 28; ET p. 27). In general, whole stories were taken from one source or the other and transmitted intact. He pointed out that it is mistaken to look for absolute consistency in a document, because each document is composed of many different elements, each retaining its own distinct characteristics (pp. 269-70; ET p. 250).

Noth's view of P is also distinctive: P was a narrator; and the legal material in P has a quite different origin from the narrative material (p. 7; ET p. 8). In spite of these reservations, however, Noth stood firmly within the boundaries of the Documentary Hypothesis. His theory (1943) of a Deuteronomistic History (comprising Deuteronomy, Joshua, Judges, Samuel and Kings) as a separate work from the Tetrateuch (Genesis to Numbers) does not essentially affect his acceptance of it, since Deuteronomy was, according to the hypothesis itself, to all intents and purposes a quite distinct document which did not undergo a process of conflation with the other documents.

R. de Vaux (1953), in an article commemorating the second centenary of Astruc's pioneering work, also defended the Documentary Hypothesis in a modified form. In some respects he was more conservative than Noth: he accepted the validity of all the criteria on which the hypothesis is based, and, in response to attacks on the whole literary-critical method *per se*, cited other examples from the ancient world and from the Old Testament itself (Chronicles, Ezra-Nehemiah) of the conflationary method of writing history. But, like Noth, he criticized the rigidity and over-minuteness of some applications of the method, and suggested (following Bentzen) that it was preferable to speak of 'parallel traditions' rather than of documents. But in attempting to combine a literary approach with an adequate recognition of the role of oral tradition, he left the reader in some confusion about his views. On the one hand he spoke of a living oral tradition continuing to develop side by side with the written tradition and continuing to influence it; on the other he maintained that J (at least) was the work of a single individual author who was responsible for arranging the material and imposing his views upon it. He concluded (p. 195): 'These conclusions agree essentially with the classical positions of the documentary hypothesis. But they are less affirmative, and in particular, they are accompanied by a double reservation: on the one hand these traditions, even after they had taken shape, continued to live and to assimilate new elements; on the other hand, they had had a prehistory which it is important to take into account.'

Fohrer (1965) accepted the four sources J, E, D and P, together with his own additional source N, and also all the classical criteria. His only substantial modification of the Documentary Hypothesis was that he avoided the term 'document' and preferred to speak of 'source strata' because, like de Vaux, he regarded the sources as more 'complex, often less tangible in wording and, on account of the use of ancient material, less the exclusive work of a single author than the term "document" suggests' (ET, p. 114). He also avoided the term 'hypothesis' as suggesting an exclusive use of a single approach to the problem, speaking rather of different 'methods' used by the compilers of different kinds of Pentateuchal material: the 'addition method' had been employed by the redactors for the combination of 'source strata'; but the 'supplement method' had been used for the gradual formation of the legal codes and for various additions to the narrative material, and the 'composition method' for the composition of each source stratum from its component traditions. This new terminology may serve the purpose of clarification, but it does not constitute a new theory: it merely puts in a new way what had always been maintained by Wellhausen and his school.

Other recent Introductions to the Old Testament such as those of Cazelles, Soggin (1976), Smend (1978) and W.H. Schmidt (1979) ought probably to be reckoned as supporting the Documentary Hypothesis, at least in a modified form. But at the same sime they serve as indications of the unease which prevails on the subject. Soggin, for example, referred to some recent trenchant attacks on the hypothesis, and was uncertain whether it can survive them. Yet, claiming (1976, p. 96) that 'it does seem legitimate to discuss the individual strata in detail', he proceeded to devote no less than fifty pages (one tenth of his book) to an exposition of their characteristics. Cazelles adopted a similar procedure, even going as far as to sketch the individual 'theologies' of the various strata. Both these writers, however, stressed the uncertainties of the present state of Pentateuchal criticism and the need for the development of new techniques. These representative works reflect a general loss of confidence in the methods and results of the hypothesis, and a tendency, even among those who might be termed its adherents, to work with it only *faute de mieux*. This point of view is summed up by Clements, who, in a recent survey of Pentateuchal study, stated that 'No detailed and convincing alternative has been able to replace the basic recognition that the major sources JE, D and P at one time existed as separate documents' (1979, p. 97).

The 'basic recognition' to which Clements referred has in fact been challenged by a considerable number of scholars for many years. Whether or not a more plausible theory can be devised, a major re-assessment of the Documentary Hypothesis is urgently needed, especially in the light of the immense amount of research which has been done in the century since Wellhausen on narrative literature in general and on the character of biblical literature in particular. Westermann in his commentary on Genesis (1974–82) and Rendtorff among others have already discussed the shortcomings of the hypothesis in some detail.

2. *Criticisms of the Hypothesis*

Every hypothesis of whatever kind must justify itself by satisfying certain tests, viz.:

a. Are its presuppositions reasonable?
b. Are its methods sound?
c. Are those methods applied logically?
d. Does it account for the data more adequately than any alternative hypothesis?

In the course of Pentateuchal criticism during the past hundred years all these tests have been applied to the Documentary Hypothesis, though few critics have applied them all in a systematic fashion. The network of arguments employed is a very complex one; but the course of criticism can to some extent be traced.

From the very beginning, two fundamental lines of criticism have been pursued: first, negatively, *the questioning of the criteria* by which the documents were identified and reconstructed; and second, positively, a plea for a greater recognition of the part played by *the development of oral tradition* in the formation of the Pentateuch. Most of the later history of Pentateuchal criticism has been based on one or other of these, or on both of them in combination, although other considerations have also played a part.

a. *The questioning of the adequacy of the criteria*
This was concerned with the second and third of the tests listed above: with the methods employed to support the hypothesis, and their application. With regard to J and E, even the early critics like Wellhausen, Gunkel and Driver admitted that one or other of the criteria, or even a combination of them all, was insufficient for the complete separation of these two documents, and that, although their existence was incontestable, it was impossible to reconstruct them completely. The various arguments about the criteria will be assessed in the next section of this book. It is the *consequences* of the doubt cast upon them which are to be considered here.

i. The difficulty of distinguishing E from J not unnaturally raised the question whether E was not an unnecessary hypothesis; and Volz and Rudolph (1933, 1938), followed by others, sought to prove that the supposed E-passages could be accounted for in other ways. This meant that in Genesis–Numbers there were only two documents, J and P. Most scholars still accepted the existence of P as a separate document, and the new simplified analysis led, beginning with von Rad's study (1938), to an intensive study of the 'theologies' of J and P. Westermann's commentary on Genesis is a recent example of this.

ii. The opposite tendency to subdivide the 'classical' documents into a larger number, also an early development, was in fact also an attack on the criteria, that is, on their application rather than their validity. For it was based on a dissatisfaction with the lack of thoroughness displayed by Wellhausen and his school: their documents were held themselves to lack internal consistency, and must therefore be composite. The latest addition to these newly proposed documents, known as 'late J' (Winnett, 1965, Van Seters, 1975, Schmid, 1976, Schmitt, 1980) throws further doubt on the hypothesis, since by postulating a very late strand in J it upsets the Wellhausenian system of dating the documents by correlating them with periods in the history of Israel, which is an essential part of it.

But these two developments—doubt about E and the multiplication of documents—led to a more radical questioning of the hypothesis. Some scholars, beginning with Mowinckel (1930; more fully, 1964) expressed the view that the documents had not been composed each in a single stage by a single individual, but had been formed gradually over many years, so that what seemed to be evidence of yet more documents was in fact the presence of *variants* within a single document (E was, for Mowinckel, simply 'J variata'). This conclusion, which has also found support in recent years (e.g. Schulte) in turn led to yet further developments:

Firstly, some scholars (e.g. Bentzen, De Vaux, 1953, Fohrer, 1965) abandoned the concept of 'documents' and substituted one of 'strata', 'strands', 'parallel traditions' and the like—terms which, although they have the advantage of permitting flexibility of treatment, are too vague to be useful or even meaningful.

Secondly, the idea that individual documents had undergone a continuous redaction raised an even more important question in the minds of some scholars: whether it was necessary to postulate continuous sources (whether or not they were to be called 'documents') at all. The possibility was raised that the whole Pentateuch might be the product of *one single continuous* process of redaction, in which the material was gradually refined and new material added. Such a view was held by Jewish scholars like Cassuto (1961) and Segal, who had never accepted the Documentary Hypothesis; but it was also put forward as a reaction to the hypothesis by Sandmel, who cited later rabbinical procedures as a possible model for the gradual composition of the Pentateuch.

Thirdly, the discovery of variants within a single document, combined with the new importance attached in certain circles to the oral tradition, suggested the possibility that some or all of these variants might have developed not in the literary but in the oral stage of the tradition; and this led by a different route again to a rejection of the Documentary Hypothesis in favour of one which regarded the written Pentateuch as mainly a later development, simply the written record of an already fully developed oral narrative tradition together with various pieces of previously written material such as certain collections of laws.

This type of theory, represented by the Scandinavian scholars Nielsen (1954) and Engnell (1962), was supported by considerations of a cultural, psychological and aesthetic character: it was argued, on the basis of increased knowledge of the ancient Near East, that the use of writing for narrative purposes was a later cultural development, resorted to only when there was a danger of the oral tradition's being lost; that the criteria of the Documentary Hypothesis were invalid because they were based on a mistaken application to ancient literature of modern western canons of consistency and order; and finally that the documentary critics, in splitting up narratives into small scraps to be assigned to the various documents, had insensitively destroyed their character as works of art—a criterion which deserved to be taken into account no less than others. Recently this final argument has received additional support from modern literary critics such as Alter.

Fourthly, another group of scholars, dissatisfied with the criteria of the Documentary Hypothesis, developed a *thematic* approach which was not dissimilar from the aesthetic approach mentioned above in that it was a protest against the splitting up of literary units. This approach was inaugurated by Pedersen (1926, 1931), who postulated the existence of a 'Passover narrative' which, he believed, was an independent narrative complete in itself having a single theme and having been composed for use in connection with the celebration of that festival. This was, so to speak, a 'vertical section' of the Pentateuch which cut completely across the 'horizontal sections' approach of the Documentary Hypothesis and so denied the existence of continuous sources. That is to say, such 'larger units' in the Pentateuch, which were, admittedly, not homogeneous, had been each built up independently of the other narrative sections and combined with them only at a later date. This approach, which was still basically a 'literary' one, was later used by those who studied the *oral* traditions, the development of these 'larger units' being regarded by those scholars as essentially an oral rather than a literary process.

b. *The study of the oral traditions*
Although this approach to the phenomenon of the Pentateuch was at first regarded as complementary to the Documentary Hypothesis rather than as an alternative to it, it tended to undercut it, especially with regard to the first and fourth of the tests listed at the beginning of this section, namely the presuppositions of the hypothesis and its claim to be the only adequate explanation of the facts.

That the Pentateuchal documents were ultimately based on legends and other traditions which had been preserved and transmitted orally was accepted by Wellhausen and the other documentary critics; but they believed that these had been completely transformed by the authors of the documents and were in any case of no great antiquity when thus committed to writing. Wellhausen wrote: 'With regard to the Jehovistic writing it is happily agreed that in language, horizon and other features it dates substantially from the golden age of Hebrew literature—. . . the period of the kings and prophets, which preceded the dissolution of the two Israelite kingdoms by the Assyrians' (1883, p. 9; ET p. 9). With such a positive view of the literary activity of the authors of the documents it is not surprising that these scholars made no attempt to investigate the pre-literary oral tradition.

The history of the study of the oral traditions will be considered in detail in Part II below. Here we are concerned with it only in relation to its effect on the Documentary Hypothesis. It was Gunkel (1901) who argued, on the basis of examples taken from the book of Genesis, that the specific features of the oral tradition had not in fact been obliterated by the authors of the documents, but that the narrative material which now forms a continuous story is the result of the combination of a large number of quite short stories or '*Sagen*' which have been little changed, and can be identified as being each complete in itself, having its own distinct form, purpose and character. This permitted him to suggest a much earlier origin for this material than the earlier critics had done: he believed that these stories, when studied individually and without reference to their present settings, reflect quite early stages in the development of Israel as a people. This meant that the period to be considered in attempting to trace the history of the composition of the Pentateuch was much longer than that with which Wellhausen worked—a period beginning not with the 'golden age of Hebrew literature' but several centuries earlier, perhaps even with the Patriarchs themselves.

This significantly enlarged the question of the way in which the material was put together. Admittedly Gunkel did not differ significantly from Wellhausen with regard to the literary stages of the process; but he thought it reasonable to postulate a much longer and more complex process, and also a more gradual one, than had been postulated by the Documentary Hypothesis. It seemed to him probable that between the short, individual *Sagen* and the earliest documents there had been an intermediate stage in which, in the process of time, stories with common features, such as those concerned with Abraham or Jacob, had been combined into 'legend-cycles'. This was likely to have occurred in the pre-literary stage, since the motives for the formation of such 'cycles' were very different from those of the 'historians' (J and E). The aim of the latter was to compose complete histories of early Israel; the legend-cycles, on the other hand, while they marked a more advanced stage of story-telling than the individual *Sagen* with their concentration on single events, had no such 'historical' perspective.

Gunkel thus pointed the way to a much broader and more flexible approach to the subject than that of Wellhausen. It is true that he saw his work as complementary to the Documentary Hypothesis rather than as an alternative to it. For him the Pentateuch—or at least, the book of Genesis, with which he was primarily concerned—had been composed, from its basic elements, in two successive and mutually exclusive stages. The oral material, already partly formed into larger units or 'cycles', had provided a common source on which J and E separately drew, and with this the further development of the oral tradition came to an end (1901, 3rd edn, p. LXXX; 1901 b, pp. 123-24). Thus Gunkel, approaching the composition of the Pentateuch from its earliest stage and working forwards did not question the arguments of the purely documentary critics who, starting from the completed Pentateuch and working backwards, had concluded that its present text could only be explained by a theory of 'documents'.

Nevertheless his new approach was bound in the end to raise the question whether the two methods were really compatible.

Nielsen and Engnell, with some other Scandinavian scholars, answered this question in the negative. They rejected documentary criticism entirely, mainly on the grounds that its presuppositions about ancient oriental ways of thinking and attitudes towards the written word were mistaken, and substituted for it a kind of 'tradition-criticism' according to which the Pentateuch (or, more properly, Genesis–Numbers) reached virtually its present form in the course of a purely oral transmission of the traditions. The supporters of this alternative hypothesis, however, have never succeeded in providing it with the necessary backing: that is, with a fully worked out history of these traditions from the earliest short units to the completed whole (see Part II, pp. 198-202 and Knight for more detailed accounts of the work of this 'school'). Meanwhile Martin Noth had worked out such a detailed 'History of Pentateuchal Traditions'; however, he, like Gunkel, retained the Documentary Hypothesis.

Von Rad (1938) and Noth (1948) were the true successors of Gunkel. It was these two scholars who, while continuing to adhere to the Documentary Hypothesis, unwittingly opened the way to an ultimate rejection of it as incompatible with the recognition of the importance of the role played by the oral tradition. Building on Gunkel's analysis of the earliest units of the tradition, they constructed detailed theories of the way in which these units had been combined which went far beyond Gunkel's analysis.

Von Rad postulated, on the basis of Deut. 26.5-10 and other texts, the existence of a 'little creed' in which the Israelite peasant recited the events of his ancestral history at the annual offering of the firstfruits of his labours to God. The 'creed' brought together a series of elements which formed the nucleus of the later Pentateuch. Noth, building on von Rad's sketch, attempted to show precisely how these distinct 'themes' or items of tradition, each of which had originally been preserved by one of the groups which combined to form the people of Israel, had been filled out with other traditions to form a common national tradition. He thus constructed a complete 'history of Pentateuchal traditions' culminating in a single work, possibly in written form, which predated J and E.

From this it was only a step to the posing of the question whether, if the basic shape of the Pentateuch was already formed at that early period, the Documentary Hypothesis, with its further, literary stages of documents and redactors, was necessary or plausible. It was Rendtorff who, after a generation of general unease with the Documentary Hypothesis, took this step.

c. *Rendtorff's* Das überlieferungsgeschichtliche Problem des Pentateuch (*1977*)
Rendtorff started from the conviction that modern Pentateuchal studies have reached an *impasse*. Most scholars since Noth had continued to accept *both* the Documentary Hypothesis in some kind of modified form, *and* the traditio-historical method, without seriously asking whether they are mutually compatible. He was convinced that the traditio-historical method is fundamental: the growth of the Pentateuch can rightly be understood only if its study begins from its earliest stage—that is, from the shortest units on which it is based. The Documentary Hypothesis, therefore, as an hypothesis related only to a particular later stage in the process—the final one—can only be acceptable if its findings are compatible with the conclusions reached on a traditio-historical basis about the earlier stages. Rendtorff was concerned to prove that this is not the case: that the Documentary Hypothesis is only one of several possible theories about the literary stage of the development of the Pentateuch, and one which does not fit the facts.

Rendtorff should be regarded as the successor of Noth, whose ideas he has attempted to carry to their logical conclusion. He is no disciple of scholars like Nielsen, Engnell, Cassuto or Segal. He has no quarrel with the *methods* of literary criticism: on the contrary, he regards them as valid, and both recommends their use and uses them himself in building his own alternative hypothesis. It is the way in which these methods have been applied by the documentary critics to establish the hypothesis of *continuous literary works* or 'documents' running right through the Pentateuch which he regards as faulty.

Noting the widely differing opinions among the documentary critics about the number, characteristics, contents and extent of the supposed documents, Rendtorff pointed out that the critics' application of the documentary criteria had clearly failed to produce a generally accepted and convincing reconstruction of them as continuous sources—even with the help of the dubious principle that it is permissible to fill them out and to fill gaps within them by assigning to one or other document passages where the criteria are entirely missing (see his remarks about W.H. Schmidt, pp. 88-89). Consequently the sigla J, E and the rest—even including P—have no basis in reality.

It was Rendtorff's contention that the documentary criteria have been misapplied. Sometimes they have been pushed too far; at other times they have not been applied with sufficient rigour. On the one hand, differences in style between various passages assigned to a particular document have been overlooked: the style of the Joseph story (Gen. 37-50), for example, is not the same as that found in any of the 'documentary' versions of the Abraham stories, and even within these there are also stylistic differences. To explain these differences on the grounds that each document is a complex one compounded of heterogeneous elements would be to render the stylistic criterion entirely useless. The differences remain to be explained. But equally, on the other hand, the supposed distinction *between* J and E in the example of the Joseph story is based on arguments which are over-subtle.

Even more serious than the misapplication of the other criteria, in Rendtorff's opinion, is the misuse by the documentary critics of the criterion of theology and point of view. Rendtorff exposed the falsity of the claim that each document has its own characteristic and consistent theology: in fact, he maintained, each is a hotchpotch of quite different ones. Here he was especially critical of those who, like von Rad, had sought to expound the 'theology of the Yahwist'. In contrast to these views Rendtorff sought to show that the only theological consistency observable, apart from that eventually imposed on the whole material by the final redactor, is to be found within each of the larger sections of the Pentateuch (corresponding roughly to Noth's 'themes'), considered separately: the Primaeval History, the patriarchal stories, the Moses (Exodus) narrative, Sinai, the sojourn in the wilderness, the settlement in Palestine. It is these larger sections rather than the documents which provide the clue to the process by which the Pentateuch reached its characteristic form; and in this process there is no room for the documents. Theologically as in other ways, the Documentary Hypothesis and the traditio-historical approach are *alternatives* which cannot be combined.

An assessment of the contribution of Rendtorff to the solution of the Pentateuchal problem from the point of view of tradition-criticism will be attempted in Part II below. Our concern here has been solely with his criticisms of the Documentary Hypothesis; but his book undoubtedly marks a new stage in the discussion in that it puts forward a real alternative to that hypothesis which purports to cover, and offer an explanation for, the *entire* history of the growth of the Pentateuch from its smallest units to its final form.

C. *Assessment of the Documentary Hypothesis*

1. *Presuppositions*

a. *Philosophical and religio-historical*

The Documentary Hypothesis was not simply an attempt to solve a literary puzzle. The criterion to which Wellhausen attached the greatest importance for the reconstruction, out of the jumble of disparate and incongruously assembled fragments, of four separate and continuous documents was that of *religious ideas and practices*: the four documents, he argued, reflected four distinct and roughly datable stages in the religious evolution of Israel. This, indeed, is the main argument of the work significantly entitled *Prolegomena to the History of Israel*, where, referring to the crucial dating of the 'Priestly Code', he maintained that only within 'the realm of religious practices and dominant religious ideas . . . can the argument be finally settled' (p. 12; ET p. 12). It was on the basis of a particular theory, current in his time, of the evolution of Israel's religion through a series of stages from the simple and 'natural', up to the high point of the teaching of the eighth-century prophets and then down again to the complex, theocratic and formalized religion (characterized by him as 'retrograde') of the post-exilic period that each piece of Pentateuchal material was evaluated and assigned to its place in one or other of the documents, and the documents themselves ranged in chronological order and dated.

This evolutionist theory is ultimately a philosophical one, and has been thought to be traceable back through the influence of the historian Vatke—to whom Wellhausen acknowledged his indebtedness—to the philosophy of Hegel. (See Perlitt, 1965 for a different view, and Kraus, 1969, p. 264 for a criticism of Perlitt.) But even if the influence of Hegelianism on Wellhausen has sometimes been overstated, it is now recognized that the religious phenomenon of Yahwism and Judaism was far more complicated, and its history less unilinear, than Wellhausen supposed it to have been, and the dating of the various Pentateuchal texts—which contain no direct references to the periods when they were written—consequently more uncertain. (See Pedersen, 1931.)

b. *Linguistic*

Much stress was laid by the documentary critics on the linguistic and stylistic differences between the various documents. For example, S.R. Driver (1904, pp. vii-xi) listed no less than thirty-four words and phrases characteristic of P. This use of differences of language and style to distinguish a late document from earlier ones is based upon certain assumptions about the history of the language of Biblical Hebrew. Yet the most recent history of the Hebrew language (Kutscher, pp. 12ff.) recognizes only three stages in its development: archaic, standard, and late. Standard Hebrew embraces all the prose works in the Old Testament with the exception of the very late books of Chronicles, Ezra–Nehemiah, Esther and Ecclesiastes. All the prose texts of the Pentateuch fall within the category of Standard Hebrew.

The earlier grammar of Gesenius–Kautzsch (ET 1910) stated that 'In the whole series of the ancient Hebrew writings, as found in the Old Testament . . . , the language . . . remains, as regards its general character, at about the same stage of development'; though it did cautiously acknowledge 'a certain progress from an earlier to a later stage' in which 'two periods, though with some reservations, may be distinguished'. The second of these began with the end of the Babylonian exile and embraced 'certain parts of the Pentateuch' (p. 16)—presumably including P. However, the only characteristic of this second period to which the authors of this grammar were able to point was its closer approximation to Aramaic than was the case with the literature of the earlier period. But it would be difficult to find evidence of Aramaic influence in the list of the characteristic words and phrases of P compiled by Driver, and he did not attempt to do so. As for the—far fewer—differences of vocabulary between J and E, there can be no question there of evidence of an earlier and later stage of linguistic development.

It would in any case be unlikely that such basic linguistic differences, had they ever existed, would have been allowed to persist in the written prose texts as we now have them. It may be presumed that the Pentateuchal narratives would have been many times recast into 'contemporary' language: that is, into the language of the various succeeding generations which received them and transmitted them. If some of these narratives originated in the patriarchal or Mosaic periods, the language in which they were first told would presumably have been either archaic Hebrew or some other Semitic language; but no trace of this remains. Even after they were committed to writing we may presume that the language in which they were written would have been systematically 'brought up to date' by the scribes who copied them. At all events, the Pentateuch, apart from the poems which are incorporated into it, is uniformly written in Standard Biblical Hebrew.

This, of course, is not to deny that there are considerable differences of style and vocabulary in the Pentateuch. It would be surprising if this were not so: it would not have been the intention of the tradents and scribes mentioned above to create a single, monotonous style for the material which they handled. Their concern was merely to ensure its intelligibility for their own generation. But once the assumption of an historical development of the Hebrew language during the period in question is removed, it becomes possible to account for these differences of style in other ways, as will be demonstrated on pp. 55-84 below.

c. *Literary*

The Documentary Hypothesis was concerned wholly with *literary* activity: with authors, scribes and copyists, and with redactors or editors who conflated existing written texts. It was assumed that no significant part of the process of composition was to be attributed to the pre-literary stage in which it was admitted that much of the material had originated. Although the study of European folk-traditions had begun as early as the publication of collections of folktales, often in variant forms, by Jacob and Wilhelm Grimm in 1812-15, the possibility that such studies might be relevant to the study of the Pentateuchal narratives was ignored. It was assumed that the only possible solution to the problems posed by discrepancies, doublets and different points of view in these narratives was to posit the combination, by editors, of earlier written texts. Wellhausen's isolationist temperament, manifested in his persistence in ignoring scholarly work in other related fields, may account for this to some extent.

A further, hidden assumption made by the documentary critics was that the creation of new historical works by the simple conflation of older ones covering the same ground was a normal procedure in the ancient literary world. It has, admittedly, been argued by such more recent scholars as Bentzen (II, pp. 61-62) and de Vaux (1953, pp. 185-86) that analogies to this kind of literary activity do in fact exist in ancient literature. With one exception, however, the examples cited by these scholars are extremely dubious. De Vaux cited the following: the works of Arabic and Syriac historians; the use of the books of Samuel and Kings by the author of the books of Chronicles; the use of earlier documents by the author of Ezra-Nehemiah; the composition of the narratives in the book of Jeremiah; the composition of Deuteronomy; and the Epic of Gilgamesh. But in none of these cases did the author conflate *continuous* sources, each covering the entire series of events and the entire period treated by the final work: rather, he quoted or adapted various written sources of limited extent which he inserted into his own narrative one after the other to form a single, extensive work. This was a method of historiography frequently employed by ancient historians; but it is in no way comparable with that postulated by the Documentary Hypothesis. In fact, it has more in common with some other theories about the composition of the Pentateuch, especially the Fragment and Supplement Hypotheses.

The only close analogy from the ancient world cited by Bentzen and de Vaux is the harmony of the Four Gospels known as the *Diatessaron*, compiled by Tatian in the second century AD. Whether the *purpose* of Tatian's work could properly be said to have been similar to that of the supposed Pentateuchal redactors is debatable; but in any case it is doubtful whether a single work produced in the early Christian era and subsequent to the work of both the Greek and early Roman historians, and unique of its kind, provides an adequate analogy to theirs.

d. *Cultural*

At the time when Wellhausen wrote his works on the Pentateuch very much less was known about the cultures, civilizations and thought-processes of the peoples of the ancient Near East than is now known. But what knowledge did exist on these subjects was mainly ignored by him and his immediate successors. Nevertheless, behind the assertions of the documentary critics there lay some very substantial assumptions about these matters. Failing to allow for the vast cultural and psychological differences between the literate and scholarly society of western Europe in the nineteenth century AD in which they lived and that of a relatively obscure ancient Semitic people of the first millennium BC, they assumed that the authors and scribes of ancient Israel would have done their work along the same lines as those on which they themselves would have worked if they had been faced with the same task.

i. *They assumed that the purpose of each of the authors of the documents was to write a consistent and continuous account of the origins and early history of Israel*, suitably adapted to the national, religious and ethical notions prevailing in their time: they were, in other words, by intention, historians. So, for example, Skinner wrote: 'Of all the Hebrew historians whose writings have been preserved to us, J is the most gifted and the most brilliant' (1930, 2nd edn, p. xiv). It will be argued later in this book that the Pentateuch *in its final form* is indeed a work of history, written according to the literary canons prevailing in the ancient world in the sixth century BC. But this is a very different matter from the concept of the author of 'J' as a brilliant historian of the early first millennium BC, at an early stage in the history of an emerging nation, writing the first great historical work of all time with no literary models to guide him. It must be asked whether this is not an anachronistic concept.

More recently von Rad has sought to support this idea with his view of the 'Yahwist' as a product of a period of remarkable 'enlightenment' in the reign of Solomon inspired by contacts with the Egyptian court and the Canaanite cities conquered by David and Solomon (e.g. 1938, p. 63; ET p. 69). This hypothesis, which assigns an even earlier date to J than that proposed by the earlier documentary critics, is hardly convincing, since on von Rad's own admission (1944, pp. 1-2; ET pp. 166-67) neither Egypt nor any other contemporary or earlier civilization had a sufficient 'historical sense' to produce works of history. He himself wrote: 'There are only two peoples in antiquity who really wrote history: the Greeks, and, long before them, the Israelites' (1944, p. 2; ET p. 167).

Nor are von Rad's three 'explanations' of the phenomenon of the 'Yahwist' (the possession by ancient Israel of a unique 'historical sense', a 'talent for narrative presentation' and a 'belief in the sovereignty of God in history' [pp. 3-7; ET pp. 168-70]) true explanations at all: they are simply conclusions reached on the basis of the presupposition of an early date for the Yahwist and drawn from the supposed phenomenon rather than arguments in support of it. It might be argued that the so-called 'Succession Narrative' in 2 Samuel and the early chapters of 1 Kings, to which von Rad pointed in his 1944 article as a supreme example of Israelite historiography of the time of Solomon, supports his point about the Yahwist; but the early date of the Succession Narrative has been questioned recently, and in any case it is not a real parallel to J, since it chronicles only a particular series of events within the span of a single king's reign.

It must then be concluded that the concept of the author of J as both a brilliant historian of the early first millennium BC and also as the earliest of all historians, the inventor of a literary genre unknown even to the finest cultures of his time, is an extremely bold assumption, and that the point made by Engnell (e.g. 1969, p. 53) and others must be taken seriously: that the documentary critics are guilty (in the cases of J and E) of a serious anachronism.

This conclusion is supported by the fact that there is no reference in the Pentateuch or elsewhere in the Old Testament to these 'histories': indeed, among all the references to written material in the Pentateuch itself there is no mention of the composition of written prose narratives or to any concern for the preservation of a written narrative tradition. It does not necessarily follow from this that no tradition of narrative prose writing at all existed before the time of the Deuteronomists; but the hypothesis that such comprehensive histories existed in earlier times is purely speculative. Although it is probable that a scribal establishment was maintained at the court in Jerusalem from at least the time of Solomon and also possibly in the Temple, with similar institutions later in the northern kingdom, the earliest indisputable references to major scribal activity of a literary, rather than merely of an administrative nature come from the time of Hezekiah and later, and these do not mention the composition of prose narrative: we learn only of a collection of proverbs compiled by royal scribes (Prov. 25.1) and of a 'book of the law' discovered in the temple at Jerusalem in the reign of Josiah (2 Kgs 22.8). Although arguments from silence cannot be regarded as completely conclusive, it is, to say the least, surprising that the very existence of books like 'J' and 'E', which could hardly have been 'private' works but must have been in some sense 'official histories' and presumably in some way normative, should have left no mark, as far as we can tell, on the religious beliefs or national sentiments of pre-exilic Israel.

For it is a fact that the contents of these works seem to have been unknown until the period of the Exile. As has frequently been remarked, the very names of Abraham, Isaac, Jacob and Moses are, with one exception, totally absent from any passage in the prophetical books which can be considered pre-exilic. Elsewhere in the Old

Testament the occurrences of these names are confined to the Deuteronomistic History and a few of the Psalms; and all, or almost all, of the former are to be attributed for various reasons to the Deuteronomistic editor, while the latter also appear to reflect post-exilic traditions. The prophet Hosea alone (12.3-5, 13-14; EVV 12.2-4, 12-13) refers to incidents in the life of Jacob which bear some resemblance to narratives in Genesis, but there are differences of detail which suggest that Hosea did not derive his information from Genesis. In fact there is no passage in any of the indisputably pre-exilic literature of the Old Testament which can be shown to refer to narratives assigned by the documentary critics to J or E.

ii. *A similar assumption seems to have been made with regard to the redactors* of the documents. For example, in the case of R^{JE}, although the documentary critics made very few explicit statements about the motives of this redactor, they appear to have taken it for granted that his motive was basically the same as that of the authors of the documents which they conflated: his intention was to produce a new 'history of early Israel'—that is, one which was an 'improved version' in that it faithfully and reverently preserved all that could be preserved of the traditions of both north and south.

But in one respect the notion of the work of the redactors entertained by the documentary critics appears to have conflicted with their own views about the original documents. The identification and reconstruction of the documents were based on the assumption that each document was consistent with itself, in language, style and theology or point of view. Without this concept of consistency the hypothesis would fall to the ground. Yet the hypothesis depends, equally, on the concept of the *in*consistency apparent in the larger works which are supposed to be the work of the redactors: that is to say, the actual distinction made by the critics between one passage or phrase and another as having originally belonged to different documents is made on the basis of the redactor's having left two conflicting passages or phrases side by side with no attempt to conceal their incompatibility.

Thus the hypothesis can only be maintained on the assumption that, while consistency was the hallmark of the various documents, *in*consistency was the hallmark of the redactors (see Cassuto, 1941, p. 67). Even if it is granted that the redactor's desire to include as much material as possible from both his sources took precedence over his desire that his completed work should be consistent, there is a serious difficulty here for the Documentary Hypothesis: for if the redactors were manifestly not primarily concerned with achieving consistency in their 'improved' history, why should it be assumed that consistency was an overriding concern of the authors of the original documents, whose purpose was more or less the same as that of the redactors? And if after all this was *not* the overriding concern of the authors, the criteria for separating one document from another lose their force.

iii. Behind the criterion of consistency which—illogically as it has now been seen to be—was employed by the documentary critics for the separation of the documents there lay *a further assumption about notions of consistency*: their application of this criterion not only made no allowances for differences in this regard between the ideas of the modern world and those of the ancient Near East, but was even more rigid than that practised by the writers of their own time, and perhaps of any other time. They assumed that a writer never makes a statement twice over, never allows himself a digression but always sticks to the point, and never contradicts himself even in the smallest matter. Any failing of this order was seized upon as evidence of a conflation of documents.

Such absolute consistency may perhaps be appropriate to the work of the scholar in his study, where meticulous attention to detail is essential; but it is not generally applicable to the literary artist, as could easily be demonstrated by the perusal of modern fiction—and, in particular, of some of the more lengthy and diffuse novels published during the same century as the early publications of the documentary critics themselves. Still less can it properly be applied to the literature of the ancient world.

This was recognized by the best of the documentary critics themselves, although they failed to perceive the full implications of this insight. Eissfeldt himself (1922, p. 5, quoted by Bentzen, II, p. 31) wrote: 'In the mind of an Israelite story-teller from the ninth or fifth century many things can lie beside one another which to us seem completely irreconcilable, and this the more as . . . we always have to do with adaptation of narrative handed down orally'. More recently it has been observed that the Temple Scroll from Qumran exhibits precisely the same 'inconsistencies' of style (e.g. abrupt changes of person, number and verbal forms) as are used by the documentary critics to distinguish different documents, although it was presumably compiled by a single author rather than over a protracted period of time. Moreover, these stylistic oscillations occur not only where biblical material has been combined with new material, but even within the new material itself (Greenberg, pp. 185-86).

That the cultural differences between ancient Israel and modern western Europe invalidate many of the judgments made by the documentary critics about what could or could not be attributed to a single author has now been widely recognized, although some scholars who continue to support the Documentary Hypothesis in its general lines (e.g. de Vaux, 1953, p. 188) argue with some justification that not all these judgments can be disposed of in this way. They argue that in the case of two different versions of the same story (for example, that of Abraham's pretence that Sarah was his sister) or of stories in which many details are repeated (for example, the story of the Flood) a duplication of material cannot be denied. This may be true; but it does not prove the existence of two separate documents later conflated, since it cannot be shown whether this duplicated material was brought together at a written or at an oral stage of composition. In any case it remains true that the work of the documentary critics is based on a misconceived application of modern—and even scholarly—principles of consistency to literary texts whose authors were entirely unaware that such principles existed. Engnell was correct in his judgment that 'Our Western desk logic fails to appreciate the Semitic way of thinking'.

It has also been pointed out (e.g. by Westermann, 1974, pp. 771-73, and Alter) that the juxtaposition of dual versions of the same event (such as Gen. 1 and 2) may be due not to a redactor's anxiety to include as much material as possible from two different documents but to a positive theological intention to present the event from two different angles, an intention which overrode such other considerations as the 'consistency' beloved of the documentary critics.

iv. *The methods attributed to the redactors* by the documentary critics also contain some hidden assumptions. Critics such as Volz and Rudolph (pp. 6, 145) and Segal (p. xii), and even some who supported the hypothesis in a modified form (e.g. de Vaux, 1953, p. 187) objected to their 'scissors and paste' methods, especially to their readiness to split texts into tiny fragments often comprising no more

than quarter-verses or even single words or phrases, in order to
assign them to different documents. These scholars argued that such
a procedure could only be 'an invention of (modern) erudition' (Volz,
p. 14) and that its attribution to ancient redactors was unwarranted
and even absurd. Volz accused the documentary critics not only of
being ignorant of ancient psychology but of projecting pure fantasy
into their work: the procedure which they attributed to the redactors
was not imaginable under any circumstances; it was not a practice
which 'occurs in real life'.

Among more recent critics, Alter, writing from the point of view of
modern literary criticism, expounded this view in more detail (pp.
133-40), asserting that when the supposed composite narratives of
the Pentateuch are studied from a literary point of view, it is possible
to find excellent literary reasons for many of the supposed
contradictions which led the documentary critics to use such
'scissors and paste' methods. The 'textual patchwork' turned out to
be a 'purposeful pattern'. Thus in Gen. 42 (part of the Joseph Story)
it is stated twice (in vv. 27-28 and again in v. 35) that Joseph's
brothers returning home from Egypt found their money returned in
their sacks. This duplication was regarded by commentators who
accepted the Documentary Hypothesis (e.g. Driver, 1904; Skinner,
1910) as due to an insertion of part of a 'J' version of the story
(vv. 27-28) into an 'E' narrative. Alter did not deny that there is a
logical contradiction here: he maintained that 'The writer was
perfectly aware of the contradiction but viewed it as a superficial one'
(p. 138). He argued that the writer's recounting the incident twice,
each time with a different emphasis, was deliberately done in order to
draw out from it its full significance: 'he reached for this effect of
multi-faceted truth by setting in sequence two different versions that
brought into focus two different dimensions of his subject' (p. 140).
Alter interpreted other so-called 'composite passages' in the same
way.

It may be pertinently observed that Alter and the documentary
critics were each making an assumption about the psychology and
literary methods of the ancient writer, that both of these assumptions
are tinged with their makers' experience of their own (modern)
times, and that neither of them can be proved. Nevertheless there is a
good deal of difference between the two assumptions. The
documentary critics could offer no reason for a redactional procedure
which, on the face of it, appears to entail a pointless and indeed

unintelligent impairment of an otherwise smooth narrative, except that the redactor was determined to include something from the other document, 'J', if he could possibly do so. They could do little more than assert that—strange as it might seem —that is the kind of thing that the redactors did. Alter, on the other hand, was able to present the 'author' of the story as it now appears in the text (he was not greatly interested in the question whether he was an 'author' or a redactor) as an intelligent and even brilliant writer who was aware of a certain inconsistency in his narrative, but whose concept of consistency was flexible and at the same time subordinated by him to another purpose which he—and presumably his readers—regarded as more important. Whether Alter's reading, as a literary critic, is correct or not, it has the merit of the perception that the reading of the documentary critics, based on the assumption that the redactors worked on the more or less mechanical 'scissors and paste' method, entailed an improbably low estimate of the redactor's intelligence.

v. *The documentary critics further assumed that it was possible to assess the aesthetic qualities of each of the documents.* Gunkel (1901, 9th edn, p. LXXXVII; ET p. 134) wrote: 'J has the most lively, vivid narratives, while E, on the other hand, has a series of moving, lachrymose stories'; the unfortunate P, on the other hand, is characterized by him (p. XCIII; ET p. 146) with the phrase 'prosaic erudition', and as one to whom, 'as to many another scholar, a feeling for poetry was denied'! Following Gunkel, almost all the later Introductions to the Old Testament have reiterated these judgments.

Aesthetic judgments are inevitably subjective, and it may be thought that such judgments about ancient literature are worthless unless, as is not the case here, the writings in question can be set in a wider literary context. But a further question can be raised about these particular judgments. They are plausible only on a very strict view of the authors of the documents as having been complete masters of their material: as having invented the stories which they relate, or at least rewritten them entirely in accordance with their own individual genius. This seems, in fact, to have been the opinion of Wellhausen himself; but many of the documentary critics disagreed with this view and regarded the 'authors' of the documents as primarily collectors of oral material rather than original writers. This opinion led them into serious difficulties with their aesthetic judgments.

These difficulties are well illustrated by the inconsistencies into which Gunkel himself was led. As a result of his studies of the individual stories in Genesis, he reached the enthusiastic conclusion that 'the *Sagen* of Israel, especially those of Genesis, are perhaps the most beautiful and the most profound ever known on earth' (p. XII; ET p. 11). But if the authors of J and E are primarily, as he believed, 'not masters, but rather servants of their subjects', whose 'prime quality was fidelity' to the oral tradition, it is difficult to speak of J as 'lively and vivid' while E is 'lachrymose'. Gunkel tried to solve this problem partly by qualifying his conception of their fidelity and partly by supposing that the two 'collectors' used different oral sources which differed in character from one another; but he was unable to explain why this should have been so. It would seem that the only way to maintain these aesthetic judgments about J and E would be to think of them as original writers who depended little, if at all, on earlier material and so were able to imprint their genius on their writings. But it is difficult to accept the view that within a comparatively short space of time there appeared in Israel not merely one, but two writers who composed original 'historical' works covering more or less the same ground in a previously unknown genre.

In more recent times the application of aesthetic criteria to sections of the Pentateuch has caused further difficulties for the Documentary Hypothesis. In particular, von Rad's treatment of the Joseph Story from an aesthetic point of view (1953) was on much surer ground than the aesthetic judgments about the various documents, since he was able to compare it with a well-known genre of Egyptian literature, the 'novella', whose aesthetic character and purpose are not in doubt. Von Rad characterized this story (Gen. 37–50) as 'a novel through and through' (1953, p. 120; ET p. 292). Yet it is clear from his other works (e.g. his commentary on Genesis) that, following the usual documentary analysis, he also regarded it as the result of the inter-weaving of J and E. He attempted to reconcile these two opinions by asserting (1956, 9th edn, p. 304; ET p. 343) that 'the redactor combined them' (i.e. J and E) 'in such a way that he . . . created an even richer narrative'!

The implausibility of this assertion reveals the fact that von Rad simply refused to admit the consequences of his study of the Joseph Story for the Documentary Hypothesis: that is to say, that that hypothesis stands in the way of an appreciation of the undoubted aesthetic qualities of those chapters. Since the chapters in question form a substantial part of the book of Genesis, the implications for the hypothesis as a whole are serious (see Whybray, pp. 522-28). Moreover, other recent writers have produced impressive arguments to show that in other parts of the Pentateuch as well, it is only when the Documentary Hypothesis is set aside that the true aesthetic qualities of the narrative can be fully appreciated.

2. Assessment of the Criteria

a. Language and style

It is to a large extent inevitable that the study of the biblical narratives should reflect the literary standards of the literary world of the critics themselves rather than those of the period in which the narratives were composed, since very little is known about the latter. Ancient Near Eastern writers of the second and first millennia BC did not, as far as is known, compose treatises on literary style. Information about their stylistic conventions, therefore, can only be deduced from the extant literary works themselves. Moreover, comparison with other Near Eastern narrative prose literature is hardly possible for the biblical critic, since few examples of comparable literature exist.

Further, although some general notion of literary conventions may be obtainable from internal evidence, this is insufficient for the purpose of establishing whether a narrative or narrative complex is composite or unitary. It cannot tell us, for example, whether an Israelite author might have varied his style and choice of words from one passage to another, whether he might have divided a lengthy narrative into more or less self-contained 'chapters', and if so, how far he might have found it necessary to provide verbal links between these, or whether he might have used the device of repetition for emphasis or for some other purpose—in short, what his *compositional* techniques were.

The principles of consistency applied by the documentary critics are therefore not derived from the texts themselves: they are modern principles derived from modern literature and imposed on the text. The documentary critic starts from the assumption, which has been commonplace since the time of Astruc, of the existence of 'documents' combined by redactors, and uses these principles to find what he is looking for. He singles out such phenomena as 'joins' and 'links', together with variations of style and vocabulary, as examples of the techniques of redactors or of multiple authorship without considering the possibility that these may in fact be the literary techniques of the biblical historians themselves.

i. One of the main criteria employed by the documentary critics to distinguish one document from another is that of consistency in the *choice of words*. Although, as we have seen, the narratives are all written in 'standard Hebrew', they observed that in some passages particular words or phrases are used with great frequency while in others they occur rarely or not at all. Lists were compiled of words and phrases held to be characteristic of the various documents; and on this basis whole narratives, and even single verses or small parts of verses, were assigned to one document or another.

A particular form of this kind of reasoning is one which is based not simply on general considerations of 'characteristic' vocabulary but more specifically on the supposed use of synonyms in different passages or sentences. Lists were again compiled of pairs of words believed to be identical in meaning and to have been used as alternatives by different writers. Thus whereas one document speaks of Sinai, another uses the term Horeb. Similar 'pairs' include Canaanite/Amorite, Reuel/Jethro (names of Moses's father-in-law), two words for 'maidservant' (in the patriarchal stories), two words for 'sack' (in the Joseph Story). Where both members of such a pair occur in the same narrative but not in juxtaposition, it was concluded that two accounts of the same incident had been combined into one.

A number of objections can be raised against the validity of this criterion.

Firstly, the concept of vocabulary 'characteristic' of the work of a particular author needs clarification. If *exclusive* use of certain words is what is meant, the use of this criterion might be justified if the narrative texts of the Pentateuch formed part of an extensive body of Hebrew prose. In fact, as Noth pointed out (1948, p. 21; ET p. 21), nothing is known of the common speech of ordinary Israelites of the period in question apart from the few texts which are available to us in the Old Testament, and these are quite insufficient to enable fine distinctions to be made between one writer and another on the basis of their choice of words. If, on the other hand, 'characteristic' means no more than occurring more frequently in the work of one author than of another, this criterion has even less validity.

Secondly, in some cases it may be questioned whether the pairs of words cited are in fact, properly speaking, synonyms. Slight nuances of meaning frequently prompt a speaker or writer to use now one, now another word in different contexts or circumstances. It cannot be proved, for example, that 'Canaanite' and 'Amorite', even if they refer to precisely the same group of persons, had exactly the same *connotation* for an ancient Israelite (it is equally impossible to prove the contrary!). It must be recognized that dead languages are never perfectly understood by those who come after, particularly when the amount of extant literature is so small, and that our present knowledge of the subtleties of ancient Hebrew is not equal to the task of making judgments of this kind.

Thirdly, the criterion is also too rigid in that it does not make allowance for another familiar phenomenon of speech: the unconscious and *apparently* motiveless and inexplicable alternation between one word and another. (There may be various hidden reasons for this; one possible cause is that at the time of speaking or writing, one word was in process of succeeding another in common speech: the oscillation by the speaker between one and another may simply reflect, without his necessarily being aware of it, a state of indecision in his mind; he is in fact in process of making the change in his own usage. This phenomenon is observable in the oscillation betwen 'you' and 'thou/thee' in the plays of Shakespeare. It is possible that the alternation between the two words for 'sack' in the Joseph Story arose in this way.)

Fourthly, behind all the discussion of consistency in the choice of words, as behind all the criteria, lies the question of the nature of the material handled by the Pentateuchal narrators. Unless it is to be supposed that they rewrote all this material entirely in their own words, they are reproducing or at least reflecting variants in the oral tradition. Certain word-pairs at least, such as Sinai/Horeb or Reuel/ Jethro, may be examples of such oral variants. But this does not prove the existence of more than one *document*.

Fifthly, many of the word-pairs occur only in a very restricted area of the Pentateuch: e.g. the pairs of words meaning 'maidservant' and 'sack'. Even if they proved the existence of two documentary sources in a particular narrative, they cannot prove the existence of longer, continuous documents. It cannot be shown, for example, that either of the words for 'sack' occurs in the same document as one of the words for 'maidservant', since the two pairs do not occur in the same narrative area. To prove that this is the case would involve the use of other kinds of evidence.

ii. As has already been remarked (pp. 23, 34, 44, 53), most Introductions to the Old Testament, including quite recent ones, set out *the general stylistic characteristics of the various documents*. These descriptions vary little from one scholar to another. J is universally depicted as a literary masterpiece. The adjectives used to describe his style include the following: noble, concrete, vivid, picturesque, graceful, delicate. P, by contrast, is arid, stiff, lacking in vividness, formalistic, fond of fixed phrases, repetitious, pedantic. The style of E appears to have been more difficult to characterize. The only characteristic of E which seems to have deeply impressed the critics is a supposed tendency, less evident in J, to depict the emotions of his characters. But the critics' difficulties in finding definite characteristic traits in the narratives they attribute to E are evident. Pfeiffer, for example (pp. 176-77), having stated that the style of E is 'subtly different from that of J', offered the opinion that E is 'more detailed. . ., more prolix' than J, citing Gen. 31.11-13 (E) in contrast with Gen. 31.3 (J); but in the next paragraph he admitted that 'occasionally, however, E is laconic to the point of obscurity'! Especially in view of the rather meagre quantity of material assigned to E, this is tantamount to saying that in this respect at least E has *no* discernible characteristics. Indeed, the contrast between prolixity and laconism, both of which Pfeiffer finds in E, would no doubt have amply sufficed to 'prove' the existence of *two* documents in this material if this had served the purposes of the documentary critics in other respects.

This inability of a distinguished documentary critic to recognize the consequences of his own analysis can only foster suspicion about the way in which the stylistic criterion is applied in general. With regard, for example, to the assertion—which commands general assent among the documentary critics—that J, in contrast to E, does not depict emotion, a story like Gen. 18.9-15 (J), which relates Sarah's bitter laughter on hearing Yahweh's promise of a child, followed by her denial, motivated by fear, that she had in fact laughed, would seem to be no less descriptive of emotion than E's account of Hagar's despair when abandoned by her child in the wilderness (Gen. 21.14-16). This is, of course, a subjective judgment; but the fact that it *is* necessarily a subjective judgment only serves to emphasize the inconclusiveness of the stylistic criterion as applied to the identification of J and E passages.

Equally damaging is the fact that the documentary critics generalized about the *uniformity of the style of particular documents* in complete disregard of the evidence. Westermann (1974, pp. 766-67) correctly drew attention to the striking differences between the styles of three stories in particular which are attributed to J: Gen. 12.10-20; Gen. 24; and the 'J' version of Gen. 37-50. Gen. 12.10-20 is a story remarkable for its brevity: all superfluous detail is avoided, leaving the bare skeleton of the events of Abraham's sojourn in Egypt for the reader to fill out. Gen. 24, on the other hand, takes 67 verses (according to the modern verse-divisions) to tell an equally simple story of Abraham's servant's journey to seek a wife for Isaac, and is generally regarded as one of the finest narratives in the Old Testament. It takes a particular delight in detail, and especially in extended dialogue. The Joseph Story with its foreign setting, complicated plot and multiplication of scenes ranging between Palestine and Egypt and covering the whole of Joseph's life, is clearly again quite different in character from either of the others. Although it is not impossible that all these narratives could be the work of the same writer, the literary techniques employed are so different that it is meaningless to try to reduce them to a single formula. To say that J was a collector who at least sometimes incorporated his material unchanged into his work is no answer to the problem, since this proposition would invalidate the stylistic argument altogether.

It is now accepted by many scholars that it is difficult, if not impossible, to distinguish J from E, at least on grounds of style. Almost all scholars, however, still maintain that a difference of style is unmistakable between the 'older material' and P. In attempting to assess this opinion it is important to observe that the only valid kind of comparison would be one which was restricted to passages belonging to the same literary genre. J and E as defined by the documentary critics are essentially narrative sources. It is true that they incorporate a certain amount of legal material; but it is generally agreed that the law-codes are not integral to the documents in which they are now set, and therefore are not to be regarded as examples of their styles.

Much of the non-legal material attributed to P may be described as formal and schematic: genealogies, lists, notes of dates and ages, headings and summaries, itineraries, etc. It has been pointed out by Rendtorff (1977, pp. 125ff.) among others that there is in fact no stylistic evidence to connect these passages with the style either of the narratives or of the laws usually attributed to P. It is true that many examples of the former, for example the series of 'toledot' formulae (e.g. 'This is the book of the generations [*toledot*] of Adam', Gen. 5.1) and chronological notes such as 'Noah was six hundred years old when the flood came upon the earth' (Gen. 7.6), are probably best understood as belonging to a structural scheme which may well be editorial; but there is no evidence to associate this with other supposed P material. Rendtorff also pointed out (p. 136) that the grammatical structure even of this material—particularly with regard to the formation of the numerals—is not uniform.

Brief notes such as these are inevitably—to use terms applied to P by the documentary critics—'formal' and 'arid' in a sense which is true of any formal record: it would be foreign to their nature and function if they were vivid or inspiring. The same is true, as Rendtorff once again pointed out (p. 125) of what are clearly summarizing or recapitulating statements such as Gen. 19.29, which marks the end of the story of Lot in Sodom. Moreover, some passages ascribed to J, such as his genealogies, have precisely the same 'arid' character as those attributed to P. For the purpose of assessing P's *narrative* style it is best to set aside the small scraps within the 'JE' narratives which are usually assigned to P, and to take as examples only complete narratives and substantial sections of narratives, where general stylistic characteristics can be clearly seen. A fact which emerges plainly from this procedure is the great stylistic *variety* which these narratives display.

The story of the creation of the world (Gen. 1.1–2.4a) is without parallel in the Old Testament. Its style has often been, rightly, contrasted with that of Gen. 2.4b-25 (J); but the two narratives are in no sense parallel. Gen. 1 is, as is generally admitted, based on one or more older, originally non-Israelite accounts whose style and structure were already fixed: there was little opportunity here for the Israelite author to give free expression to his own style.

Gen. 23, the account of Abraham's purchase of the cave of Machpelah from Ephron the Hittite, also has features which make it unique among the narratives of the Old Testament. It has been argued that it shows an interest in legal matters which is characteristic of P, the bulk of whose material consists of laws; but Rendtorff pointed out (p. 129) that only one verse (17) is couched in legal style; moreover, unlike the cultic laws, it is a 'profane' story in which God does not appear. In other respects its style is reminiscent of 'J': in its prolixity it resembles chapter 24 (in both cases a simple incident is told in great detail with extensive dialogue, a trait supposedly quite unlike P's normal brevity); and in the prominence which it gives to a dialogue between two persons which is fundamentally an attempt to secure a bargain it most resembles 18.22-33 (Yahweh's dialogue with Abraham about the fate of the cities of the plain), which is itself unique among the narratives attributed to J.

In the story of the Plagues (Exod. 7–11) some substantial passages (7.1-13; 8.5-7, 15-19; 9.8-12; 11.9-10) are attributed to P; but from the stylistic point of view there is nothing to distinguish these from the remainder of the narrative: the whole sequence has its own very distinctive style consisting of constantly changing variations on a basic structure.

These examples, to which others could be added, show that 'P', like the other supposed 'documents', has no distinctive narrative style of its own. The narratives which have been attributed to it vary considerably in this respect, and some of them might with equal plausibility have been attributed to J. This fact is generally unperceived, ignored or implausibly explained away by writers on this subject. Thus McEvenue, in the most detailed study of P's style yet to appear, rejected Gen. 1 and 23 as being untypical of P and so unsuitable for his purpose, and lamely accounted for this inconvenient fact by remarking that P 'used sources' at these points in his work (p. 22). Instead McEvenue chose to analyse three passages: the 'P' elements in the Flood story (Gen. 6–9) and in the 'spy story' (Num. 13–14), and the account of the oath sworn by God to Abraham (Gen. 17). These passages were chosen on the grounds that here it is possible to compare the style of P with corresponding material from JE. There is, however, a circular argument here, since he had first to make the assumption—following one or other of the earlier documentary analyses, themselves partly based on stylistic arguments— of the existence of separate JE and P narratives which can be clearly defined.

It was admittedly not McEvenue's purpose to prove the existence of P as a continuous source running through the Pentateuch: his aim was merely to confirm and add precision to earlier assessments of P's style. However, his method was inadequate even for this limited aim, since he confined his analysis to only three passages. Nothing short of an analysis of the whole of 'P'—or at least of its narrative sections—could have defined the style of the work.

That there are stylistic links between many of the passages generally ascribed to P cannot of course be denied. It would be idle, for example, to deny that the description in Gen. 6.20 of the animals entering the Ark as 'every beast according to its kind, and all the cattle according to their kinds, and every creeping thing that creeps on the earth according to its kind' echoes the language of Gen. 1.20-26; and there are many other instances of this sort. But such stylistic links can be explained in a number of ways apart from the hypothesis of P as a separate document running through the Pentateuch, a hypothesis which cannot be demonstrated on the basis of a stylistic analysis.

Aesthetic considerations. As has been stated above, the documentary critics based their analysis to a large extent on supposed unevennesses and incongruites within the narratives. These they attributed to the clumsy work of the redactors, who had conflated originally separate narratives and narrative complexes, sometimes disrupting them by the insertion of entire narratives from one document into another, and at other times conflating two parallel narratives to form a new one in a process which involved splitting each into small pieces and then reassembling the fragments in a new way. The criteria employed by the critics to detect this operation will be dealt with in detail below. Our present concern is with the stylistic aspect of their work: with its *aesthetic implications*.

The critics' separation of the documents was made partly on the basis of an aesthetic judgment: it was believed that the redactors had destroyed the aesthetic qualities which had been present in the original documents. All the Introductions to the Old Testament which accepted the Documentary Hypothesis contained sections emphasizing the superior qualities of J and E as literary compositions, and, at least by implication, the lack of aesthetic perception shown by the redactors (and usually also the inferior literary quality of P). As recently as 1973 Cazelles was still expressing this view:

> The work of literary criticism, if it is carried out with sensitivity, makes it possible to reintegrate fine harmonious compositions in all their artistic polish, whereas the narrative in its present form fails to satisfy all the requirements either of art or of psychology (p. 102).

The opponents of the Documentary Hypothesis, however, advanced precisely the same arguments as these against it. Thus Cassuto, commenting on the dismemberment of Gen. 27 into J and E, wrote that this story (of Jacob's obtaining the blessing from Isaac by deceit) is

> a classical example of oustandingly beautiful narrative art, and by dismembering it we ... destroy a wonderful literary work (1961, p. 96).

Volz and Rudolph made this point again and again in their study of Genesis; and Noth, although he remained in general a supporter of the Documentary Hypothesis, acknowledged that

> Volz and Rudolph undoubtedly deserve the credit for having wrested from customary literary criticism the literary unity of many a beautiful story (1948, p. 24; ET p. 24).

Similarly Segal argued that documentary analysis

> has broken up many a charming old tale into ... fragments ... and has thus destroyed the beauty and symmetry of the tale and the coherence and logical sequence of its parts (p. 20).

Clearly what is beautiful to one scholar is a shambles to another. In the face of these diametrically opposed opinions we are bound to consider whether the aesthetic criterion has any value at all. Licht (quoted with approval by Moberly, pp. 25-26) deserves attention when he writes:

> One should never use one's aesthetic observations to evaluate the ... integrity of a passage. ... It is far too easy to find some aesthetic perfection when we look for it *because* one needs it as an argument to establish the integrity of a given story (p. 146).

The argument cuts both ways. But it seems that we must draw the conclusion that only if it were possible to establish some objective criterion of literary merit would it be safe to use aesthetic arguments either to prove or to disprove the Documentary Hypothesis. It is evident that no such criterion has been discovered; and, despite the efforts of writers like Alter—who has no axe to grind in this respect— to extract from the text itself tangible evidence of literary art, it seems unlikely that there will ever be sufficient unanimity to use this kind of argument effectively.

iv. *The criterion of the use of different names for the Deity* properly belongs to that concerning distinctive items of vocabulary. It is here singled out for special treatment, however, because it has played a particularly important part in the history of Pentateuchal criticism. The claim has even been made for it (Volz in Volz and Rudolph, p. 16; Segal, p. 10) that it is the primary criterion by which the whole Documentary Hypothesis stands or falls.

God is referred to in the Pentateuch by a number of different names or epithets; but two of these—Yahweh and Elohim—are the predominant ones, and it was on the basis of the occurrence of these in different Pentateuchal texts that the Documentary Hypothesis was first put forward. It was the observation that in some narratives in Genesis God is called Elohim while in others he is known as Yahweh which led to the surmise by Astruc that two originally separate documents had been combined to form the text of Genesis. These came to be known as the Yahwistic and Elohistic documents. Later, however, the situation was complicated by investigations which led to the conclusion that the Elohistic document was not unitary: that there were in fact not one but two documents in which God was called Elohim and not Yahweh. One of these corresponds to what is now generally known as P. The criterion of the divine names is obviously not applicable to the problem of distinguishing E from P, and can at best do no more than help to distinguish J from the rest of the material.

There is another limitation to the application of the criterion: it has no validity beyond the book of Genesis and the first few chapters of Exodus. From that point onwards Elohim as a name for God ceases to be commonly used in *any* of the material: *all three* documents, as identified by means of other criteria, normally use only one name—Yahweh—for God. This change of terminology by E and P in the course of their narrative was explained by the critics as due to the peculiar view of these two 'theologians' about the time when Yahweh first revealed his true name Yahweh to mankind. Whereas J placed this event very early in the history of mankind (Gen. 4.26), E and P both state that the name was first revealed to Moses (Exod. 3.13-15 and 6.2-8 respectively), having previously been totally unknown. The critics believed that E and P for this reason avoided the use of the name Yahweh in that part of their narrative which preceded this revelation to Moses.

This theory is hardly convincing. Since both the authors of E and P and their readers would themselves have been familiar with the name Yahweh, there is no reason why these writers should not from the very outset have used this proper name of God except when quoting the words of their characters. There is, for example, no reason why Genesis could not have begun with the statement that in the beginning *Yahweh*—rather than Elohim—created the heavens and the earth. Some other explanation for the relatively frequent use of Elohim in Genesis as compared with the rest of the Pentateuch seems to be required.

However this may be, the fact that the criterion of the divine names applied, on the basis of their own theory, only to a limited part of the Pentateuch did not prevent the documentary critics from making full use of it. They used it in Genesis as the basis for establishing the other criteria, and then applied the latter to the analysis of the other books.

The criterion has been positively assessed by several modern scholars (e.g. Noth, de Vaux, Cazelles) as a useful contributory tool. Yet in fact even in Genesis the textual evidence does not always support it. Even Eissfeldt admitted that 'sometimes an *Elohim* has intruded into a *Yahweh* stratum, and a *Yahweh* into an *Elohim*' (1934, 4th edn, p. 242; ET p. 182). This is the case in Gen. 5.29; 17.1; 20.18. But there are other passages—e.g. Gen. 15.1-6; 22.1-14; 29.31–30.24; 32.23-32—where the divine names either do not 'match' the documentary analysis or pose insoluble problems for it. Eissfeldt is hardly convincing when he explains these exceptions by saying that it is not strange that 'the two strata should occasionally have exerted a mutual influence upon one another in respect of the divine names'. Once the possibility of such an editorial alteration has been admitted, the case for the criterion is seriously weakened.

Westermann (1974), although he cautiously entertained the criterion on the grounds that no generally accepted alternative to it has yet been found (!) (p. 767), indicated a further limitation of its use: he pointed out (p. 768) that in very substantial sections of Genesis (e.g., in Gen. 1–11 alone, 4.17-24; 9.18-24; 10.1-32 [apart from verse 9]; 11.10-32) there are no references to God at all. In these passages documentary analysis must rely on other criteria. Westermann also provided an interesting example of the way in which different scholars can draw entirely different conclusions from the same distribution of divine names in a passage considered by the documentary critics to be the result of the conflation of two documents. The story of the Flood (Gen. 6.5–8.22) is regarded by most critics (including, in recent times, Eissfeldt, de Vaux and

Cazelles) as a classical example of the value of the criterion of the divine names for unravelling a composite passage. Westermann, however, (pp. 768-70) singled it out as the one passage in Gen. 1–11 where although both the names Yahweh and Elohim occur, the criterion is entirely valueless. Although he admitted on other grounds that two narratives (*Erzählungen*) have been woven together here, he stated emphatically that the choice of the divine names in the passage (leaving aside the 'P' epilogue in 9.1-17) has been made completely at random ('*beliebig*').

This opinion of Westermann's brings out what is perhaps the most serious weakness of this criterion: its assumption that the authors of the three documents (J, E and P) were *necessarily* consistent in their use—and in their avoidance—of the names: that is to say, that the use of either Yahweh or Elohim in a particular Pentateuchal document precluded its author from using the other. It is on this assumption that the criterion is based.

Now it has already been observed that in the Pentateuchal text as it stands there are clear exceptions to this rule. Not only do some passages in Genesis contain the 'wrong' name, which has to be explained away; but even the very first narrative attributed to J (Gen. 2–3) breaks the rule by referring throughout to the Deity by the *double* name Yahweh Elohim, which *combines* the two supposedly mutually exclusive appellations. The name Yahweh Elohim occurs virtually nowhere else in the Old Testament, and its occurrence here has never been satisfactorily explained. A satisfactory explanation is, however, an urgent necessity for those who accept the criterion of the divine names.

There is a further matter which requires an explanation. As has been observed above, the documentary critics themselves postulated that E and P *did* vary their own usage with regard to the names in the course of their narrative: they used Elohim before Exod. 3 (or 6), and Yahweh from that point onwards. This admission, which is essential to the critics' argument because it explains why the criterion cannot be used after Exod. 3 or 6, is alone sufficient to weaken their assumption about consistency of usage, since if these authors were prepared, on what seemed to them to be sufficient grounds, to alter their usage on one occasion, they may have had other grounds, unknown to the modern critic, for altering it at other points in their work.

The likelihood that there was in fact no such strict rule as is assumed for Gen. 1 to Exod. 6 by the documentary critics may be confirmed by an investigation of the use of divine names in a series of wider contexts: the Pentateuch as a whole, the Old Testament literature as a whole, and the religious literature of the ancient Near East.

With regard to *the usage of the Pentateuch*, we find that there is no consistency of usage, at least as regards 'E'. Although, like 'P', E normally refers to the Deity as Yahweh after the revelation of this name to Moses, this is not always the case. In a number of passages universally ascribed to E (e.g. Exod. 13.17-19; 19.3, 17-19) the name Elohim is used: God is called sometimes Yahweh and sometimes Elohim, as though the two names were interchangeable. These are not passages where a non-Yahwist is speaking (as in Exod. 18.13-23), nor is Elohim used descriptively: it is used as a *name* of God.

These passages, then, show clearly that E, at any rate after Exod. 3, was not bound by any principle restricting him to the use of only one divine name. But this fact has important implications also for the use of the criterion of divine names *before* Exod. 3. For if E was not restricted to the use of a single divine name after Exod. 3.16, it may be assumed that J, who states that 'men began to call on the name of Yahweh' as early as the lifetime of Adam (Gen. 4.26) had the same freedom from the very beginning of his work, and might well have referred to the Deity as Elohim from time to time even in Genesis. Thus the criterion of the use of divine names, based on the picture of a 'J' who never used Elohim as a name of God and of 'E' and 'P' who could not have used the name Yahweh in Genesis appears not to be supported by the evidence of other parts of the Pentateuch.

The use and distribution of Yahweh and Elohim (and of other divine names) in *the remainder of the Old Testament* have been studied in detail by Cassuto and Segal. Important for the present purpose is Segal's demonstration that a variety of biblical authors of texts where a plurality of documentary sources is out of the question use both Yahweh and Elohim interchangeably. For example, in the course of a short narrative section in Jonah (4.1-11), where there is no discernible reason for the alternation such as the inclusion of a speech by a non-Yahwist, the author refers to the Deity by no less than four appellations: Yahweh, Yahweh-Elohim, Elohim and ha-Elohim. Alternations between Yahweh and Elohim can also be found in the historical books.

In his extended discussions of this subject (pp. 1-14, 103-23) Segal made a further point of considerable interest with regard to the alternation of *human* names in Old Testament narratives. For example, in some episodes in the so-called Succession Narrative (2 Sam. 15–20) *David* is referred to in three different ways: as 'David', as 'the king' and as 'king David'. It must be supposed that this alternation is to be accounted for on purely stylistic grounds: it is done for the sake of variety. Comparison with the similar alternation of *divine* names, as in the passage from Jonah referred to above, suggests that a similar desire for literary variety may lie behind both usages.

Finally, it is well known that in *the religious literature of the ancient Near East* a god or goddess might be called by many names, and that both in mythical texts and in hymns to the various deities more than one name might be applied to a single deity in the same text. There are of course no exact parallels in the extant literature of the ancient Near East to the narrative texts of the Pentateuch; but a partial parallel exists in the poetical narrative texts from Ras Shamra, where in the texts relating the activities of the god Baal, that god is often referred to not only by a variety of decriptive epithets, but by two distinct proper names: Baal and Hadad. The two names sometimes occur as alternatives in the same episode, and may even appear as parallel pairs, as in the line 4 vii. 36 (Gibson, p. 65):

> The foes of Baal clung to the forests,
> the enemies of Hadad to the hollows of the rock

It is interesting to observe the similarity here to Num. 23.8, where Balaam (using the name El ['God'] rather than Elohim) asks:

> How can I curse whom El has not cursed?
> How can I denounce whom Yahweh has not denounced?

These investigations taken together strongly suggest that there is likely to have been far more fluidity in the use of the names Yahweh and Elohim by the Pentateuchal writers than the documentary critics supposed. But there is also another possibility, which may throw doubt on the criterion of the divine names from another angle: that there was equally fluidity of usage on the part of either redactors or copyists—in other words, that we cannot be sure that one divine name was never substituted for another in the course of either the redaction or the transmission of the written text.

This question has been widely discussed, but no consensus of opinion has been reached. The textual evidence was reviewed early in this century by a number of scholars, and most thoroughly by Dahse, in particular with reference to the Septuagint. Dahse noted a number of verses (among them Gen. 4.1, 4, 16; 12.17) where in place of the 'Yahweh' (in Greek, ὁ κυριος) of the standard text the principal LXX manuscripts read ὁ θεος ('God'). The number of these verses could be substantially increased if secondary LXX manuscripts were taken into account. Dahse also found the reading 'Elohim' for 'Yahweh' in some Hebrew manuscripts. He attached great weight to the LXX readings: he believed them to be faithful renderings of a Hebrew original rather than the invention of the LXX translators. And if this were the case, he argued, then in the case of the divine names there could be no certainty that the standard Hebrew (MT) text was reliable.

Dahse's thesis was, however, strongly attacked by Skinner. Skinner defended the superiority of the Hebrew (MT) text as against a handful of LXX readings which did not all represent the best LXX tradition, and which were in any case probably due rather to a lack of concern for exact translation on the part of the LXX translators than to their following a different Hebrew text from MT. He also argued that little weight should be attached to the testimony of a few late Hebrew manuscripts, and he pointed out that the Samaritan Pentateuch supports MT in almost every case cited by Dahse. (More recently the Qumran fragments have provided further testimony to the trustworthiness of the MT.) Although Skinner's arguments have been gratuitously ignored by some of the more trenchant opponents of the Documentary Hypothesis (e.g. Engnell), most recent scholars have agreed with Skinner. Even Volz, whose attempt to disprove the existence of E as a separate document would have been assisted by Dahse's conclusions, regarded the testimony of the LXX as dubious.

Nevertheless, however insubstantial Dahse's thesis may be, most scholars now recognize that it is impossible to be sure that the Pentateuchal redactors and copyists never substituted one name for another. There is, indeed, some indirect evidence on this point from another part of the Old Testament. Westermann, in discussing this question (1974, p. 768), cited, as an example of such redactional activity, the case of the so-called 'Elohistic Psalter' (Pss. 42–83). In this group of psalms, in complete contrast to the usage of the rest of the Psalter, God is almost always called 'Elohim' and only rarely Yahweh. There is general agreement among scholars that this phenomenon is due to redactional or scribal activity: a redactor or copyist has at some time systematically substituted 'Elohim' for an original 'Yahweh'. Such action might be explained as due to a well-attested late post-exilic tendency to avoid the sacred name Yahweh. It is therefore possible that similar alterations may have been made at various stages in the transmission of parts of the Pentateuch as well, although clearly the process—as in the case of the Psalter!—was not carried out throughout the work.

Thus although direct proof that there was a fluidity in the use of the divine names in the course of the early transmission of the text of the Pentateuch is lacking, the more cautious critics, including some who are inclined to accept the Documentary Hypothesis in general, recognize that it is unwise to accept without qualification a criterion which makes the assumption that the textual transmission was so completely faithful that no changes can possibly have been made by copyists or redactors in the transmission of the divine names.

Enough has been said to show that for a variety of reasons the criterion of the use and distribution of the divine names Yahweh and Elohim in the Pentateuch is, to say the least, not a reliable indication of diverse authorship. Moreover, the objection that there is no other satisfactory explanation of the variations in the use of the names is not well founded. For even if it be allowed that the traditional Hebrew text (MT) is so totally reliable that it is impossible that one name might sometimes have been substituted for the other in the process of *scribal transmission* before the establishment of a standard text, and even if it be equally allowed that there is no possibility of wholesale alteration by *redactors* of the names originally written in the 'documents', it has now been demonstrated that the *writers of the documents themselves* did not regard themselves as bound to confine themselves to one name or the other. It is therefore *not necessary*, as writers like Cassuto have tried to do, to attempt to discover *why* they used now one name and now the other, although it is interesting to make that attempt.

It is generally agreed by critics of all schools that there are some cases where the occurrence of the word Elohim is not an indication of documentary provenance but is due to the employment by all the writers of the Pentateuch of a common linguistic usage which they all shared. In many passages, for example, Elohim is not used as a divine name but simply as a word denoting the class 'god', whch included the God of Israel. Thus Abraham's servant spoke of 'Yahweh, the god of my master Abraham' (Gen. 24.12). In other passages Elohim occurs in what appear to be fixed formulae or phrases which are probably older than Yahwism and which correspond to similar expressions in the religious literature of other Semitic peoples. Such phrases, for example, as 'house of God' (Gen. 28.17) and 'fear of God' (Gen. 20.11), were hallowed by long usage and not to be lightly altered. Again, Elohim might be used in an explanation of a place-name which included a theophoric element, as in Gen. 32.31 (EVV v. 30) in an explanation of the meaning of Penuel, 'face of God'. Further, Elohim is used in conversations with non-Yahwists, for example in Gen. 31.42, 50.

Such specialized usages are indications that the authors of the Pentateuchal narratives were sensitive to the appropriateness or inappropriateness of one or other of the divine names in particular cases. Opponents of the Documentary Hypothesis such as Cassuto sought to extend this principle of sensitivity to cover the whole Pentateuch. They argued—and this view would receive some support from modern linguistic studies—that the two divine names Yahweh and Elohim, although they refer to the same deity, are not in fact synonymous: that each has a slightly different nuance, giving prominence to a particular aspect of Yahweh's nature and role rather than to others: for example, 'Elohim' suggests God's universality while 'Yahweh' draws attention to his role as God of Israel.

That this theory as an explanation of *all* the occurrences of the divine names is at best no more than partially convincing must be obvious to any unbiased reader of the Pentateuch. It may well be possible to make out a case for it in a limited number of passages where one name is used consistently throughout a narrative, though even here Cassuto's arguments contain as much special pleading as those of the documentary critics themselves. But in passages where both names are used frequently in the same narrative—for example, in the story of the Flood—it is highly improbable that the author should have deliberately intended to bring out different aspects of God's nature by turns. Cassuto (in particular) tried to prove too much.

But his elaborate argument is in fact not necessary. Far more convincing is that put forward by Segal (pp. 13-14):

> The use of *Elohim* . . . reflects a popular usage in the contemporary spoken Hebrew. The frequent interchange between the appellative common noun *Elohim* and the proper noun *YHWH* is practised by

the narrator for the purpose of variety in expression which is a standing feature in all Hebrew narrative style, and particularly in the designation of names of persons. Compare for example the interchange between "Jethro" and "the father-in-law" in Exodus xviii, between "David" and "the king" in II Samuel xvi, and many more such cases in the biblical narrative.

Cassuto and Segal thus offer two alternative explanations of the interchange of divine names: that it was done for theological reasons (the two names having each its own peculiar nuance), or for stylistic reasons (the two names being identical in meaning). There is a third possibility: if the two names were completely or virtually identical in the minds of the narrators, the alternation may well have been *unconscious*. Such unconscious variations in the choice of words occur frequently in ordinary speech, and also in modern books. For example, the very same names—God and Yahweh—are quite frequently unconsciously interchanged in modern lectures on the Old Testament, and even in published works. (The apparently motiveless variation in the *transcription* of YHWH [e.g. יה and יי] and the use of a variety of circumlocutions in references to him in the same text and even in the same paragraph in some mediaeval Hebrew manuscripts are examples of the same kind of phenomenon.)

In fact these three types of 'non-documentary' solution to the problem are not mutually exclusive. Not only may any of these three influences have been operative on the Pentateuchal writers at different points in their work; they may even have sometimes been operative simultaneously. Thus stylistic and theological considerations may have sometimes coincided, and some of the decisions taken may have been taken instinctively—that is, to some extent at least by the unconscious mind. In many cases, too, there may have been subtle reasons for the decision to use one name rather than the other which are bound to remain beyond the ability of the modern reader to discover. But it can be safely concluded that, if the solution proposed by the documentary critics is set aside, the alternative explanations of the phenomenon of the alternation of divine names in the Pentateuch are amply sufficient.

b. *Repetitions, duplications and contradictions*
The basis of this criterion is the observation that the Pentateuch, although ostensibly a single, long, connected narrative, does not run

smoothly but is full of irregularities such as duplications both of small details and of whole stories, contradictions of fact, and digressions, all of which appear to have no *raison d'être*. These irregularities, it was supposed by the documentary critics, can only be accounted for on the supposition of the combination or conflation by redactors of separate and originally independent literary works, which have not been harmonized so as to conceal their separate identities, but which can easily be identified by a critical reader. These tell-tale phenomena are not all of the same kind. They may be roughly classified in the following way:

Double accounts of the same event (commonly known as 'doublets'), e.g. two accounts of the creation of the world (Gen. 1 and 2), two stories in which Abraham passed off his wife as his sister (Gen. 12.10-20 and 20.2-18), two calls of Moses by God (Exod. 3 and 6).

Repetitions within a single story. This phenomenon, which occurs frequently, may be illustrated by Gen. 7.21-23: 'And all flesh *died* that moved upon the earth. . .; everything on the dry land . . . *died*. He *blotted out* every living thing that was upon the face of the ground. . .; they were *blotted out* from the earth.'

Contradictions of fact, e.g. the statements that *two* of every kind of animal entered the ark (Gen. 6.19) and that *seven* pairs of clean animals did so (Gen. 7.2); that the earth became dry after the Flood on the first day of the first month (Gen. 8.13) and on the twenty-seventh day of the second month (Gen. 8.14); that all the Egyptians' cattle died (Exod. 9.6) and that shortly afterwards they were still alive (Exod. 9.19).

These indications of literary irregularity were not, of course, supposed by the documentary critics to constitute in themselves proof of the existence of continuous documents running through the whole Pentateuch: it was only possible to link together these isolated—though numerous—examples to form continuous documents if the verses and passages in question could be shown by means of the other criteria (for example, the use of different divine names) to possess common characteristics pointing to a common provenance. If this could not be done, they merely provided evidence of a negative kind: that in each case considered individually the two (or more) repeated or inconsistent statements or incidents could not be the work of a single author. It was, of course, claimed by the documentary critics that the various criteria did in fact support one another in this way. The validity of this claim will be considered below.

It should be noted that the documentary critics found it necessary to suppose that the redactors of the documents employed, at different points in their work, two quite different methods of compilation: in some cases—in the double accounts of the same event—they preserved the two accounts separately and placed them either side by side (e.g. Gen. 1 and 2) or at different points in the total narrative (e.g. Gen. 12.10-20 and 20.2-18), while in others they interwove the two (or more) accounts to form a single composite narrative (as in the story of the Flood), being apparently indifferent equally to the resulting incongruities of reiteration and of contradiction (the story of the Flood contains both types of incongruity, e.g. in Gen. 7.21-23 and 8.13-14).

A further point to be observed is that the documentary critics in their use of the criterion of literary irregularities employed two opposite criteria: those of likeness and unlikeness. That is to say, they held that there must be two documents involved if *identical* statements occur twice, because duplication is not permissible in a single narrative; while on the other hand there must be two documents involved if *contradictory* statements are made, because inconsistency also is not permitted. The only narrator whom they could accept as a genuine single author would therefore be one who never repeated a detail and was never guilty of an inconsistency. Repetitions and inconsistencies, on the other hand, *were* permitted—and on a grand scale—to redactors!

i. *Double accounts of the same event ('doublets').* Terms like 'double account' and 'doublet' have been used to cover a wide variety of pairs of narratives, ranging from some which have little more than their basic theme in common to others which resemble one another so closely that they are clearly different versions of the same basic story. This fact is of some importance for the assessment of this criterion.

The two so-called 'creation stories' (Gen. 1.1-2.4a and 2.4b-25) were regarded by the documentary critics as a clear example of a doublet. Although they were to a considerable extent complementary in content it was asserted that they could not both have belonged to the same document because they both purport to describe the same event—the creation of the world—and because they differ in some respects in the order of events within the total creative action.

This unanimous conclusion of the documentary critics is based on a number of misconceptions: first, they assumed, quite arbitrarily, that the biblical writers were slaves to an obsession with literal accuracy which could not tolerate the slightest discrepancy of fact, and which outweighed all other considerations; secondly, they failed to appreciate the true character of the stories: they did not see that, far from being intended to give an accurate account of the facts (!) correct in every detail, the stories are poetical in character and concerned to teach religious and theological truths; thirdly, they paid insufficient attention to the quite different purposes of the stories, especially to the fact that Gen. 2 is not primarily an account of the creation of the world, and, in addition, is part of a longer narrative (Gen. 2-3) which must be considered as a whole; and fourthly, they did not envisage the possibility that the stories may be intended to complement one another. It must be concluded that these two stories are not 'doublets' in any real sense; and that there is no obstacle whatever to the simpler view that one and the same writer selected and made use of two traditional stories, refraining from an attempt to harmonize them.

The two stories of the expulsion of Hagar from Abraham's household and her divine encounter in the wilderness (Gen. 16.1-16, attributed, with some additions from P, to J, and Gen. 21.9-21, attributed to E) form an entirely different kind of pair. In spite of differences in detail it is difficult to dismiss the striking similarities between these stories (as Alter, p. 49, appears to do) as due to the influence upon the author of the narrative conventions of the so-called 'type-scene', since it is evident that they are not simply similar stories perhaps made more closely similar in the telling, but *the same story* told twice with variations, at different points in the total Abraham narrative. Is it possible to account for the duplication in other ways than that of documentary analysis? The answer to this question cannot be the same as in the case of Gen. 1 and 2.

It has been suggested that one of the versions of the story is a deliberate rewriting of the other, carried out in order to give expression to particular ethical or theological concerns: in other words, the second version is a supplement to an older documentary source, rather than part of a second major document. This raises the question why the author of the 'improved' version did not simply substitute it for the other and so avoid duplication. Volz, who adopted this explanation of the duplication, confessed his inability to answer this question, and other scholars (e.g. Noth, 1948, pp. 22-23; ET p. 22) regarded the difficulty as insuperable. Recently Sandmel has pointed out that the kind of procedure in question has an analogy in the practice of rabbinic 'improvers', who pursued a policy which may be described as 'neutralizing by addition', but also had a 'disinclination to expunge' which resulted in similar duplications to those in the Pentateuch.

There is, however, another way of accounting for the duplication: to understand it as a deliberate literary device. The two versions of the Hagar story have been placed, the one preceding and the other following the section (Gen. 17.1-21.8) which contains, among other matters, the accounts of the promise of the birth of Isaac and of the fulfilment of that promise in the birth itself. By placing the story of the miraculous birth of the true heir between the two stories about Hagar and Ishmael, the author may have intended to draw attention to the way in which God faithfully and effectively overcame, on two separate occasions, the threat to the true succession to Abraham caused by human entanglements and muddle. The pattern of the narrative in chapters 16-21 is not a simple one, and other explanations of the placing of the Hagar stories are possible; but the mere fact that what is virtually the same story has been repeated in this way is hardly sufficient to justify the assertion that there must be a combination of two separate literary sources here. A place must be given to the possibility of literary ingenuity on the part of a single author and to the possibility of deliberate repetition on his part.

The two stories in which Abraham passed off his wife as his sister (Gen. 12.10-20—J—and 20.2-18—E—) constitute another example of a genuine doublet. There is, however, a further complication in this case: there is yet a third variant of the story (Gen. 26.6-11), in which not Abraham but Isaac practised the same deception with *his* wife, the occasion being (as with Abraham in 20.2-18) a stay in Gerar. This third version, however, is attributed not to E, whose version is also set in Gerar, but to J. All three stories, despite the variation in the participants and in the location, are clearly versions of the same story, and two of them are attributed to the same document J.

This occurrence of a doublet in the same document naturally created difficulties for the Documentary Hypothesis, and the supporters of the hypothesis were obliged to explain it away in one way or another. Thus Wellhausen (1899, p. 23) was forced to adopt a supplement hypothesis at this point: 12.10-20, he suggested, was not part of the original J but was a later addition, modelled on 26.6-11. Other critics, who had concluded on other grounds that J was too full of inconsistencies to be a single document and postulated an additional document preceding J, took this doublet as supporting their theory and assigned 12.10-20 to this earlier document (e.g., Eissfeldt assigned it to 'L', Van Seters to a 'pre-Yahwist source'). But all these critics based their theories on the assumption fundamental to the Documentary Hypothesis that the presence of doublets in 'original' documents is inconceivable, although full licence to include doublets was given to redactors.

As in the case of the Hagar stories there are various other ways of explaining the presence of these three variants in the text of the Pentateuch. It is possible, for example, that two of the versions are 'improvements' of the third, added in 'rabbinic' style to an older text. But once again, a simpler explanation is available if the prejudice against doublets in a single document is set aside: the reiteration of the incident may be a deliberate literary device.

It should be noted that the theme of these stories—a threat to the lives of the ancestors overcome by divine intervention—is closely connected with the promises given by God to Abraham (Gen. 12.1-9) and renewed to Isaac (26.1-5) of divine blessing, becoming a great nation and inheriting the land of Canaan. The stories recount how God showed his faithfulness to his promises from the very first moment, saving the promised race from extinction and delivering the prospective ancestors from the consequences of the actions to which folly or human necessity had driven them. They occur at crucial points in the total narrative: in chapter 12 the promise to Abraham is immediately followed by a crisis in which God's promise is put to the test, and the same is true of the story in chapter 26. That in chapter 20 also occurs at a dramatic point, after the announcement that Sarah will bear a son to Abraham, and immediately before the account of that birth, which is the climactic point of the whole Abraham cycle of stories. Here the incident in Gerar provides a dramatic suspense.

These stories, then, emphasize, at crucial moments, how God began to fulfil his promises. But to say this is to state only part of their function. The *repetition* of what is basically the same story is integral to the literary effect intended by the author. He was deliberately drawing attention to the theme by informing his readers that God intervened *not once but three times* to ensure that the fulfilment of the promise of progeny, on which all the promises depended, should not be thwarted by human wickedness or folly.

It is one of the strange inconsistencies of the documentary critics that while they paid great attention to some doublets and used them to distinguish one document from another, they paid no attention at all to others, which appear side by side in the same document in their analysis. In fact, the literary device of repetition, expressed in the form of duplicate or thematically similar stories, may be said to have been a leading characteristic of the narrator's art, and the separation of all the pairs of stories in the Pentateuch into different documents would have been an impossibility for the Documentary Hypothesis.

In Gen. 37.5-11, for example, Joseph tells his brothers of not one, but two dreams which foreshadow his eminence over them. The dreams are clearly doublets but both are attributed by the Documentary Hypothesis to J. Later in the Joseph story, Pharaoh similarly dreams two duplicate dreams. This passage is attributed to E (41.1-8). There are other examples of such repetition in the Joseph story. Joseph's comment on Pharaoh's dreams (41.25-28) that they are in fact 'one' is another way of saying that the purpose of doublets is to emphasize or confirm. It is significant —to say the least—that in these passages the documentary critics not only allow the existence of doublets within a single document, contrary to their principle which they apply elsewhere, but, by attributing one *set* of dreams to J and the other to E, at the same time implicitly concede that both authors employed precisely the same technique at almost the same point in their narrative, a coincidence for which no explanation is offered.

The narrative of the plagues of Egypt (Exod. 7ff.) offers further examples of duplication for the sake of emphasis and dramatic effect, for the mere logic of the story would have been adequately maintained if only one sufficiently terrifying plague had been recorded. Here the ten plagues are attributed to three documents (J, E and P), resulting in not merely doublets but triplets at least to each, however the analysis is carried out. In style and treatment these are all genuine duplications comparable with the stories of the wife passed off as sister.

In the examples given above the doublets referred to differ from those used by the documentary critics in that the two (or more) stories succeed one another with no other material intervening. Such is not the case, however, with the numerous stories of rebellion in the wilderness in the books of Exodus and Numbers. In these chapters, while the most obvious doublets (e.g. the two stories of the sending of the manna and the quails [Exod. 16 and Num. 11]) are attributed to different sources by the documentary critics, no amount of documentary analysis can produce a result which negates the extraordinary profusion of constantly reiterated motifs or the heavily charged atmosphere of constant rebelliousness on the part of the Israelites in the wilderness. In fact the intricate intertwining which characterizes these stories posed greater problems for documentary analysis than anywhere else in the Pentateuch: Noth's attempt at this analysis is studded with footnotes indicating uncertainty or modification of the principles of the Documentary Hypothesis at various points without which it could not be made to work.

With some possible exceptions, these stories are not doublets in the strict sense of that term: they are not based on a common narrative source. Nevertheless many of them possess common features at least as striking as do, for example, Gen. 1 and 2; yet, as in the case of the plague stories, there are duplications in each 'document'. No less than six times, for example, it is recorded that the rebels complained against their lot on the grounds that life in Egypt had been preferable to their present miserable state (Exod. 14.10-12; 16.1-3; 17.3; Num. 11.4-6; 16.13; 20.5). It is, of course, possible to argue that such common features are often secondary elements, added at a later stage to produce greater coherence in the series of stories of rebellion in the wilderness. But this is impossible to prove. However these complexes of stories on this theme (in Exodus and Numbers) may have been put together, to distribute the stories among three written documents later combined fails completely to do justice to their complexity.

The documentary critics claimed that it is the *frequency* of the phenomenon of doublets in the Pentateuchal narratives which constitutes the strength of this criterion. Thus Noth, who regards the criterion of doublets as the only one which is 'really useful' and 'adequate', defines it as 'the *repeated occurrence* of the same narrative materials or narrative elements in *different versions*' (the italics are those of Noth). 'This phenomenon', he wrote, 'can hardly be explained in any other way' than by the Documentary Hypothesis

(p. 21; ET p. 22). In other words, an occasional isolated example of a doublet might be explained as an isolated secondary version which was added later to an older continuous narrative, but a large number of such phenomena would require a more general solution. In fact, as has been seen above, there are many more doublets and parallel stories in the Pentateuch than the documentary critics took into account; and it is their very frequency which, far from supporting the Documentary Hypothesis, shows it to be inadequate.

ii. *Repetitions within single stories*. In many of the Pentateuchal stories certain details are given twice: e.g. in the story of the Flood it is twice stated that all the human beings and land animals which did not enter the Ark died (Gen. 7.21 and 22); Jacob at Bethel twice comments on the presence of God there (Gen. 28.16 and 17); God twice tells Moses that he has heard the cry of the oppressed Israelites (Exod. 3.7 and 9). By themselves, such repetitions would hardly have been sufficient to generate the hypothesis that these stories are composite: that the repetitions are the consequence of the dovetailing of two originally distinct versions of the same incidents. This hypothesis was built mainly on other supposed evidence: variations in vocabulary and style, discrepancies and inconsistencies, and—to some extent—differences of point of view. But once it had been concluded on such grounds as these that a narrative was composite, the critics sought to support their hypothesis by attempting to reconstruct the two (or more) versions in as great detail as possible. It became necessary to demonstrate that the versions ran parallel to one another: in other words, it was a *requirement* of the hypothesis that there should be, in the final version of such a story, as many repetitions as possible, which could then be assigned to the different versions.

In this search for repetitions little attention was given to alternative ways in which their presence might be explained. Moreover, there was a tendency to ignore the existence of *other* repetitions in these stories which did not suit the reconstruction of the separate sources. For example, in the story of the Flood, attributed by the critics to two documents (J and P), the coming of the waters on the earth is reported not twice but four times, that is, twice in each document (Gen. 7.10 and 12 [J]; 6 and 11 [P]). The uncertainty of the criterion of repetitions for documentary analysis could not be better demonstrated.

Repetition within narratives is in fact a literary device which is found in literature of many kinds, and is particularly common in the literatures of the ancient Near East. It is also particularly employed in *oral* literature, since in the course of oral transmission the memory of the audience needs frequent refreshing if the thread of the story is not to be lost. Thus in the case of the Pentateuchal stories repetition could be explained as due to their earlier history as orally transmitted stories, or to purely literary considerations, or to both.

As has already been observed, the biblical writers, unlike the authors of the classical world of Greece and Rome, have left to posterity no account of the techniques of their literary art. Consequently the only source from which the modern student of biblical narrative can acquire any knowledge of these matters is the narrative text itself. A full understanding is therefore—to say the least—unattainable, and many of the reasons for the use by the biblical writers of the device of repetition inevitably remain unknown. Nevertheless, an intelligent study of the text combined with some knowledge of the uses to which such repetition has been put in other and later literature does provide sufficient explanation of the majority of cases in the Pentateuch without recourse to documentary surgery.

The chapter in Alter's book entitled 'The Techniques of Repetition' (pp. 88-113) is a particularly perceptive discussion of repetitions in Old Testament narrative. Drawing on a wide knowledge of both ancient and modern literatures, Alter approached the subject from a point of view which is precisely the opposite of the documentary critic: he regarded the repetitions in biblical narrative not as indications of literary insensitivity or ineptitude (on the part of redactors) but of consummate literary skill. Such repetitions were to be expected: 'At least some parts of a whole spectrum of repetitive devices are bound to be present wherever there is pattern in narrative, from Homer to Günter Grass' (p. 91). Although a few examples in the Old Testament narratives might be due to other causes such as glosses, variant traditions and the like, Alter found that 'most instances of repetition prove to be quite purposeful' (p. 89): 'What we find... in biblical narrative is an elaborately integrated system of repetitions' (p. 95).

The cause of some of the repetitions, according to Alter, may lie in folkloric convention or in the exigencies of oral delivery. But 'If the requirements of oral delivery and a time-honored tradition of storytelling may have prescribed a mode of narration in which verbatim repetition was to be expected, the authors of the biblical narratives astutely discovered how the slightest strategic variations in the pattern of repetition could serve the purposes of commentary, analysis, foreshadowing, thematic assertion' (p. 91).

Alter made a further point which seems to have escaped the notice of the documentary critics: he pointed out that the use of repetition for such literary purposes can hardly have been unfamiliar to the writers of the biblical narratives, since, in the form of parallelism, repetition—with variations—was one of the main characteristics, if not the principal characteristic, of biblical *poetic* composition: 'the conscious or intuitive art of poetic parallelism was to advance the poetic argument in seeming to repeat it—intensifying, specifying, complementing, qualifying, contrasting, expanding . . . .' (p. 97). So also in the case of prose—and, one may add, especially in the elevated prose which is characteristic of biblical narrative—the reader or listener 'is expected to attend closely to the constantly emerging differences in a medium that seems predicated on constant recurrence'.

To test the correctness of Alter's approach to the question of repetitions would require a detailed analysis of all the cases of repetition within every relevant narrative in the Pentateuch, a task too vast to be undertaken here. Moreover, it would probably be impossible to devise an objective criterion for assessing whether, in particular cases, the aesthetic solution which he proposed is sufficiently plausible to account for what to the documentary critic seemed like a clear case of the redactional dovetailing of two parallel accounts of the same incident. What is important about the aesthetic or literary approach is that it offers an alternative explanation of the phenomenon and lays the burden of proof on the documentary critic: since it cannot be denied that repetition is a recognized literary device, the critic who wishes to use its occurrence in Pentateuchal narratives as a proof of multiple authorship must demonstrate in each case that the text as it stands manifests a gross implausibility or absurdity, and that the two or more documentary strands into which he proposes to divide it manifest a literary quality superior to that of the original.

It should also be noted that in order to throw doubt on the validity of the criterion of repetition as an argument for documentary analysis it is not necessary for the literary critic to show that *every* case of repetition can be accounted for in literary terms. The documentary argument depends to a large extent on the *frequency* of repetition within a single story, since if the existence of parallel accounts is to be demonstrated, at least the main features of the story must be shown to occur twice. If it can, on the other hand, be shown that a large number of the repetitions are best explained as integral parts of a single narrative, the case for conflation of parallel accounts falls to the ground, for although the present text may well contain some isolated repetitions due to glosses, variants and the like, these would be insufficient to demonstrate the existence of complete, parallel, continuous documents lying behind it.

The story of the Flood (Gen. 6–9) offers a good example of a narrative where the presence of a large number of repetitions has been a major factor in documentary analysis. Here almost every incident in the story is repeated; but it is repeated not once but several times. God's intention to destroy the inhabitants of the earth is stated four times (Gen. 6.5-7, 11-13, 17; 7.4). Four times it is recorded that Noah and his companions entered the Ark (7.7-9, 13-14, 15, 16). Three times the coming of the rain is recorded (7.6, 10, 11-12). The prevailing or increasing of the waters of the Flood is mentioned five times (7.17, 18, 19, 20, 24), and their abatement similarly five times (8.1, 2, 3, 4, 5). It is illogical on the basis of these repetitions to analyse the story into *two* documents (J and P). On the other hand the dramatic effect of this portentous constant repetition in the text as it stands cannot be denied. The terror of this most crucial disaster in the history of the world and the sense of relief when at last the danger began to recede are both expressed *through* the solemn repetitions which run through the whole story. (On the inner coherence and artistic patterning of the story see especially Wenham.)

Exod. 3.7-8 and 9-10 (assigned to 'J' and 'P' respectively) provide a further example of repetition which can be explained on literary grounds without a need for documentary analysis. Here God twice states that he has seen the oppression of Israel by the Egyptians, that he has heard their cry, and that he intends to bring them out of Egypt. As in the story of the Flood, the moment is a critical one, and marks a new beginning (this time for the people of Israel) brought about by God out of a situation of despair. God's solemnly repeated statement about his care for his people and his intention to deliver them stresses the significance of the new direction of events. But there is also progression as well as repetition here: whereas in verses 7-8 the emphasis is entirely on the fact that God cares and will save, in verses 9-10 it is the means which he will use to save the people which is stressed: he will save them through the medium of Moses. The two phrases '*I* have come down to deliver them . . . and to bring them out of that land' (v. 8) and 'that *you* may bring forth my people . . . out of Egypt' (v. 10) are not alternatives pointing to two variant versions of the story now conflated into one, but have been deliberately chosen by the author to express a theological truth concerning God's *modus operandi* in history, and also to confirm Moses' authority as God's instrument. This is made even more plain in the succeeding exchange between Moses and God in vv. 11-12: 'Who am I?' and 'But I will be with you'.

In some cases the documentary critics' conviction on other grounds of the duplicate character of a narrative led them to discover the presence of repetitions when in fact there are none. For example, in the story of the theophany experienced by Jacob at Bethel (Gen. 28.10-22), which was believed by them to be the result of the dovetailing of J and E, Jacob's reflections on awaking from his dream—'Surely Yahweh is in this place; and I did not know it', and 'How awesome is this place! This is none other than the house of God, and this is the gate of heaven' (vv. 16-17)—were regarded as a case of repetition arising from the duplication of the story. But in fact the two reflections, separated as they are by the sentence 'And he was afraid, and said . . .', are not mutually exclusive but mark a progression in Jacob's reactions from surprise and awe to fear, and together prepare the ground for the cultic action and naming of the place as Bethel, 'house of God', which follow. (See Rendtorff, 1982, pp. 517-18 for a similar assessment.) There are many other instances of the arbitrary designation of consecutive events or speeches as alternatives, that is, repetitions, to serve the cause of the Documentary Hypothesis.

iii. *Contradictions of fact*. That there are numerous formal and material discrepancies within the Pentateuchal narratives and laws with regard to matters reported as facts is indisputable. A few examples of this phenomenon will suffice as illustrations. According to Exod. 2.18-21 Moses married the daughter of a priest of Midian whose name was Reuel; yet in Exod. 3.1 and 18.1 his father-in-law is stated to have been Jethro, priest of Midian. (In Judg. 4.11 he is given a third name, Hobab, and is said to have been not a Midianite but a Kenite.) Clearly there is a discrepancy here: the sequence in which the narratives are arranged does not permit the possibility that Moses might have married two Midianite girls and so be the son-in-law of two Midianite priests! Besides discrepancies concerning names, there are discrepancies in the sequence of events: for example, according to Gen. 35.7 Jacob named Bethel after his return from Mesopotamia; but according to Gen. 28.19 he had already named it while on his way to Mesopotamia, after his theophanic experience there. Similarly according to Gen. 32.28 it was at Penuel, after he had wrestled with the angel, that Jacob's name was changed to Israel, but according to Gen. 35.10 the change of name was made on a later occasion. Such examples could easily be multiplied. There are also examples of discrepancies within the legal parts of the Pentateuch, especially between laws which appear in different collections such as Exod. 20–23 and Leviticus.

There are no grounds for postulating the existence of separate continuous documents on the basis of cases such as those cited above, where the discrepancies occur in separated, often widely separated, narratives or groups of material. For it is not disputed that the Pentateuch has been composed from a number of different traditions which have not been completely harmonized. Unless some other kind of connection can be discovered between the various examples of discrepancy, these inconsistencies are most naturally explained as belonging to isolated double traditions about particular events or to independent collections of laws. Discrepancies of fact *within single narratives*, however, are another matter.

It is the contention of the documentary critics that such inconsistencies or contradictions of fact within single narratives are the result of the conflation of originally separate written versions of the same story in which the redactor, in his desire to include as much as possible of the text of both versions, has included in the final version two (or more) references to the same incident or circumstance, even when the two versions contain details which are mutually incompatible. The criterion of discrepancies of fact is thus closely linked with that of repetitions within a story: what we have, according to the documentary critics, is cases of repetition (in a broad sense) in which there is discrepancy of detail.

Once again, as in the case of some criteria already dealt with, the documentary critics assumed that the mentality of the redactors was quite different from that of the authors of the individual documents. Certainly whoever was responsible for the text in its present form did not regard the discrepancies as significant in comparison with the importance, as he saw it, of preserving as much as possible of the material which was available to him. It seems clear that at some stage in the history of these narratives elements of two—or more—traditions or versions have been combined. But it may be asked whether it is more probable that this conflation took place in a redactional process or whether it occurred earlier: either in the course of oral transmission, or at the point when the stories were committed to writing for the first time.

Unless there is other evidence to support the theory of documentary conflation, the burden of proof would seem to lie entirely on the shoulders of the documentary critics: for their hypothesis is the only one which necessarily presupposes the existence at some period of more than one *complete* (in the sense of continuous and coherent) version of the stories in question. If the discrepancies were created at an earlier stage, it would be necessary only to suppose that a single main account had at some time been expanded with some isolated motifs from other traditions. But for the documentary critics it is necessary to prove that there once existed two or more complete versions, because such versions are only parts of longer continuous histories, in which, originally, there can have been no gaps. But in fact these stories in their present form do not, in general, contain sufficient material for the reconstruction of two complete versions. This may be illustrated from what is often considered to be the most convincing example of a composite narrative formed by the conflation of two sources, the story of the Flood.

In this story, in addition to the repetitions referred to above, there are a number of obvious contradictions of fact which no amount of subtle argumentation has been able to disguise. The most obvious of these concern the inner chronology of the story and the number of each kind of animal taken into the Ark. There appear to be two distinct chronologies, that in Gen. 7.4, 10, 12, 17; 8.6-12 being attributed to J and 7.6, 11, 24; 8.3-5, 13, 14 to P. The statements about the numbers of animals have similarly been attributed to the two sources, 7.2-3, 8-9 to J; 6.19-20; 7.14-16 to P. In fact these distinctions are not entirely clearcut, and additions by the redactor and the interpolation of small groups of words from one source into another have to be postulated in order to make the scheme work.

It is true that—in contrast with some other supposedly compound narratives—these indications of documentary sources are here supported by other kinds of evidence: the alternation of the names of God and of language and style (especially with regard to certain phrases held to be characteristic of P) seems to coincide with the evidence provided by the discrepancies of fact. Nevertheless the story in its final form does not contain sufficient material for the reconstruction of two complete versions: some of its essential elements are recorded only once. While the version attributed to P makes a coherent story, there are serious gaps in that attributed to J. In particular, there is only one version (attributed to P) of God's speech to Noah in which he tells Noah of his intention to destroy mankind, commands him to build an ark and instructs him how to build it (6.13-22). Indeed, in the J account there is no reference whatever to the building of an ark before God's command, 'Go into the ark' (7.1). Secondly, at the conclusion of the story it is not recorded in J that Noah and his companions left the ark when the Flood had subsided. The J story, in fact, is a torso.

The documentary critics made light of these serious gaps in the J narrative. Thus Skinner remarked , 'The resolution of the compound narrative into its constituent elements in this case is justly reckoned amongst the most brilliant achievements of purely literary criticism, and affords a particularly instructive lesson in the art of documentary analysis'. Of the redactor he stated that 'Of J he has preserved quite enough to show that it was originally a complete and independent narrative; but it was naturally impracticable to handle it as carefully as the main document'. He elaborated this statement by admitting that 'the middle part of the document . . . has been broken up into minute fragments, and these have been placed in position where they would least disturb the flow of narration. Some slight transpositions have been made, and a number of glosses have been introduced; but how far these last are due to the Redactor himself and how far to subsequent editors, we cannot tell. . . . Duplicates are freely admitted, and small discrepancies are disregarded'. In spite of these admissions of the manipulations required to produce the semblance of a credible J document, Skinner was so confident of the legitimacy and validity of such methods that he could conclude, in a manner characteristic of the documentary critics: 'This compound narrative is not destitute of interest; but for the understanding of the ideas underlying the literature the primary documents are obviously of first importance' (1910, pp. 147-50).

The question of the cumulative effect of different kinds of evidence supplied by the application of different criteria to the same passage, which is sharply raised in the case of the story of the Flood, will be discussed on pp. 116-17 below. Here we are concerned only with the question of the most probable explanation of the contradictions which exist within this passage, considered by themselves. Although it is clear that these contradictions are due to some kind of combination of two (or more) traditions, there is, as we have seen, no proof that these traditions originally took the form of two complete and parallel written narratives which have been subsequently combined.

That there are alternative solutions to this kind of problem may be illustrated from another text in the Primaeval History: Gen. 2 and 3. This narrative also contains contradictions, of which the most obvious is the inconsistent appearance of the tree of life beside the tree of the knowledge of good and evil. The tree of life is mentioned early in the story (Gen. 2.9) as standing in the middle of the garden together with the tree of knowledge. Yet it plays no part at all in the subsequent narrative: when God tells the man of what trees he may and may not eat the fruit, only the tree of knowledge is mentioned as forbidden (2.16, 17), and it is this tree of knowledge (referred to in 3.3 as 'the tree which is in the midst of the garden') the eating of whose fruit by the woman and the man leads to God's anger. Yet at the end of the story (3.22, 24) the tree of life reappears, and it is made clear that it is of the greatest importance to God, for he takes every possible precaution to protect its fruit from being eaten, although he had earlier issued no prohibition against this.

There is a very serious inconsistency here, and it is clear that the motif of the tree of life is an addition to the original story, the references to it having been at some time interpolated into it. This situation closely resembles that of the story of the Flood, where also a narrative complete and coherent in itself has been confused by the addition of alien motifs. In the case of Gen. 2-3, however, the documentary critics did not attempt to analyse the narrative into documentary sources, but attributed the whole to J. Some, however, (e.g. Skinner), recognized the existence of the inconsistencies, and concluded that the references to the tree of life are due to the interpolation into a main narrative of small fragments of a different account. Subsequent attempts at documentary analysis subdividing J into two documents have been unsuccessful because not enough of the second account is preserved.

The contradictions in the story of the Flood are no greater than those in Gen. 2-3, and do not, by themselves, justify a documentary analysis which can only be made to work by means of the assumption of the omission by a redactor of important elements in one of the two postulated documents. The incorporation of fragmentary motifs from another tradition into an otherwise consistent and coherent narrative seems, as in the case of Gen. 2-3, to be the most probable solution of the problem, though it remains uncertain at what point in the history of the Flood story this interpolation occurred.

In the story of the Flood the two documents supposed by the documentary critics to have been combined are J and P. In the remainder of Genesis the sections deemed to be composite are mainly attributed to a combination of J and E. As has already been pointed out, E has always posed problems for the Documentary Hypothesis, mainly because the passages which were believed to belong incontrovertibly to E were insufficient in quantity to permit the reconstruction of a plausible alternative to J as a continuous document. It was therefore supposed that (a) large sections of E had been omitted in favour of the J account, and (b) in many places J and E had been so skilfully merged as to make source division uncertain or even impossible. Such skilfully combined passages naturally did not manifest a large number of palpable contradictions. One other section of Genesis, however, was regarded as an example of an easily analysable composite narrative: the story of Joseph (chs. 37ff.).

The beginning of this narrative (ch. 37) in particular seemed to offer plentiful evidence of the existence of two alternative versions, especially from verse 19 onwards (together with 39.1), where the account of the behaviour of Joseph's brothers which led to his being taken to Egypt and sold there is a somewhat complicated one. Of the various supposed inconsistencies in these verses, the apparently alternative roles played by the Ishmaelite and Midianite traders in the affair (37.25-29, 36; 39.1) seemed to provide the clearest case of a double account. Attempts have been frequently made to fit both Ishmaelites and Midianites into a single coherent account; but even if it is concluded that there is a real contradiction here, it still remains to be proved that the story of Joseph as a whole provides evidence that there were once two complete versions of the story which have been combined. Even those critics who believed this to be so admitted that the case would not be convincing apart from the general presupposition of the Documentary Hypothesis that there must have been such a dual version. So Driver: 'The narrative of Joseph cannot be judged entirely by itself; it must be judged in the light of the presumption derived from the study of JE as a whole. And this presumption is of a nature which tends to confirm the conclusion that it is composite' (1904, p. 20). There appears to be a circular argument here. Further, with regard to the analysis of the major part of the story (chs. 39ff.) Driver made two serious admissions: that nothing like two parallel versions can be re-constructed, and that the evidence for distinguishing one source from the other is often inconclusive: 'The narrative of Joseph in c. 39ff. consists, as it seems, of long passages *excerpted alternately* [my italics] from J and E, each, however, embodying traits derived from the other' (p. 18).

The narrative of the Plagues (Exod. 7.14–11.10) is held by the documentary critics to be composed of three documentary sources, J, E and P; but this conclusion is based on differences of language and of theological point of view supposedly detectable in various narrative elements which recur—though not consistently—in the accounts of the individual plagues, rather than on the presence of contradictions. The actual contradictions in these stories are few; and where they do occur (for example, with regard to the Egyptians' cattle, which all died according to 9.6 but were still alive according to 9.19) they do not provide evidence for documentary analysis: both the verses referred to above are attributed to J. That the plague narrative has undergone a complex history which has left its mark on the present text is probable; but since each account of a single plague differs considerably in form from all the others, it is clear that a simple analysis of the whole into the three 'classical' documentary sources fails to account for its complexities.

The same is true of the story of the rebellion of Korah, Dathan and Abiram in Num. 16–17. Here there are clear inconsistencies which appear to be due to the combination of two originally separate stories concerning Korah and his associates on the one hand and Dathan and Abiram on the other; but here again conventional documentary analysis does not solve the problems of composition. The documentary critics agreed that the evidence for a separate E strand here is of a very insubstantial nature: the analysis of J and E 'can only be carried into detail in the most tentative way' (Gray, p. 190). Yet on the other hand they agreed that the remainder, although attributed to P, is not straightforward and can best be explained on the hypothesis either of a double source or of a later redaction of an original P. Thus the discrepancies in this narrative seem to suggest the presence not of the three 'classical' documents but rather of a quite different set of elements or traditions peculiar to this chapter, the history of whose composition remains obscure.

c. *Differences of culture, religion and theology*
For Wellhausen and his contemporaries this criterion was the most important of all for the solution of the composition of the Pentateuch. Later reflection, however, has led to a more cautious attitude towards it, even on the part of the supporters of the Documentary Hypothesis. So Eissfeldt, while maintaining its validity in general, acknowledged that the criterion lacks precision: 'there may often be very divergent opinions as to whether a particular conception does or does not accord with the whole outlook of a stratum as it may be established in other respects. . . . The spiritual make-up of each individual person is a *complexio oppositorum*, and so too a narrative work will reveal many points of tension'. This, Eissfeldt believed, was particularly true of the authors of the Pentateuchal documents, since they were not the creators of their own materials: although for him they were indeed 'authors, not collectors', they were 'authors who shaped or reshaped materials which were . . . centuries old' and which had already undergone a development of their own: consequently 'it is naturally difficult to draw conclusions of literary lack of unity from the presence of elements belonging to different spiritual levels' (1934, pp. 206-207; ET pp. 185-86).

Of the points made by Eissfeldt—the necessity to make allowances for theological tensions (whether acknowledged or unconscious) in the minds of the individual authors, and the persistence in their works, despite 'reshaping', of the religious and theological diversity of the material which they used—the latter especially has been expressed with greater emphasis by other scholars. Already in 1931 Pedersen had argued that the fact of diversity of religious levels within the supposed documents made the entire system of documentary criticism untenable. The idea of four successive documents, J, E, D and P, each representing a distinct stage in the development of Israel's religious notions, and of their successive incorporation, step by step, to form a single work was a reflection of nineteenth-century concepts of cultural and religious development. Once it was realized that these supposed documents each contained material of different religious and spiritual levels, they ceased to provide evidence for any such progress. This meant, first of all, that it was impossible to distinguish two documents, J and E, since the material in each case was equally diverse. D and P could admittedly be distinguished from JE and from each other because their contents were distinctive; but they, like J and E, also contained material from different periods and stages of religious thought. All the documents, therefore, were undatable in the sense intended by the documentary critics: they were all equally the products of many periods, and they had developed not in chronological succession but simultaneously and side by side.

But Pedersen went further than this. He maintained not only that P and D, which were generally held to be *late* sources, contain material *earlier* than the dates usually assigned to them, but also that JE, though basically a collection of *early*, pre-exilic material, contains elements which must be regarded as *late*, that is exilic or later—for example, the emphasis on individual obedience to the will of God, or the theological discussion in Gen. 18.22-33. In other words, these so-called documents were *all* post-exilic in their final form, and their combination to form the present Pentateuch was entirely a late phenomenon. It might admittedly be possible to date individual passages; but the collections themselves had no specific theological characteristics. They witnessed to the great diversity of Israel's religious life. Consequently the 'theological criterion' was useless. There was no evidence of the existence of actual documents at all— the Documentary Hypothesis was an 'illusion'.

Another kind of attack on this criterion came from Volz, who pointed out that it involved a circular argument (Volz and Rudolph, p. 20): passages were assigned to one or other of the documents on the grounds of their conformity to the supposed basic character of that document, but that character was itself determined on the basis of the material which had already been assigned to it. Volz insisted that the theological description of a document could not be given until its contents had previously been determined by other—that is, by literary—methods. Later scholars (e.g. Rendtorff, 1975, p. 5) echoed this opinion.

In fact, theological congruity, even if it could be adequately defined, would by itself be insufficient to prove the existence of continuous documents. It is one thing to assemble a collection of literary fragments which appear to manifest common theological characteristics; it is another to prove that these once belonged to a single continuous document. This could only be done by showing that together they form a literary unity which as a whole and in all its individual parts manifests a single, purposive theological theme. In recent discussion attempts have been made to do this, particularly in the case of J. On the other hand, it has been argued that the theological themes which find expression in the Pentateuch do not correspond to the documentary strata at all, but developed separately and independently before being combined at a late, possibly 'Deuteronomic' stage.

The theology of the Yahwist

It was mainly on the basis of religious ideas and practices and the supposed affinities of these with particular stages in the religious (and political) history of Israel as reconstructed from other Old Testament books that the various Pentateuchal documents were assigned both relative and absolute dates by the documentary critics. In this way J and E were assigned to the earlier period of the monarchy, D to the later period, and P to the period of the Babylonian Exile or later. With regard to J and E, the chronological priority of the former over the latter was almost universally accepted on the grounds that E reflected a higher, and therefore later, religious and ethical standard than J. Opinions differed on the question of the influence of prophetic teaching upon the authors of these two documents, but both were most commonly dated within the period from the ninth to the early eighth centuries BC.

An entirely new approach to these criteria was initiated by von Rad (1938). Whereas earlier scholars had seen the authors of J and E as either collectors and arrangers of traditional material or, at most, as historians who to some extent coloured the material with religious notions of their time, von Rad's 'Yahwist' was a historian who dominated his material and made it serve a precise and all-embracing politico-theological purpose. He was a theologian and writer of genius; and his work, written during the reign of Solomon, reflected the confident atmosphere of the court of the united Israelite kingdom. He was concerned to encourage the belief that the spectacular success of David in winning independence and political greatness for Israel was due to Yahweh's faithfulness to his promises. 'The datum upon which he based his entire work', wrote von Rad, 'was, it seems to me, an historical one: not just the success-story of Israel's settlement in Canaan, but the further fact that in his subsequent dealings with Israel God had manifestly continued to show the same kind of favour towards them. In this way God had set his seal afresh upon the ancient creed' (p. 77; ET p. 70).

At the same time the Yahwist was, for von Rad, an original and even revolutionary theological thinker. Although the traditional material, originally preserved in connection with the cult, which formed the basis of his work, represented God as one who intervened spectacularly and miraculously, but sporadically, at crucial points in history, the Yahwist wove these together to present a much more 'spiritual' view: 'The spiritual atmosphere in which the Yahwist moves is almost unparalleled in the history of Old Testament religion' (pp. 66-67; ET p. 69). For him, 'God's dealings are not experienced only intermittently . . . through the deeds of a charismatic leader. . . . God's activity is now perhaps less perceptible to the outward sight, but it is actually perceived more fully and more constantly because his guidance is seen to extend equally to every historical occurrence, sacred or profane, up to the time of the Settlement. It is a history of divine guidance and providence to which the Yahwist bears witness' (p. 78; ET p. 71).

Von Rad further maintained that the Yahwist's theological understanding of the divine control of history was determinative of the whole subsequent development of the Pentateuch (or Hexateuch): 'The Elohist and the priestly writer do not diverge from the pattern in this respect: their writings are no more than variations upon the massive theme of the Yahwist's conception, despite their admittedly great theological originality' (p. 82; ET p. 74). The correctness or otherwise of von Rad's view of the Yahwist has frequently been debated (see W.H. Schmidt, 1981 and the references there); but there is a wide agreement that, as Rendtorff pointed out (1977, p. 86), the question of the Yahwist's theology is crucial to the whole problem of the composition of the Pentateuch. For it is, for the Documentary Hypothesis, the only possible reference-point for the discussion of later theological developments within the Pentateuch. If in the end it turns out that it does not make sense as a coherent work, then the hypothesis as a whole does not make sense, and some other model for the formation of the Pentateuch must be sought.

Rendtorff, however, paradoxically saw in von Rad's heavy emphasis on the theological importance of the Yahwist not a confirmation of the Documentary Hypothesis but a shift away from it of which von Rad himself was not fully aware. According to Rendtorff, the 'Yahwist' for von Rad was not really identical with the earliest of the four documents: 'his "Yahwist" has hardly anything to do with the "Yahwist" of the documentary hypothesis'. 'Von Rad was too much a child of his own time and could not easily free himself from the traditional view of the division of sources. So when he had to choose a name for the theologian who had carried out this work of composition, he spoke quite naturally of the "Yahwist"' (1975a, p. 160; ET pp. 3-4). But in fact, according to Rendtorff, von Rad's conception of the 'Yahwist' as the theologian who carried out the fundamental work of forming the Pentateuch out of a number of complexes of tradition (Primaeval History, patriarchal history, Exodus tradition, Sinai tradition, Settlement tradition) makes the Documentary Hypothesis, with its four (or, in Genesis to Numbers, three) documents each with its own substantial contribution to make to the whole, irrelevant and unnecessary. The two theories are mutually incompatible.

Rendtorff's assertion that von Rad's Yahwist 'has hardly anything to do with the "Yahwist" of the documentary hypothesis' is an exaggeration: it is quite clear from von Rad's article that E and P, as well as D, were realities for him, and that when he spoke of the Yahwist he was referring to a document which exists side by side with them in the Pentateuch and is more or less the 'J' of the hypothesis. Nevertheless, for him the contribution of J was so great that its importance dwarfs the others; and it is in this sense that Rendtorff was correct when he asserted that von Rad's view of the Yahwist as the single-handed architect of a unified Pentateuch is incompatible with the Documentary Hypothesis. To say this is, of course, not to prejudge the question whether von Rad's view is correct: this still needs to be examined. Rendtorff's point is that, whether he was conscious of it or not, von Rad was in fact offering an alternative to that hypothesis.

Though it may be true in one sense that von Rad's thesis undermined the Documentary Hypothesis, he was ostensibly a supporter of it, since what he was proposing was a defence of the credibility and cohesion of one of its documents, J: for him, J was not just a collection of heterogeneous material but a unified theological work. But it is precisely this rationale of von Rad's Yahwist which has come under attack in recent years. The questions have been raised: Is von Rad's estimate of that theology correct? Is there a single theological point of view observable throughout the J material? Can J be as early as von Rad believed it to be?

The first question which presents itself in this connection is that of the correctness of von Rad's estimate of the Yahwist's theological purpose. Unlike Noth, who ten years later argued that the various traditions existing among the pre-Israelite tribes were already integrated before the settlement of those tribes in Canaan, von Rad regarded this integration as the work of the Yahwist, who worked during the period of the United Monarchy. By laying great emphasis on the promises to Abraham, repeated to Isaac and Jacob, that he— that is, his descendants—would become a great nation, inherit the land and be a blessing for the nations of the earth (Gen. 12.1-3 and a few other passages, which von Rad regarded as original contributions by the Yahwist himself) the Yahwist was able to weld all his material into a whole which showed how God, despite the obstacles presented by human sin (Gen. 2–11 and many later passages), guided and preserved the ancestors of Israel (Gen. 12–50), delivered them from Egypt and from various vicissitudes, bound them to obedience to his righteous will (Sinai) and finally, as he had promised, brought them to the land of Canaan and gave them possession of it (J, for von Rad, continues into the book of Joshua).

Von Rad's thesis was clearly a *tour de force*. So diverse are the elements which compose the picture that the interpretation which von Rad gives of it can be no more than one of several possible ways of looking at it, each of which seems equally plausible. It is not clear, for example, that either the Primaeval History with its picture of sin and its consequences, or the Sinai pericope with its note of rigorous divine demand is particularly well suited to the Solomonic scenario for which von Rad argues. The presence of both these sections could be more plausibly explained in terms of a much later period in Israel's history, while the theme of the divine promises, especially that of the possession of the land, would be of at least as great significance for the Israel of the exilic period, longing to repossess the land and in need of some kind of divine assurance, as for the self-confident Israel of the Solomonic era which might be taking its possession for granted. Moreover, the very comprehensiveness and richness of the total theological content of J would seem to be more appropriate to an Israel which had experienced disappointment and suffering than to a much earlier Israel in its heyday.

These observations may be extended further. Von Rad's account of the Yahwist's theology is no more than a brief sketch; and even if we take into account his later writings on the subject (e.g. his commentary on Genesis) the question arises whether the theological unity of purpose which he claims for it can be demónstrated when its contents are considered in detail. Von Rad was not greatly concerned with these matters of detail, since he believed that the Yahwist's method consisted mainly not in any direct contribution which he made to the *contents* of the individual narratives either by additions of his own or by reshaping the narratives themselves, but in his *arrangement* of the narratives which he selected in a way which would create out of the disparate material a single, continuous story which demonstrated the working out of a consistent divine purpose. By this process, according to von Rad, he invested the various narratives with new meanings derived from their new contexts. Although he made some 'occasional' but significant additions of his own—'sections which, as can be seen relatively easily, do not go back to ancient tradition but represent short bridges between early narrative material', such as Gen. 6.5-8; 12.1-9; 18.17-23 (1956, 9th edn, ET p. 23)—'in shaping the individual narratives he probably did not go beyond some trimming of the archaic profiles and making definite fine accents' (p. 37).

This view of the Yahwist's method of working seems at first sight to provide a satisfactory explanation of any unevennnesses, contradictions or irrelevancies which the scholar may find in J, a problem of which von Rad was aware when he wrote:

> Naturally one cannot expect complete thematic consistency in a composition that joins together the most varied ... materials. Occasionally the narratives are even unyielding toward one another. In the stories of Laban, for instance, one cannot help feeling that the individual traditions to which the Yahwist was bound by the history of tradition had resisted thematic permeation more than others. ... And yet the plan for a thematic synopsis cannot be misunderstood (p. 39).

This last assertion seems an exaggeration. Although the story of the deceits and trickeries practised mutually by Jacob and Laban (Gen. 29-31) will no doubt have entertained the original readers of these stories as much as they had entertained their predecessors who knew them in some other and earlier context, the serious theologian whom von Rad presents to us under the name of 'Yahwist' would surely have done better to omit them, as presumably he was free to do, as distracting from, and irrelevant to, his main theme.

This point has been made by a number of scholars (e.g. Sandmel, pp. 116-18). Even more serious, however, are the criticisms which have been made about the consistency and coherence of the Yahwist's supposed theology. Following Sandmel (pp. 118-19), Westermann (1974, p. 775; 1981, pp. 17-18), with regard not only to von Rad's thesis but to all attempts to find a consistency in any of the documents, insisted that it would be possible to speak of a 'theology' of J or P only if the same theological standpoints could be found *throughout* the document in question—which he believed to be impossible, given the fact that the authors of the documents were primarily 'tradents' of the earlier material. Westermann pointed out (1974, p. 775) that to draw conclusions about the theology of P simply on the basis of Gen. 1 or to maintain that J had an anthropomorphic view of God solely on the basis of Gen. 2-3— as has often been done—would be entirely unjustified. As with the other criteria for the identification of the documents, the theological criterion must be based on a full examination of all the material.

It was Rendtorff (1975, 1977) who offered the most serious and thoroughgoing criticism of such theological constructions, and in particular of von Rad's 'theology of the Yahwist'. He accepted, in general, von Rad's and Noth's traditio-historical approach to the material, which viewed the Pentateuch as the result of the combination of originally separate complexes of tradition, but differed from them in regarding this approach as incompatible with the Documentary Hypothesis. Whereas for von Rad and Noth all these traditions had coalesced at an early stage—the period of Solomon for von Rad, earlier for Noth—into a 'pan-Israelite' account of origins which already during the early monarchy took the shape of comprehensive written documents (J and E), Rendtorff found no trace of such a stage of literary development until much later. He was not prepared to date this late stage precisely, but he found evidence of both priestly and Deuteronomic editorial work.

Rendtorff maintained that before this late stage no comprehensive account of Israel's origins existed. Rather, the individual traditions each underwent a long and complex process of development in which they progressed from the smallest units to more substantial 'medium-sized' ones and then to larger ones before their final combination into a single continuous account (e.g., in the case of the patriarchal traditions, from individual stories to the separate 'histories' of Abraham, Isaac and Jacob, and finally to the fully integrated 'larger unit' of the 'patriarchal history' which was itself eventually combined with other 'larger units' to form the Pentateuch). Rendtorff thus proposed a complete *alternative* to the Documentary Hypothesis.

Rendtorff's thesis depends partly on purely literary considerations; but it is his theological argument which is its most significant element. In contrast to the attempts of von Rad and his predecessors to construct 'theologies' of the various supposed documents, he attempted to show that each of the 'larger units' has its own character and 'theology', and that these theologies differ from one another: each of them has been edited and organized in such a way as to give expression to a single dominant theological theme. Von Rad and Noth, who in turn were partly dependent on the work of earlier scholars such as Pedersen, had already provided much of the groundwork for this; but they had held that these separate theologies or theological themes had been to a large extent overridden, or at least transformed, by the more comprehensive theologies of J and E (or, in the case of Noth, of an even earlier source, G) when they used this material to create their continuous 'histories' of early Israel.

Rendtorff set himself the task of showing that a theology of J (or E) must be an illusion, because, with the exception of the later editorial material (Deuteronomic and priestly) there is no continuity between the various blocks of material (the 'larger units') of which the Pentateuch is composed: that the differences between them are so great that they cannot have been composed by the same person or with the same theological intention. The creator of each of these separate theologies worked in isolation from and in ignorance of the others. In view of the vastness of the task, Rendtorff concentrated on one theme in particular: the patriarchal stories of Abraham, Isaac and Jacob. He attempted to show that the 'theology' of Genesis was unknown to those who were responsible for the composition of the other 'larger units', and in particular to those who composed that which immediately follows it: the Moses or Exodus 'larger unity' of Exod. 1–14.

In his assessment of the predominant theme of the patriarchal stories Rendtorff did not differ basically from von Rad, who had recognized the crucial importance of the divine promises made to the patriarchs. But, following Westermann (1964, 1976), he concluded from the form and contents of these promises that they had not been formulated at a single stroke (e.g. by von Rad's 'Yahwist'), but had reached their final, complex shapes (promise of land, progeny, blessing, guidance; extension of the scope of the promise from Abraham alone to include his progeny, etc.) through an extended process of theological development, which had gone hand in hand with the editorial process which gradually bound the stories together into a single 'larger unit'. The passages in which the promises were contained were mainly not integrally related to the main narrative material, but were the work of its editors: it was here that the theological theme of this section of Genesis was most clearly expressed.

Where Rendtorff differed radically from his predecessors, however, was in his assertion that this 'promise' theme was not the central theological theme of a Yahwistic history which ran through the entire Pentateuch, but was confined to the patriarchal stories. In other words, although they anticipate a fulfilment which their audience presumably recognized as having occurred in the life and experience of later generations of the descendants of their original recipients, and although the Pentateuch in its *final*, post-exilic form has bound all the 'larger units' together so that the Exodus and subsequent events are represented as showing the promises in process of fulfilment, these 'larger units', including the story of the sojourn in Egypt and the Exodus which form the early chapters of the book of Exodus, had, until a comparatively late date, undergone a long process of development entirely independent of the patriarchal stories, and had been edited with entirely different theological ends in view.

One of the considerations in favour of Rendtorff's thesis was the fact that the series of divine promises, at any rate in the form in which they appear so prominently and so frequently in addresses to the patriarchs in Genesis, comes to an end—except in material generally regarded as late—with the book of Genesis. Von Rad and Noth had noted this fact but had made a virtue out of it. Von Rad, writing of Gen. 12.1-3 and specifically of the promise to Abraham that in his descendants all the families of the earth should be blessed, maintained: 'It was sufficient that it should be expressed at one point in the work with programmatic clarity. . . . The contribution of the J writer is to be seen primarily in the composition itself, that is, in the way in which the material has been put together' (1938, p. 75; ET p. 67). Noth, also writing about Gen. 12.1-3, which he regarded as looking both backwards and forwards, as a bridge passage joining the Primaeval History to the patriarchal narratives and as a crucial pointer to the rest of the Pentateuch, somewhat similarly asserted that 'The entire weight of the theology of J rests upon the beginning of his narrative. . . . It was enough for him to have said plainly at the beginning how he intended to understand everything beyond that' (1948, p. 258; ET p. 238).

Rendtorff agreed with von Rad and Noth that each of the 'larger units' in Exodus to Numbers has its own distinct theological theme. But whereas they regarded the promise theme in Genesis as an all-embracing Pentateuchal theme which was the creation of the Yahwist, and which overrode all the others and bound them into one, Rendtorff maintained that there are no backward-looking allusions to the promise theme of Genesis in any of the other 'larger units' in material earlier than the final redaction of the Pentateuch. In particular, while agreeing with von Rad and Noth that the basic theme of Exod. 1-14 (with its climax in the poems of Exod. 15) is that of divine salvation—the act of grace by which God saved his people from their oppressors and led them out of Egypt, and the grateful acceptance of this by Israel in the form of a confession of faith—he argued that there is no evidence of a 'Yahwist' who combined the theme of promise with that of salvation and confession.

Rendtorff maintained—and this is a crucial point in his argument —that Exod. 1-14 is basically the work of an editor who knew nothing of the patriarchal traditions as they are found in Genesis. That is, apart from the additions made by the final editor who created the Pentateuch in its present form, there are virtually no allusions in Exod. 1-14—or, indeed, in the subsequent 'larger units' in Exodus-Numbers—to the promises made to the patriarchs, nor does the material in Genesis look forward to the events narrated in Exod. 1-14 (sojourn of the sons of Israel in Egypt, plagues, Exodus). Even where there would have been an obvious opportunity to make such a connection, as in Exod. 1.7, where Israel's growth into a numerous and powerful people might seem to be an obvious fulfilment of the corresponding promise to Abraham, or Exod. 3.8, where the promise to Moses of guidance into the land of Canaan might be expected to contain a reference to the earlier promises of the land to the patriarchs, there is no mention of those promises or of the patriarchs. On the contrary, the promise of the land is expressed in entirely new terms (specifically as 'a land flowing with milk and honey') which suggest that such a land was previously unheard of. There are admittedly a few references in this part of Exodus (2.23-25, and even in chapters 3-4) to the patriarchs, but the fact that these do not refer to the promises and do not correspond to the accounts in Genesis confirms the general point. The passages which, in the present text, provide cross-references between the two 'larger units' (Gen. 15.13-16; 50.24; Exod. 1.6, 8—and 5b?—; 32.13; 33.1; Num. 14.23; 20.14-16; 32.11) come from the final redactor, and are generally easily identifiable by the fact that they are not integral to the main narrative but can be removed from it without disruption.

Most of the passages regarded by Rendtorff as late were attributed by the documentary critics to J, E or JE. Rendtorff is not alone, however, in assigning them to a later stage of composition: with the exception of Exod. 1.6, 8 it has long been suspected that they belong to a later, Deuteronomic or proto-Deuteronomic stage (see Perlitt, 1969). Exod. 1.6, 8, which refer back to Joseph and his high position in Egypt, are part of a section (1.1ff.) whose present function is to join together the patriarchal narratives (not only the Joseph story) and those of Moses and the Exodus. Some uncertainty now prevails among the critics with regard to its composition (see W.H. Schmidt, 1974-7, pp. 7-26). Rendtorff, as has already been said, regarded verse 7, which in a single sentence telescopes the history of several generations from the seventy sons of Joseph to the existence of Israel as a great and strong people, as belonging to the early material because it does not refer back to the corresponding promise to Abraham.

It would perhaps be better to regard the entire section, in its present form, as a late editorial bridge passage between the two larger units. It attempts by a gradual change of terminology to smooth over the abrupt transition. The phrase *bᵉnē yiśrā'ēl*, which means literally Jacob's sons in verse 1 (cf. verse 5), has an ambiguous meaning in verse 7, and then unequivocally means 'Israelites' in verses 12, 13 and the following narrative, being equivalent to the term 'the *people* of the Israelites' (*ᶜam bᵉnē yiśrā'ēl*) in verse 9 and later verses. From that point onwards there is no further thought of the family of the man Jacob or of the life and work of Joseph. This careful linking passage between two otherwise unconnected and thematically distinct 'larger units' gives the impression of being a later construction. Although Rendtorff did not interpret this passage in this way, such an interpretation would seem to strengthen his argument: here is a clear editorial join between two otherwise distinct 'larger units'.

A further confirmation of Rendtorff's thesis is provided by the curious silence, already referred to above (pp. 48-49), of the pre-exilic writings about the patriarchs, and indeed about the Pentateuch as a whole. As is well known, the name of Abraham does not occur in the pre-exilic prophets at all; and the only two passages in the entire Old Testament in which it occurs which *may* be pre-exilic are Elijah's prayer in 1 Kgs 18.36, where God is addressed as 'Yahweh the God of Abraham, Isaac and Jacob', and Ps. 47.10 (EVV v. 9), where Israel is called 'the people of the God of Abraham'. There are no references in these passages to any of the narratives of Genesis. Isaac and Jacob (as personal names) are not otherwise mentioned at all, except in Hos. 12, and even here the version of Jacob's activities known to the prophet seems to have been different from that preserved in Genesis. With regard to Moses, the only references in passages which may possibly be pre-exilic are three references to him in the book of Judges (1.16, 20; 4.11) as the son-in-law of Hobab, the ancestor of the Kenites, and a further reference to him as the grandfather of Jonathan, Micah's priest (Judg. 18.30); Ps. 77.21 (EVV v. 20), where Moses and Aaron are identified as having led the people through the experiences of the Exodus, and Ps. 99.6, where Moses is associated with Aaron and Samuel as a famous intercessor. Not all these passages are certainly pre-exilic, and Ps. 77, the only one which refers to the Exodus tradition, is regarded by some scholars as dependent on Deutero-Isaiah.

With regard to Abraham, it is particularly significant that, after the total silence of the pre-exilic prophets about him, he suddenly sprang into prominence in prophetic circles at the time of the Exile as the person to whom the land was given and so as one from whom Israel, now deprived of its land and inclined to believe that God had permanently withdrawn from them, might derive encouragement: God, according to these prophets, had not forgotten his promises to Abraham and his descendants, but would again bless, lead, guide and prosper them, make them a strong and powerful people and above all give them (once more) the land which he had promised to give them (Isa. 41.8-10; 51.1-3; Ezek. 33.24). At this period, then, we find for the first time what appears to be a fairly comprehensive knowledge of the Abraham traditions, not merely as isolated stories but in a theologically developed form. In other words, the evidence which we have suggests that the exilic period was the period when the theological importance of the promises to Abraham was first drawn out.

Rendtorff was cautious about the use of this evidence: he believed that it would be overstating the case to argue that the patriarchal and the other Pentateuchal traditions were entirely unknown before the Exile; but he argued (1977, pp. 169-73) that his view of the late date of the formation of the Pentateuch helps to explain what has long been an unsolved problem: the failure of the pre-exilic literature and especially of the pre-exilic prophets, for whom God's activity in history was so important, to make use of this material. That the material was in existence in some form long before the Exile is of course possible; but it is reasonable to conclude that before the Exile it had not yet been co-ordinated to form a central, much less an 'official', record of Israel's origins such as the documentary critics' picture of a 'Yahwist' or of a 'JE' would suggest.

Rendtorff's study of the question of the 'larger units' of the Pentateuch was mainly confined to the patriarchal narratives and their relationship to the sections which follow, though he hinted at the lines along which the study of the other 'larger units' should proceed, and noted—following von Rad, Noth and others—that the Primaeval History, the Exodus material, the Sinai pericope, the wilderness narratives and the Settlement traditions have each its own special and to a large extent 'self-contained' character. Little work has yet been done to substantiate this view, and it is possible that some of these sections may have been less independent of one another than Rendtorff believed: for example, the figure of Moses, which dominates the whole Pentateuch from the early chapters of the book of Exodus onwards, remains a problem. Although the paucity of references to Moses in the pre-exilic literature suggests that the traditions concerning him were not of central importance in that period, Noth's extreme radical view that Moses originally figured only in one (at the most) of the Pentateuchal 'themes' has provoked a strong reaction; and, if the 'themes' or 'larger units' remained entirely independent of one another until a late date, as Rendtorff believed, his sudden rise to dominance in every one of them becomes even more difficult to account for.

A beginning along similar lines has however been made in the case of the Primaeval History. Crüsemann (1981) has carried out a study of this 'larger unit' and its affinities and concluded, largely on theological grounds, that its point of view is quite foreign to that of the patriarchal narratives and to Gen. 12.1-3 in particular: the latter does not constitute a bridge between the two sections and does not look backwards. The two sections remained separate until they were joined together by the genealogical link of 11.27-32, which is entirely late.

In selecting the patriarchal narratives as a test case, Rendtorff has perhaps chosen for his thesis the area which lends itself most easily to his approach; but it should be stressed that, from a logical point of view, his analysis of this one major section of the Pentateuch, if correct, is—though such studies as that of Crüsemann will help to confirm it—by itself sufficient to establish his thesis: if the main narrative materials in Gen. 12-50 and in Exod. 1-14 do not have a common authorship, the hypothesis of a Yahwist document running through the whole of Genesis–Numbers falls to the ground.

The main criticism of Rendtorff's position with regard to the theology of the Yahwist has been that he has not wholly succeeded in establishing the independence of the larger units: his dating of the cross-references to which he alludes is disputed, and he has been accused of neglecting others. This is largely a matter of judgment rather than of fact. Otto further suggested that his arguments are too theologically oriented and too abstract: he does not pay sufficient attention to historical and sociological changes which may have forged links between the themes of the Pentateuch at a fairly early stage without necessarily leaving tangible evidence in the form of interpolated 'cross-references': it was, after all, in that way that the medium-sized units such as the Abraham stories took shape in their earlier stages.

But although there is as yet no consensus of opinion in favour of Rendtorff's thesis, and the supporters of the Documentary Hypothesis in one form or another remain unconvinced, other scholars writing about the same time as Rendtorff have independently reached conclusions similar to his.

H.H. Schmid's book on the Yahwist was published (1976) before that of Rendtorff, but after the latter's article (1975a), in which he had already presented the most essential points of the argument which he was to develop two years later. Schmid, therefore, was able to take account of Rendtorff's position and to express his agreement

with much of it. He had, however, worked independently of
Rendtorff, a fact which makes the substantial agreement between the
two the more impressive.

Schmid's study, *Der sogenannte Jahwist* ('The So-Called Yahwist')
was entirely concerned with the question of the Yahwist's theology.
His intention was in fact not to deny the existence of the Yahwist but
to put forward an interpretation of the character of that work which
was completely different from that of the Documentary Hypothesis,
and also different from those of von Rad and Noth. It also differed
from that of Rendtorff, but this difference was mainly a matter of
terminology. Whereas Rendtorff spoke of a '*Bearbeitungsschicht*' or
'editorial stratum' closely related to Deuteronomic ideas in which, at
a relatively late stage, the 'larger Pentateuchal units' were for the
first time combined into a single work of history, Schmid continued
to use the term 'Yahwist' for the concluding stage of a similar
editorial process, but brought this 'Yahwist's' activity down to a date
at least as late as that postulated by Rendtorff for his '*Bearbeitungsschicht*'. For Schmid, the 'Yahwist', by his editing and
arrangement of the material, was expounding an entire 'theology of
history', and one which was only conceivable at a period when
Israel's national history (in the political sense) was at an end and
could be viewed and reflected upon as a whole: that is, the post-exilic
period. His 'Yahwist', moreover, was not, like von Rad's, a single
'collector, author and theologian'. Rather, the Yahwistic work was
the result of an '(inner-)Yahwistic process of redaction and interpretation' of the deposit left by the mainly oral development of
traditional materials in the pre-exilic period.

The arguments used by Schmid to substantiate his case for a 'late
Yahwist' differed from those of Rendtorff. The latter was concerned
above all to demonstrate the differences of purpose and approach
between the 'theologies' of the various 'larger units' and the lack of
cross-references between them in any but the latest redactional stage.
Schmid (p. 170) did not entirely agree with Rendtorff on this latter
point; instead he developed a line of argument which he reproached
Rendtorff for having neglected, but which led to somewhat similar
results: like Pedersen at an earlier period, he made a comparison
between various ideas and expressions which occur in the 'Yahwistic'
material and theological ideas and forms occurring elsewhere in the
Old Testament (especially the prophets and the Deuteronomistic
History) which demonstrate the dependence of the former on the

latter. Thus he found that the account of the call of Moses in Exod. 3-4 is modelled on the call narratives of the eighth- and seventh-century prophets and reflects a theology of the divine calling and mission which not only cannot be earlier than the period of the pre-exilic prophets but which, moreover, is expressed in terms which recall the later Deuteronomic or Deuteronomistic picture of prophecy.

Similar conclusions were reached by Schmid about other parts of the Yahwistic material. In the plague narratives in the book of Exodus the use of the 'messenger formula' ('Thus says Yahweh, the God of the Hebrews') and the so-called 'recognition formula'('... that you may know that I am Yahweh') is cited as modelled on prophetic usage; the words of Moses to the people in Exod. 14.13-14 before the crossing of the Sea ('Fear not, stand firm, and see the salvation of Yahweh'; 'Yahweh will fight for you, and you only have to be still') are compared with Isaiah's words to Ahaz in Isa. 7.4, 9; the theological treatment of the stories of Israel's disobedience in the wilderness belongs to a period not anterior to Jeremiah. In the Sinai pericope, following Perlitt, Schmid found no genuine 'Yahwistic' narrative at all but only a Deuteronomic composition made out of small traditional units and expressing a developed covenant theology which can only be post-Deuteronomic; and finally in the patriarchal narratives the promises of a strong and numerous people and of the gift of the land are only understandable as coming from a period when Israel had already lost both political independence and the possession of the land, while the promise of blessing could only be derived from the kingship theology at a time when this was no longer a practical reality. All in all, Schmid found in the Yahwistic work as a whole a fully developed 'theology of history' which was not to be found in the traditional individual stories or even in the pre-exilic prophets, but which is comparable to that of the Deuteronomistic History.

What Schmid has done, then, is to find in the work of the 'Yahwist' a theological scheme which is no less comprehensive and coherent than that proposed by von Rad, but which is entirely different and points to a date of composition several centuries later. The fact that two such opposite conclusions could be reached about the same material is in itself sufficient to raise doubts about the entire enterprise. Schmid discussed von Rad's thesis (pp. 13-16) and put forward some telling reasons for rejecting it, especially the theory of a tenth-century 'enlightenment'; on the other hand, Schmid's own dating of the Yahwist could be criticized at several points, particularly for its undue dependence on Perlitt's controversial thesis of the late introduction of the covenant concept into Israel's theological thought. If von Rad assumed an early profundity of theological thought in Israel for which there is little other evidence in the Old Testament, Perlitt and Schmid can be equally criticized for making the opposite assumption: that what is not positively known to be early must be late. The truth is that despite the immense labour of reent generations in the fields of ancient Israelite religion and theology, it is still as difficult as it was in the time of Wellhausen to plot the course of the history of religious ideas in Israel with sufficient precision to pinpoint the moment at which this or that theological notion arose. Indeed, the Wellhausenian confidence with regard to this matter has given way to a state of great uncertainty.

Nevertheless it is clear that between them Rendtorff and Schmid have succeeded in demonstrating the fragility of the theological criterion for the defence of the Documentary Hypothesis, for they have at least demonstrated—as von Rad and Noth failed to do—that there are alternative ways of accounting for the phenomena which have the advantage of situating the development of a comprehensive theology of history in Israel in a period (after 587 BC) when it is known that such an interpretation of the past was needed, and when the opportunity for such an interpretation of the past was present in terms of Israel's past historical experiences, and was in fact being attempted in a somewhat different way by the Deuteronomists in the Deuteronomistic History. It is also interesting that the conclusions drawn from their theological arguments are similar to those reached by means of purely literary arguments by Van Seters and others. In contrast, the arguments of the documentary critics for the existence of J and E as 'documents' (i.e. books) and of R^{JE} as a literary redactor presuppose a high degree of theological reflection as well as of literary skill in a period from which these are hardly to be expected.

The theology of P

The use of the theological criterion to identify P as a continuous Pentateuchal source is rendered extremely difficult, if not impossible, by the widespread lack of agreement about the literary problems.

Wellhausen himself was aware that the legal material in P contains old material and that it was brought together and expanded over a long period of time. But inconsistencies and incongruities in the narrative material were also discovered: von Rad (1934a) postulated the existence of a double source (P^A and P^B) for the whole work, both laws and narrative. A pericope which provides a clear example of an attempt to harmonize two originally distinct presentations of the same event is the creation story (Gen. 1), which preserved two different numerical schemes and two separate sets of formulae in its account. Although such inconsistencies are now more frequently explained in traditio-historical terms than in terms of documentary criticism, they have theological implications which militate against the notion of a single 'theology of P'.

The preponderance of legal material and the relatively small amount of narrative in P also raised the somewhat different question whether the two had ever belonged together in a single unitary work, and the further question whether 'P' was essentially a lawgiver or a narrator. Noth (1943, 1948) saw P as an essentially coherent narrative work. But Volz (Volz and Rudolph, 1933, pp. 135-42), Cross (1973) and Rendtorff (1977), among others, came to the conclusion that there is no P narrative running through the Pentateuch at all. Volz studied the material in Genesis attributed to P by the Documentary Hypothesis, and concluded that P was not a narrator. He pointed out that Gen. 23 (the story of Abraham's purchase of the cave at Machpelah) is the only extended narrative in Genesis attributed to P (and the only one not paralleled in the earlier 'sources'), and that the supposed evidence for its attribution to P is entirely inferential and runs counter to the actual characteristics of the story: it is quite unlike the other 'priestly' narrative material in Genesis, which is very laconic; it contains nothing of P's language or theological point of view; and it has all the liveliness and vividness of a typical 'J' story which are generally supposed to be lacking in 'P'. Otherwise the 'P' material in Genesis consists entirely of theological material such as Gen. 1 and 17 which are not real narratives at all, brief summary and linking 'historical' statements, genealogical and chronological notes, and a few interpolations (e.g. into the older Flood narrative). Cross, much later, reached similar conclusions.

It was Rendtorff who made the fullest investigation of the question of P as narrator. To the fact—acknowledged by all scholars—of the extreme brevity and colourlessness of the historical notices attributed to P in Genesis he added the observation that after Exod. 6.9 this kind of narration ceases altogether. He agreed with Volz that there is no reason to attribute Gen. 23 to P. Although—as is generally acknowledged—the 'historical' notices and the sequence of events in P are based on the J (JE) material with which P was familiar, they do not make up a continuous narrative even in Genesis and early Exodus: there are gaps which are impossible to account for if P was attempting to write a continuous narrative parallel to JE. For example, P has no story of Joseph, nor does he introduce Moses to the scene but has him appear abruptly in Exod. 6; he also has no account of the departure of Israel from Egypt except a brief notice in Exod. 12.41. Moreover, even the chronological notices are not all composed in the same style. P is in fact not a document but a 'redactional strand' (*Bearbeitungsschicht*), not even in itself unified, which interpolated various brief genealogical, and chronological, notices and some additional theological interpretation and helped also to unite the patriarchal narratives with the early chapters of Exodus, but in this role went no further than Exod. 6. Rendtorff's main object in his consideration of P was to show that P is not a continuous narrative source observable throughout the Pentateuch, with the corollary that—contrary to the beliefs of certain recent scholars—it cannot be synonymous with the final redaction of the Pentateuch. He did not deal in detail with the mass of material attributed to P in Exodus–Numbers, a question which deserves further investigation but which was not strictly necessary to his theme.

A further difficulty in the way of the construction of a 'theology of P' is that there is no consensus about the point at which it concluded. According to Noth and others, it concluded with the account of the death of Moses in Deut. 34, a passage which has been separated from the rest of P by the insertion of the book of Deuteronomy. Others (notably Mowinckel, 1964b) continued to maintain that P extended into the book of Joshua and contained an account of the conquest of Canaan. As in the case of the other 'documents', the question whether P ended with the death of Moses or with the settlement in the land substantially affects its perspective, and is of vital importance for an assessment of P's theological purpose.

Noth (1948, p. 259; ET p. 239) issued a significant warning to those who attempt to construct a theology of P:

> It is much more difficult to perceive the basis of the theology of P than it is in the case of J. This is primarily due to the fact that in P

the theological content is not found in the graphic portrayal of events or conversations but rather in the use of particular *termini technici* for objects and institutions. It is no longer completely clear, and probably never will be, what views and ideas were implied when these terms were mentioned.

This was Noth's judgment; and it should be noted that he was referring not to the laws in P, which he believed not to have originally belonged to it, but to the narratives—presumably mainly to the narratives in the Sinai pericope and in Numbers. Noth nevertheless proceeded to give his own account of the purpose and theology of P. He is, however, only one of many scholars who in the last fifty years have attempted the same task, among them von Rad (1934), Elliger (1952), Zimmerli (1960), Mowinckel (1964), Cross (1973) and Rendtorff (1977). The conclusions reached by these scholars have varied to an astonishing degree in accordance with their estimates of the date and historical situation of the writer and of the contents and extent of the work.

Others, more cautious, have expressed doubts about the enterprise. Westermann, for example (1974, p. 775) pointed out that P, like the other 'documents', was a tradent rather than an original writer and warned against the danger of expecting to find a consistent 'theology' in P, especially of reading the 'theology' of a particular passage—e.g. Gen. 1—into the rest. Childs (1979, p. 123) spoke of 'the great variety within the P material and the divergence of function within the strand', citing as an example Gen. 12–25 compared with Gen. 1– 11. The very great variety of views about the character, function, unity and date of P in recent scholarship inevitably raises serious doubts about the possibility of applying to it the 'documentary' criterion of theological standpoint.

The theology of E

The use of the theological criterion in the case of E is beset even more by the weakness of the other criteria than in the case of P. Whereas in the latter case the documentary critics were able to piece together passages and fragments which could at least with some plausibility be represented as a continuous narrative beginning with the creation of the world and ending with the death of Moses or even later, it has been universally recognized since the early days of the Documentary Hypothesis that not merely is the Elohist in his matter and in his manner of looking at things most clearly akin to the Jehovist; his document has come down to us, as Nöldeke was the first to perceive, only in extracts embodied in the Jehovist narrative (Wellhausen, 1883, p. 8; ET pp. 7-8).

Moreover in much of the Pentateuch, especially from the book of Exodus onwards, Wellhausen and his successors found it impossible to separate the two documents and assigned a large number of texts—apart from those attributed to P—simply to the 'Jehovistic history', i.e. to an undifferentiated 'JE'.

The extant 'E' material, then, is, by universal agreement, not a complete document. At best, it is a torso. 'E' as a document has no actual existence, but is merely an hypothesis constructed on the basis of a series of narratives and smaller fragments, which cannot be fitted together to form a whole. In these circumstances the criteria of language and style, even if admissible in this case, cannot prove that it was ever a continuous whole, nor can the existence of doublets in the Pentateuchal text. Noth (1948, p. 247; ET p. 228) admitted that its original existence as the work of a single author 'can only be assumed on the analogy of the other two sources'. This is as true of the theological criterion as it is of the others.

It is generally agreed that all the Pentateuchal writers are, at least to some extent, tradents or collectors, and that they are not entirely homogeneous in their allusions to religious practices or theological notions: they have not entirely obliterated in favour of their own theological purposes the traces of earlier religious beliefs and practices inherent in the material which they used. In view of this, it would be difficult to demonstrate the existence in the 'E' material of a specific theology or religious standpoint of its own substantially different from that of the 'J' document in which it is supposed to be embedded, unless that theology were extremely coherent and distinctive to a degree which exceeded the theological fluctuations likely to exist within 'J' itself. If it could be shown that this is the case, there would be good reason to speak of an Elohistic theology.

But even so, nothing would have been proved at all about the existence at any time of a continuous 'E' document. The theological phenomena could easily be accounted for in other ways: for example, by the hypothesis of an 'Elohistic school' (or even a single 'Elohistic' editor) who supplemented the older material by the piecemeal interpolation of passages and smaller additions representing this 'new' theological point of view. It is the *lack of continuity* in the 'E' material which (quite apart from the uncertainty where 'E' begins and ends) stands in the way of the use of the theological criterion; for in the absence of an extant continuous work it is quite impossible, without resort to dubious conjecture about what its original contents might have been, to discover—as, for example, von Rad attempted to do in the case of J—what the distinctive theological thrust and purpose of the work as a whole might have been.

Objections to the E hypothesis such as those suggested above were first systematically put forward by Volz and Rudolph (1933 and 1938). These scholars, after a detailed examination of Gen. 12–50 and (by Rudolph alone) of Exodus–Numbers, divided the material ascribed to E roughly into three classes: first, in many passages they found that there were insufficient grounds for suspecting the existence of two separate documents unless the investigator was first persuaded that this must be so. Second, with regard to doublets, they argued that these were the result of the policy of J as a collector, who deliberately incorporated double versions of incidents into his narrative for various reasons including the desire to illuminate certain events from more than one angle. Finally, the remaining 'E' material could be accounted for as the work of editors who had inserted it piecemeal into J. Much of their argument is concerned with purely literary phenomena: they maintained that the theological criterion was too weak to stand on its own, and had been introduced by the documentary critics only secondarily in an attempt to support what had already become, on literary grounds, the 'dogma' of dual documentary sources (Volz, pp. 19-21). Although the views of Volz and Rudolph about E were vigorously attacked in the years following the publication of their work, several scholars have more recently reached similar conclusions (e.g. Mowinckel, 1964 and Westermann, 1964 and 1981).

The majority of Introductions to the Old Testament up to the present time have, however, continued to defend the existence of E as a distinct document, being mainly content to repeat from one generation to the next and with little variation the list of the religious and theological characteristics of E which had been drawn up during the early days of the Documentary Hypothesis. Other scholars, however, while supporting the E hypothesis, have had reservations about the validity of using the theological criterion for doing so. Von Rad—who devoted only three pages (82-84; ET pp. 74-76) of his

'Problem of the Hexateuch' (1938) to E—acknowledged that E is 'theologically less clearly . . . differentiated than J'. For Noth (1948), writing about 'JE', 'a particular stratum can no longer be separated from other elements on the basis of a marked peculiarity in speech, style and thought-world' (p. 20; ET p. 20). The only valid criterion, he believed, was that provided by the existence of doublets. In view of the fragmentary nature of the E material, 'one will have to be very cautious in making judgments about the particulars of its content and about the "spirit" of the E narrative work' (p. 40; ET p. 37). The construction of a theology of E is hardly possible 'not only because the material of this source is preserved so fragmentarily, but above all because both the introduction and the transitions are lacking in which most likely the theology of E would have been expressed' (pp. 255-56; ET p. 236). Another recent writer who rejects the theological criterion is Van Seters: for him the only valid criteria are the doublets and the variations in the use of the divine names.

No doubt because of the insubstantiality and fragmentariness of E, there has been comparatively little original study of its theology in recent years. Von Rad and Noth devoted little attention to it in comparison with the other documents, nor did Rendtorff (1977) discuss it, although he devoted much of his work to attacking the Documentary Hypothesis with regard to J and P. The most significant study devoted exclusively to E in recent years is that of Wolff (1969). Wolff, while admitting that only fragments of E have been preserved, defended its claim to be a distinct document on both literary and theological grounds. 'The Elohistic fragments in the Pentateuch point toward an originally independent source, with its own technique of composition and an independent message' (p. 161). As far as the theology is concerned, he made out an impressive case, selecting *one* of the features which commonly appear in the lists of theological characteristics repeated in so many Introductions to the Old Testament, and giving it the status of the central theme. This theme is the *fear of God*:

> The most prominent theme of the Elohist is the fear of God. By means of the traditional materials from salvation history the Elohist wanted to lead the Israel of his day through the events in which they were tempted and to bring them to new obedience.

The period in the history of Israel which, according to Wolff, is most likely to have called forth the E document was the century between Elijah and Hosea, when Israel was especially tempted to abandon the fear of the God of Israel and serve the Canaanite gods.

Wolff's analysis of the theme of the fear of God in the E material, which he finds especially in Gen. 20 and 22, the Joseph Story, the story of the midwives in Exod. 1.15-21, the account of the call of Moses (Exod. 3.6b), the 'godfearing' character of the men chosen by Moses to be judges (Exod. 18.21), and Moses' address to the people before the mountain in Exod. 20.18b-21, is probably the most convincing argument yet advanced for a theology of E. Yet, as has been pointed out above, the discovery of a few passages here and there in the Pentateuch with a common theological theme does not in the least constitute proof of the existence of a continuous document. Evidence is needed that these fragments are the remains of what was once a coherent and connected literary work; and for this it is necessary to find in them some connecting links: not merely common theological traits, but something like cross-references or other traces of a narrative thread. Wolff was well aware of this. He cited, as evidence of such a thread, a number of passages in which reference is made by one of the Patriarchs or by Moses to events earlier in the story. Most of these, however, are confined to Genesis; and the examples from the later books are imprecise and so less convincing.

But Wolff also offered a further argument: he laid stress on certain passages (especially Gen. 42.21; 50.16-17) which appear to refer to earlier incidents which are *no longer* preserved in the present text. From these he concluded that E must once have contained material which was suppressed when E (or rather, selections from it) was merged with J. This argument, however, is not conclusive, since the incidents which he claims are missing (Joseph's brothers' refusal to be merciful to him when they had put him in the pit, and Jacob's supposed plea to Joseph before his death to forgive his brothers), although they are not actually related in the earlier narrative, could well be simply an elaboration or interpretation of what had happened by speakers recalling the past but remembering it in such a way as to present themselves in a favourable light or to protect themselves. It is not required by the narrative that these details should appear explicitly: this is a deliberate narrative technique which needs no further explanation, and indeed enhances the quality of the narrative art.

It cannot be said, therefore, that Wolff has made out his case on literary gounds for the existence of a connected E narrative; and in consequence his theological argument, though impressive, also fails to establish his case. The same is true of two other treatments of the Elohist, those of Jaroš (1974) and Klein (1977). The article by Schüpphaus (1975) relies too much on the supposition that the legal texts of the Decalogue and the Covenant Code belong to E, a feature of the Documentary Hypothesis which is now widely rejected.

The Elohistic fragments, then, may well point to the work of an 'Elohistic' editor or supplementer, but not to a connected narrative document running from Genesis to Numbers.

3. *The Application of the Criteria*

The rejection of the Documentary Hypothesis in favour of some other approach such as the traditio-historical one does not necessarily entail the rejection of all the *critical methods* of the documentary critics: Rendtorff, for example, has endorsed the methods, and used them in an analysis of the compositional history of Gen. 28.10-22 (1982). His rejection of the hypothesis is based on the view that in the attempt to prove the existence of *continuous documents* these methods have been *misused* and held to prove more than they are capable of proving.

The question of the validity of the methods in themselves has already been sufficiently examined in the foregoing pages. But the further question raised by Rendtorff concerning their misuse when applied to the larger canvas of the Pentateuchal narratives needs further discussion.

a. *The claim that the force of the criteria is cumulative*
This claim is based on what are sometimes known as 'constants': that is, features of the narratives brought to light by the use of the various criteria, which supposedly appear consistently throughout a particular document. The documentary critics claimed that these constants have a cumulative force: that the regular occurrence of not one but several constants together in a group of passages confirms beyond any doubt that these passages all belong to the same document.

This claim was clearly enunciated by Driver: 'The literary differences [i.e. differences between literary sources] . . . are frequently accompanied by differences of treatment or representation of the history, which, when they exist, confirm independently the conclusions of the literary analysis' (1909, p. 5). Thus the existence of P is confirmed 'by a multitude of convergent indications' (p. v.). In

Genesis, the linguistic indications of documentary differentiation 'are not isolated, nor do they occur in the narrative indiscriminately: they are numerous, and reappear with singular persistency *in combination with one another*' [Driver's italics]; and he claimed that the same is true, at least for P, 'in the following books to Joshua inclusive' (p. 10).

This claim has been echoed in much more recent times: De Vaux (1953), writing about the criterion of divine names, maintained that 'this alternation of the divine names coincides with variations of vocabulary, literary form, purpose and teaching' (p. 191) throughout Genesis; and that as far as the distinction between P and JE is concerned the other constants still function in this way in Exodus and Numbers. Again, Soggin (1976), referring to the various linguistic arguments for distinguishing between J and E, and admitting that each of these by itself is 'indicative rather than definitive', claimed that their effect is cumulative: 'it is their number rather than their quality which makes the division between J and E probable' (p. 100). Further, the additional factor of theological characteristics seems 'to put the scholar on firmer ground'.

It will be observed, however, from the above quotations that even the most enthusiastic supporters of the Documentary Hypothesis such as Driver recognized that the cumulative argument was not available in every case: the distinguishing marks of a literary nature were only 'frequently' accompanied by theological ones; the latter can, naturally, only be used to confirm the former 'where they exist'. The fact is that there are many narratives in the Pentateuch where there is no combination of 'constants'; and the documentary critics made no attempt to disguise this despite their assertions of the value of this argument.

b. *The analogical argument*
Indeed, far from denying that the cumulative argument could not always be used, the documentary critics admitted that there are many passages which contain *no indications at all* in themselves of their belonging to one document or another. In order to overcome this difficulty they invented what may be called the 'principle of analogy': that is, on the basis of their contention that the existence of separate documents each with its special characteristics could be proved in the case of *some* parts of the Pentateuch, they thought it legitimate, by analogy, to assume that these documents must have

run continuously through the *whole* of it. Wellhausen was particularly frank about this. Referring to the Joseph story (Gen. 37-50), he wrote: 'It must be assumed that this work is composed from J and E: our earlier results force us to this belief and would be shaken (*erschüttert*) if it could not be proved' (1899, p. 52). He admitted that there are particular difficulties involved in the dissection of what had been described as 'this smooth-flowing story', but he did not shrink from the task: to undertake the dissection, he maintained, was 'not mistaken but as necessary as the "decomposition" of Genesis' in general.

Noth (1948) echoed the views of Wellhausen stated half a century earlier. Admitting that 'literary-critical analysis can never presume to solve all individual problems', he argued that in the study of passages which did not seem to yield to documentary analysis, such as Gen. 15; Exod. 19; 24; 33; Num. 22-24, 'it must always suffice to offer a *possibility* for explanation on the basis of those results of literary-critical analysis which have proved adequate elsewhere'. 'Those who oppose the literary-critical study of the Pentateuch or specific literary-critical theses. . . can gain an all too easy victory by pointing to the absence of any certain and acknowledged result in the analysis of such passages' (p. 6; ET p. 6).

These remarks of Noth were particularly directed against the work of Volz and Rudolph (1933). In particular, Rudolph had (p. 147) quoted Wellhausen's remark with regard to the Joseph Story to which reference has been made above, and, very reasonably, had taken it as the expression of a principle, which he held to be fallacious, lying at the basis of much of the work of the documentary critics: the principle that, in the case of material which did not at first sight seem to present evidence of belonging to one or other of the documents, it was methodologically acceptable to presuppose the existence of such evidence before looking for it. Driver's remarks about the analysis of the same Joseph Story well illustrate, in greater detail than Wellhausen's remark, the operation of this principle. Although obliged by his investigation of these chapters to note the very curious problem facing the documentary critic that 'The narrative of Joseph in c. 39 ff consists, as it seems, of long passages excerpted alternately from J and E, *each, however, embodying traits derived from the other*' (p. 18, my italics), he nevertheless, in common with other critics, proceeded to brush the problem aside by postulating a most unusually substantial intervention by R^{JE}, in the following way (pp. 19-20):

In the history of Joseph the harmonizing additions which the analysis attributes to the compiler may be felt by some to constitute an objection to it. In estimating the force of such an objection, we must, however, balance the probabilities: is it more probable, in the light of what appears from other parts of the Pentateuch, that the work of one and the same writer should exhibit the incongruities pointed to above, or that a redactor in combining two parallel narratives should have introduced into one traits borrowed from the other?

There is a real question here which ought to be answered on the basis of internal evidence. Yet the answer which Driver gave to his own question is derived *a priori*, from outside the passage:

> The narrative of Joseph cannot be judged entirely by itself; it must be judged in the light of the presumption derived from the study of JE as a whole. And this presumption is of a nature which tends to confirm the conclusion that it is composite.

It was against the validity of such a 'presumption' that Volz and Rudolph protested. Their method of work was to begin (as far as J and E were concerned) without such presuppositions and presumptions, to examine the text in detail for itself, and to reach literary-critical conclusions on that basis alone. Whether their solutions to the various 'incongruities' in the text of the Joseph story referred to by Driver, and which undoubtedly exist, can all be accepted is beside the point: the question which they raised was one of principle—of a correct methodology. The documentary critics were arguing in a circle.

Recently Rendtorff (1982) reaffirmed the principle on which Volz and Rudolph took their stand in his literary-critical analysis of Gen. 28.10-22, in which he pointed out the circular nature of the method employed by the documentary critics. Using precisely the same literary-critical methods but without any presuppositions about the necessity (or otherwise) of finding the documentary sources in this passage, he concluded that this passage, believed by the documentary critics to be the result of the combination of two accounts of the same incident by J and E, is indeed composite, but that there are not two distinct accounts here which could be attributed to two 'documents': rather this is a single story which underwent editorial expansion during the process of the combination of the various individual patriarchal stories into a coherent whole. Once again, Rendtorff's analysis is not necessarily definitive and is subject, like any other, to criticism; but it is important as a demonstration of a *method* which, rather than beginning with presuppositions about the Pentateuch as a whole and then seeking to find confirmation of what has been assumed from the start, begins from the individual unit and bases its conclusions solely on internal evidence. More recently still, Moberly has applied the same principles and methods to Exod. 32–34, although he has reservations about Rendtorff's approach to the composition of the Pentateuch as a whole.

The kind of analysis of particular passages in the Pentateuch exemplified in these studies of Rendtorff and Moberly clearly raises new problems with regard to the composition of the Pentateuch, which will be discussed later in this book. The point to be noted here is that serious doubt has been thrown by a succession of scholars on the way in which the documentary critics used the literary-critical methods of studying texts. The particular texts referred to above are intended only as examples. Much recent investigation shows that there are many other narratives in the Pentateuch which have been attributed to the 'documents' mainly on the basis of the presumption of the existence of continuous documents rather than on the basis of their own internal evidence.

4. *The Role of the Redactors*

The role played by the redactors—especially R^{JE}, R^D and R^P—is an important and essential part of the Documentary Hypothesis. Their main contribution to the formation of the Pentateuch, it was believed, consisted in their selection, arrangement, and, occasionally, re-ordering of the material which they took from the documents with which they worked. Their role was essentially conservative: they retained as much of the older material as possible, and made only rather minor additions to it of their own. It was in fact precisely this conservatism which, according to the documentary critics, made it possible (though not in all cases) to distinguish the various documents which were held to underlie the Pentateuch in its present form. Nevertheless it was believed that the redactors did make some literary contribution of their own, mainly in order to harmonize their material and to conceal joins between one document and another, but also on occasion to 'correct' or supplement where they thought this necessary. But their contributions were on a modest scale.

References to the role of these redactors in the works of the documentary critics are, however, mainly sporadic. In view of the fact that the Documentary Hypothesis depends entirely on the assumption that such redactional activity took place, it is remarkable that they do not appear to have thought it necessary to substantiate this assumption by clearly defining the redactors' motives or by discussing in general terms the extent and character of their additions to the material on which they worked. If the theory of redactional activity is to be adequately assessed, however, it is necessary to ask these questions.

With regard to the *motives* of the redactors, some of the sharpest criticism of the hypothesis came from Sandmel, who, writing about R^{JE} (pp. 106-107), asked what reason there can have been for dovetailing two works covering the same ground to form a single work if nothing essentially new was created as a result. He rejected the frequently used analogy of Tatian's harmonizing of the four Gospels in his *Diatessaron* on the grounds that the Gospels had already been canonized: to unite their conflicting accounts into a single harmonious one while losing nothing essential from any of the original books may have been seen as an apologetical necessity. But there was no such necessity in the case of J and E, and Sandmel could find no satisfactory motive for the work of R^{JE}. It is true that it has been frequently suggested that the motive was the combination of the traditions of Judah (J) with those of northern Israel (E). However, apart from the fact that doubt has recently been expressed about the correctness of the attribution of these two documents to south and north respectively, it is not at all clear that either party would have accepted a new version of Israel's origins which both omitted parts of its own traditions and also introduced new material unknown to it, especially since the documentary critics themselves maintained that each version had its own bias which was in some respects unfavourable to the other group. In fact the historical circumstances which could have inspired the work of R^{JE} are extremely difficult to discover.

The alternative solution to the problem proposed by Sandmel, that one writer composed a new version of an earlier work incorporating new material of his own, is not open to the same objections. At all events, the question of the motive which inspired the work of R^{JE} has not been adequately thought through; and the same is true of R^{P}. Gunkel's suggestion that 'The attempt of P to supplant the older tradition had proved a failure; accordingly a reverent hand produced a combination of JE and P' (1901, 3rd edn, p. xcix; ET p. 158) is pure guesswork: there is no evidence of a historical situation which would have given rise to such a need; and it is just as easy, and less complicated, to suppose that P himself incorporated the older material into his own work, or, rather, provided the older material with his own framework.

Secondly, if the redactors postulated by the Documentary Hypothesis are to be credible, it is necessary to show that their *methods* or modes of operation were consistent. With regard to the way in which they are supposed to have handled their documentary sources, Driver's statement that 'J and E . . . were combined into a whole by a compiler, sometimes incorporating long sections of each intact (or nearly so), sometimes fusing the parallel accounts into a single narrative' (1909, p. 20) accurately sums up the conclusions of the documentary critics. Yet no satisfactory reason has ever been given why a single redactor (R^{JE}) should have employed these two entirely different methods of compilation at different points in his work. If he was intent on harmonizing his material in some instances, why did he prefer in others to set two different versions of a narrative side by side? One would have expected that the documentary critics, with their insistence on the criterion of consistency of style when it came to separating one document from another, would have drawn the conclusion that there must have been not one, but two separate redactors of J and E, each with his own literary methods.

With regard to the redactors' own *additions to the material*, despite Driver's remark that 'the documents can generally be distinguished from one another, *and from the comments of the compiler*' (p. 5, my italics), there was in fact considerable divergence of opinion about the *extent* of these 'comments'. More significantly, the critics were no more successful in discovering consistency or a clear policy on the part of the redactors with regard to the additions which they made than they were with regard to their handling of the older material. Indeed, they hardly attempted to do so. Wellhausen for example, in his detailed study of the texts (1899), contented himself with occasional *ad hoc* comments that a phrase has been added here or a section rephrased there. He did not gather these additions and alterations together and consider them as a whole. It is difficult to resist the impression that the redactor in his guise as author is only called in when the documentary critic finds himself faced by material which he cannot fit into his documentary analysis. Van Seters is justified in claiming that 'In the actual practice of literary criticism the redactor functions mainly as a *deus ex machina* to solve literary difficulties' (p. 129).

Many of the additions attributed to R^JE were regarded as having a harmonistic aim; but even these do not prove that the redactor had a consistent purpose, since he clearly did not carry through his attempt at harmonization in a consistent way. It is precisely the *lack* of any attempt at harmonization in a large proportion of the Pentateuchal narrative which lies at the basis of the critics' distinction of two documents. The same considerations apply to R^P. Further, the problem of distinguishing the additions made by the redactors is made more difficult by the fact that the function attributed to them is not unlike that attributed to J and E themselves, since, as some of the documentary critics themselves recognized, J and E were collectors and 'harmonizers' of older material, whose 'comments' are not readily distinguishable from those of their redactor (see Koch, 1967, p. 62 and n. 1; ET p. 58 and n. 1). Again, if following the 'newer' or 'newest' version of the Documentary Hypothesis, the number of documents is increased by the recognition of J¹, J², L, E¹, E², P^A and P^B etc., the difficulties are even greater, since it then becomes necessary to distinguish between the work of a very large number of redactors.

R^D. That JE was, before the addition of P, combined with Deuteronomy by a 'Deuteronomist' redactor (R^D) is a fundamental feature of the Documentary Hypothesis. It would be natural to suppose that this redactor would not have left the JE part of the new work (i.e. Genesis–Numbers) untouched, but would have re-edited it to bring it into conformity with 'Deuteronomic' theology. Yet the documentary critics could find no sign in Genesis–Numbers of a comprehensive Deuteronomic edition. Only a few passages, they believed, could be assigned to D, and indeed no clear concept of the role of R^D emerged at all. In a number of passages Wellhausen admitted that it was difficult to distinguish R^D from JE, since the former was 'dependent on the Jehovistic source for many of his expressions' (1899, p. 74; cf. p. 86). He also wrote of JE's 'spiritual affinity with Deuteronomy' (p. 94 n. 2).

This anomalous situation of a 'Deuteronomic' Pentateuch most of which (Genesis–Numbers) contained virtually no sign of Deuteronomic influence provided the starting-point for Noth's revolutionary theory (1943) of a separate 'Deuteronomistic History' beginning with the book of Deuteronomy, which originally had no connection with Genesis–Numbers. This entailed the rejection of the concept of R^D as understood by the documentary critics.

Recently a number of scholars (especially Perlitt, 1969, Schmid, 1976, Rendtorff, 1977, Weimar, Smend) have put forward yet another theory which differs from both the Documentary Hypothesis and that of Noth: using an entirely new set of criteria, they have suggested that there may, after all, have been a thorough Deuteronomic redaction of Genesis–Numbers (see pp. 21, 98–108 above): much of the narrative material in those books has been cast in a 'Deuteronomistic' mould. Mayes has now gone further still with a suggestion that Genesis–Numbers never existed as an independent work at all: it 'was composed primarily as an introduction to the already existing deuteronomistic history' (p. 141). This type of theory is not, however, as might at first seem to be the case, a revival of the R^D of the Documentary Hypothesis, for it dispenses with 'J', 'E', and 'JE' altogether: the Deuteronomist now becomes the earliest Pentateuchal author, before whom there was no comprehensive literary work in existence at all.

The theories referred to in the above paragraph have not gone unchallenged. They have, however, raised new questions (or, it might be truer to say, revived old ones). But none of these is of a kind which can be solved in terms of the Documentary Hypothesis. One of the most hotly debated of these questions is that of the criteria for determining whether a passage is to be regarded as 'Deuteronomic' (or 'Deuteronomistic': it is not possible to distinguish the two terms in this connection). On the question of style, it has been increasingly doubted (e.g. by Brekelmans) whether there is a truly Deuteronomic style: it is held by some scholars to be unlikely that a new prose style should have suddenly come into existence in the seventh century BC without a period of gradual development. Consequently, from the stylistic point of view considered by itself, the supposed Deuteronomic (R^D) passages in Genesis to Numbers may well have been composed earlier than the period of Deuteronomy. (The terms 'proto-Deuteronomic' and 'early Deuteronomic' have been devised to characterize them.) In view of this uncertainty, Rendtorff, while noting the Deuteronomic affinities of the passages which he regards as indications of the first complete redaction of the older material, is cautious about the use of the term 'Deuteronomic' (1977, p. 79).

Other scholars have pointed out the affinities of these passages to E (Brekelmans) or have claimed that they are closely associated with 'late J' (Van Seters, Schmid). With regard to the theology of such passages, the case for their Deuteronomic character obviously depends on the view which is taken of the nature of the Deuteronomic movement, and in particular of Perlitt's view that 'covenant theology' was first introduced by the Deuteronomists. This view, if correct, would entail the attribution of a good deal of 'JE' material to D. However, Perlitt's thesis has met with considerable opposition, and the question remains unsolved.

Thus the documentary critics' original concept of R^D has been swept away by the subsequent discovery of a host of new and complex problems—not least by recent research into the complicated redactional history of the book of Deuteronomy itself—which have not yet been resolved, but which clearly call for more complex solutions.

R^P. The *raison d'être* of the postulation of a 'priestly redactor' (R^P) has never been entirely clear. It is difficult to avoid the conclusion that it was due to a fixed notion of the documentary critics that the entire process of the composition of the Pentateuch must have been achieved through the combination by redactors of a series of independent literary works rather than, for example, by a series of 'new editions' involving the addition of new material to the old by editors. In the case of P the hypothesis requires that, with a few exceptions, all the material which cannot be ascribed to the other documents must, despite its heterogeneous character comprising brief 'historical' summaries, theological constructs like Gen. 1, genealogical and chronological notes, and (in the later books) an overwhelming preponderance of laws, have constituted an independent work, P; and this in turn necessitated the postulation of a final redactor, R^P, who combined P with JED, thus (with allowance made for a few even later additions) completing the Pentateuch virtually in its present form. P, it was claimed, then became the framework or skeleton on which R^P hung the remainder. This view, almost universally held by the documentary critics, was endorsed by later writers including Noth.

It was one of the most important insights of the Scandinavian 'tradition-historians' Engnell and Nielsen, followed by Cross, that the hypothesis of R^P is unnecessary: it is more natural to see P as having been, as it were, his own redactor. Some documentary critics had, it is true, already suggested something of the kind, for example Pfeiffer: 'P was compiled for the purpose of being united with JED, which enjoyed a certain canonical authority at the time, so as to bring that older work into harmony with the tenets of Judaism in the fifth century' (1941, p. 286). Unless there is overwhelming evidence for regarding P as once having been a coherent and independent work, a view of this kind is difficult to contest: it has the virtue of simplicity.

The only substantial argument in favour of a separate R^P is summarized by Bentzen:

> It is generally stressed that it is impossible that P himself should have incorporated the old sources in his work. P seems to be too polemical against much of the material of his predecessors. . . . P must have intended to *replace* the earlier works by his own collections. . . Authors like D and P, who take up a polemical position, cannot be believed to overlook the discrepancies between their own basic ideas and those of the predecessors whom they want to supersede (II, p. 71).

Whether P's intentions were in fact more polemical than those of, let us say, 'J' when he (according to the documentary critics) imbued his previously disparate traditions with a strong theological and political flavour is a matter of opinion; and, in view of the little we really know about the history of the religion of Israel, likely to remain so. But the real fallacy in the kind of argument summarized by Bentzen is that it simply transfers the 'impossibility' of reconciling P's notions with those of the rest of the Pentateuch to an even more shadowy figure, 'R^P', who, it is supposed, was able for some undisclosed reason to do what P himself could not do. Once again, we are in no position to place the hypothesis of R^P in a clearly defined religio-historical context. The simpler hypothesis, which does away with R^P altogether, seems to be the more probable.

D. *Comparison With Other Literary Hypotheses*

It has often been pointed out that the Documentary Hypothesis was not regarded even by its most enthusiastic supporters as providing a complete explanation of the composition of the Pentateuch. It was always recognized that the Supplement and Fragment Hypotheses were needed to account for some of the phenomena. In fact, as Fohrer pointed out, the use of the term 'hypothesis' in the discussion is probably unfortunate: it implies that these approaches are mutually exclusive, whereas what are in fact being compared are three different possible methods of composition. There is no reason to rule out *a priori* the possibility that they may all have been employed in different parts of the Pentateuch or at different stages in the process of composition.

With regard to the supplement method, Wellhausen himself recognized that it had been used in the formation of the laws of P: 'The Priestly Code consists of elements of two kinds, first of an independent kernel. . . and second, of innumerable additions and supplements'; it has a historical unity of a kind, but it is 'no literary unity' (1883, p. 384; ET p. 385). In fact, Wellhausen's view of the Code is a combination of both the Supplement and the Fragment Hypotheses, since he also recognized that it incorporates earlier written law-codes such as the 'Holiness Code' (Lev. 17–26).

There was also general agreement that similar literary processes lay behind the formation of the Covenant Code (Exod. 20.23–23.19), attributed to JE, and the Code of Deuteronomy (Deut. 12–26). With regard to the latter, Wellhausen suggested that 'the priests may before this time have written down many of their precepts. . . . Deuteronomy presupposes earlier compositions, and frequently borrows its material from them' (1883, p. 401; ET p. 402). Other examples of the fragment method recognized by the documentary critics include Gen. 14, which was generally admitted not to belong to any of the main documents (Wellhausen, 1899, pp. 24-25), and similarly Gen. 49 (p. 60).

Not only the composition of the legal codes in the Pentateuch— which constitute roughly one half of the entire work—but also the relationship of these codes to their narrative contexts constituted a problem for the Documentary Hypothesis, sometimes involving the critics in contradictions. For example, the Covenant Code was assigned by them to JE; yet Wellhausen admitted that the 'Jehovistic work' was 'originally a pure history-book' (1883, p. 343; ET p. 345), and that its legal sections had 'invaded the narrative' (p. 341; ET p. 342): in other words, they were originally separate 'documents' added after the rest of JE had been completed. (Such examples invite the question 'What is the difference between a "fragment", a "document" and a "supplement"?' No clear distinction seems to have been made between these three terms; nevertheless, it is clear that such a composition as the Covenant Code, despite its length, is not a 'document' in the Wellhausenian sense of a source running through the whole Pentateuch.)

It is remarkable that, with the exception of the book of Deuteronomy, there has been little discussion, either in the time of Wellhausen or since, of the relationship of the legal to the narrative parts of the Pentateuch. The law codes themselves have been studied and compared with one another, giving rise to a large body of specialized literature; but this has been done mainly in isolation from the problems of their setting in the narrative framework. Noth, in a major study of 'The Laws in the Pentateuch' (1940) summarized the critical position of the time in the following way:

> The Pentateuch . . . is a long narrative composition assembled from diverse elements . . . into which laws—admittedly in large quantities—have been inserted at particular points . . . Law is present in a series of different *literary units*. . . . All these were originally independent units, existing in their own right, each having its own purpose and sphere of validity (1940, pp. 14-16; ET pp. 5-7).

This is a clear admission that the way in which the law-codes have grown and developed points to the use of both the fragment and the supplement methods of composition. But otherwise Noth had nothing to say, in a work entirely devoted to the laws in the Pentateuch, about the process by which they were incorporated into the narrative material, or about the reasons why it was decided that narrative and law *should* be combined in this way—a procedure that is by no means self-explanatory.

Clearly this subject requires further study; in any case it raises important questions about the validity of a documentary theory: for if it cannot be determined how the laws are related to their contexts, there can be no grounds for attributing them to the particular 'documents' in which it is supposed that they are embedded. The Pentateuch then becomes not a work composed of a small number of documents combined step by step in an orderly fashion by a few definable redactors, but an amalgam of a large number of written units which may have been put together in quite a different way, possibly at a very late date.

At first sight, compared with the Supplement and Fragment theories, the Documentary Hypothesis appears to have the advantage of simplicity and clarity. It also appears to fit with admirable precision into the background of the political and religious history of

Israel, with each document corresponding to a particular stage in that history. Even when fashions in the understanding of the history changed, and Noth proposed the pre-monarchical period as the time when the foundations of Israel as a nation were laid, or von Rad moved the date of the Yahwist back from the ninth century to a supposed period of 'Solomonic enlightenment' in the tenth; or when modifications were made to the hypothesis with the addition of new documents such as J^1, L etc., a plausible correlation between it and the data of Israelite religious history seemed still to be a possibility.

By contrast, neither the Fragment nor the Supplement Hypothesis can offer such precise results: for here the critic is dealing with short or comparatively short units, and the motives for their combination are more difficult to define than where there is a substantial 'document' whose features, and therefore whose motivation, can be analysed. Each example has to be studied in isolation, and the results may be very meagre. Nevertheless, as has been demonstrated above, the Documentary Hypothesis has feet of clay. It rests on false assumptions and methodological errors which render it fundamentally untenable.

In recent years Pentateuchal criticism has entered a new period in which new literary theories are being tentatively put forward. Some of these could be described as new versions of the Fragment and Supplement Hypotheses. They will be considered later in this book. First, however, we shall turn to consider a different kind of approach to the problems: that of the proponents of theories of oral tradition and tradition-history.

E. *Summary and Conclusions*

1. Many different explanations could be given of the process by which the Pentateuch attained its present form. The Documentary Hypothesis in its classical form is a particular and elaborate example of one main type of literary theory, which has predominated for many years. It relies on a complexity of converging arguments, each of which needs examination.

2. Its supporters claimed that it accounted for almost all the material in the Pentateuch. But in practice Wellhausen himself admitted that certain sections—notably law-codes—could not be satisfactorily accommodated within it. It was also universally admitted that the distinction between the earliest documents, J and E, was frequently blurred.

3. The hypothesis was unduly dependent on a particular view of the history of the religion of Israel.

4. The authors of the documents are credited with a consistency in the avoidance of repetitions and contradictions which is unparalleled in ancient literature (and even in modern fiction), and which ignores the possibility of the deliberate use of such features for aesthetic and literary purposes. At the same time, the documentary critics were themselves frequently inconsistent in that they ignored such features *within* the documents which they had reconstructed.

5. No allowance was made for the possibility that repetitions, doublets and inconsistencies might have already been present in the oral stage of the transmission of the material used by the authors of the written text.

6. The breaking up of narratives into separate documents by a 'scissors and paste' method not only lacks true analogies in the ancient literary world, but also often destroys the literary and aesthetic qualities of these narratives, which are themselves important data which ought not to be ignored.

7. Too much reliance was placed, in view of our relative ignorance of the history of the Hebrew language, on differences of language and style. Other explanations of variations of language and style are available, e.g. differences of subject-matter requiring special or distinctive vocabulary, alternations of vocabulary introduced for literary reasons, and unconscious variation of vocabulary.

8. The hypothesis depends on the occurrence of 'constants', i.e. the presence *throughout* each of the documents of a single style, purpose and point of view or theology, and of an unbroken narrative thread. These constants are not to be found. The use of the analogical argument to claim otherwise 'neutral' passages for one or other of the documents, and the making of assumptions about 'missing' parts of a document are dubious procedures.

9. The fact that the authors of the pre-exilic literature of the Old Testament outside the Pentateuch appear to have known virtually nothing of the patriarchal and Mosaic traditions of the Pentateuch raises serious doubts about the existence of an early J or E.

10. Subsequent modifications of the Documentary Hypothesis have not increased its plausibility. The postulation of additional documents, which are of limited scope, marks the breakdown of an hypothesis which is essentially one of *continuous* documents running through the Pentateuch. Attempts to make the hypothesis more

flexible by speaking rather vaguely of 'strata' and the like rather than of documents are essentially denials of a purely literary hypothesis.

11. The Supplement and Fragment Hypotheses have suffered neglect for many years, but have recently been revived in new forms and need to be reassessed.

A. *The New Approach*

It was Hermann Gunkel who, in his commentary on Genesis (1901),
first explored the possibility of going back behind the literary
formulation of Israel's 'historical' traditions in the earliest written
sources (J and E) to discover how these traditions had originated and
taken shape in an earlier, preliterary period. His starting-point was
the suggestion made by earlier scholars, notably Heinrich Ewald,
that these written sources were based on oral material analogous to
the *Sagen* or folk tales of non-literate European peoples whose
collection and scientific study had begun in Germany in the
eighteenth century. Some of these *Sagen* were simply 'fairytales'
about a purely magical world; but others purported to preserve the
memory of actual events in a remote ancestral past. They were,
however, far removed from 'history': each *Sage* was a tale complete
in itself, narrating a single event or simple chain of events without
reference to any wider historical context and with no concern for
accuracy of detail. The events which the *Sagen* described were
somewhat dimly perceived, and—although formally they were in
prose rather than poetry—they had a certain 'poetical' quality.

Gunkel went far beyond his predecessors in his use of the concept
of the *Sage* as the key to the understanding of early Old Testament
narratives. To the Introduction to his commentary (3rd edn, 1910) he
boldly gave the provocative title 'Die Genesis ist eine Sammlung von
Sagen' ('Genesis is a collection of *Sagen*'). Using comparative
material from the folklore of other peoples, he attempted to analyse
and classify the individual stories, and to determine the situations
and circumstances in which they had arisen (their *Sitz im Leben* or
'life-setting') and in which they had been transmitted.

In using the word 'collection' of the book of Genesis Gunkel did
not, of course, mean that the book is no more than an assemblage of

unconnected stories like the 'fairytales' which the brothers Grimm had collected and published. It was obvious that Genesis in its present form purports to offer a single continuous account of events from the creation of the world to the death of Joseph. But he contended that this continuous narrative had been put together, in the course of a long period of growth, from *Sagen* which had originally existed independently. This process had taken place in two stages: a period of *oral* composition followed by one of *written* composition. In the first of these stages the original *Sagen* had been combined, step by step, to form 'complexes of *Sagen*' (*Sagenkränze*). This process was already at a fairly advanced stage when the first committal to writing took place. The authors of the 'documents' were in fact collectors of already formed material rather than creative writers. Their contribution to the process had been to join the *Sagenkränze* together into single continuous accounts. Precisely how much of the work of compilation was to be attributed to the oral stage and how much to the written was, however, difficult to determine.

In attempting to identify and characterize the different types of story in Genesis Gunkel relied to a large extent on his feeling for atmosphere: these stories seemed to him to be for the most part— though there were exceptions to this—simple, naive tales comparable to the *Sagen* of other peoples and characteristic of an early stage of cultural development. But he did not rely entirely on vague feelings of this kind: he analysed the formal characteristics—language, style, structure—of the different kinds of story as well as their contents and drew conclusions about their specific types (*Gattungen*) and their original functions and purposes. To a considerable extent he made use of the work of 'folklorists' such as Axel Olrik, whose theories will be discussed below. But as far as the Old Testament is concerned he was a pioneer. The new method of study which he introduced, now generally known in English as 'form criticism' (in German, *Gattungsforschung*, *Gattungskritik*, or *Formgeschichte*) has been, and remains, one of the most widely used, although also one of the most frequently abused, in the study of the Old Testament. (It should be added that Gunkel himself applied it with great success to other forms of Old Testament literature, especially the Psalms.)

But it was not only as a '*form*-critic' that Gunkel was a pioneer. In attempting to go beyond the single narrative units of Genesis to suggest how these might have been progressively combined into larger oral collections before the composition of J and E, he may be said to have been the initiator of a further type of research, to which he himself gave the name by which it has since been generally known: the study of the *history* of traditions (*Überlieferungsgeschichte*). He himself went no further than to sketch the outlines of the 'tradition-history' of Genesis. But later scholars—notably Hugo Gressmann, Albrecht Alt, Gerhard von Rad and Martin Noth—took up his method, applied it more intensively to solve particular problems, and extended its application to the whole of the narrative material in the Pentateuch.

Martin Noth, in his *Überlieferungsgeschichte des Pentateuch* (ET A *History of Pentateuchal Traditions*), 1948, pushed the use of the new method to its extreme limits. This work, which will be examined more fully later in this book, was nothing less than an attempt to describe the entire process of the composition of the Pentateuch in all its minute details: it opens with the statement that 'The growth and formation of the large body of traditions now found in the extensive and complicated literary structure of the Pentateuch was a long process, nourished by many roots and influenced by a variety of interests and tendencies. . . . It is the task of a "history of Pentateuchal traditions" to investigate this whole process from beginning to end' (p. 1; ET p. 1). Like Gunkel, he understood the process as having taken place in two consecutive stages, an oral followed by a written one. Since, however, the latter had already been 'thoroughly treated', he announced that the 'major interest' of his own study would be 'the origins and first stage of growth', that is, the oral stage. All subsequent research in this field has taken Noth's work as its starting-point.

It is important to notice that these scholars were not solely concerned with solving the problem of the composition of the Pentateuch. They saw the traditio-historical method as a means of elucidating questions concerning the historical origins of Israel and of Israelite religion. Just as Wellhausen and the documentary critics had regarded the succession of the documents J, E, D and P as material for the reconstruction of the religious history of the later, *literate* period, so this new generation of scholars regarded their traditio-historical conclusions as material for reconstructing the history and religion of the Israelite tribes in the *pre-literate* period, a period about which very little direct evidence was available. For them, each stage in the process of oral composition reflected some development in the formation of the people of Israel or of its religious beliefs and practices. In this way their traditio-historical studies have come to form the basis of modern historical and religious study of Israelite origins. It is, for example, no accident that the author of *Überlieferungsgeschichte des Pentateuch* was also the historian who had already in 1930 put forward a new theory of Israelite origins as a tribal league or 'amphictyony' (*Das System der zwölf Stämme Israels*) and in 1950 published the first edition of a History of Israel, in the earlier chapters of which all these aspects of his earlier work were combined to form a coherent whole. The same combination of interests is to be seen in the work of Alt and von Rad, to whose insights Noth was indebted.

B. *The Meaning of 'Tradition'*

In this book we are concerned solely with the question of the process by which the Pentateuch was composed. Although, as we have just seen, it may not be possible to divorce this question completely from its *historical* and *religious* implications, it is a question which can only be solved by *literary* arguments, that is, arguments based on the actual text of the Pentateuch. Moreover, if the Pentateuch is to be used as a basis for historical reconstructions, the literary question— that is, the question of composition—must be solved *first*. Consequently if the traditio-historical method proves to be faulty, any historical conclusions based upon it fall to the ground.

First, however, it is necessary to enquire what is meant in Pentateuchal studies by the terms 'tradition' and 'history of traditions'. This is particularly important because in recent study of the Old Testament these terms have been very confusingly used in somewhat different senses.

In ordinary contemporary English a tradition is understood to be a *custom* or a *belief* which has been transmitted within a particular group—such as a family, church, sect, society, nation, people or tribe—for a considerable time (usually for several generations) and which is accepted and handed on by each generation to its successor. In this sense, the tradition-history of ancient Israel is to a large extent synonymous with the history of Israelite religion, which is the sum of Israel's religious traditions. Historians of Israelite religion regularly use the term in that sense.

Most religious beliefs or 'traditions' exist independently of any verbal account which may be given of them. It is true that they may be associated with particular verbal expressions or technical terms, but they are not dependent on these. Religious beliefs like the holiness or the glory of God, or the special relationship between God and Israel, for example, may be expressed verbally in a number of different ways: the beliefs themselves and the verbal expression of them are distinct, and it is the task of the historian of religion to study these various verbal expressions in order to define the nature of the belief or 'tradition' itself. With *historical* traditions, however— that is, with traditions or beliefs held by a particular people about supposed *events in its past history*—the situation is different. For in this case the tradition is a wholly verbal one: it is itself a *narrative*. In a sense, this kind of tradition *is* the form of words in which it is expressed, and cannot be dissociated from it.

For this reason the terms 'tradition' and 'tradition-history' have a special meaning when used in connection with the kind of narrative which is found in the Pentateuch. Thus Noth's work entitled 'A History of Pentateuchal Traditions' is in fact a history of the Pentateuchal *narratives*—that is, of the *words* in which these traditions are expressed in the Pentateuch. Although the precise wording of these narratives may have gradually been modified in the course of centuries of oral transmission, and although their contexts and even their meaning may have changed, there is still a *continuity* of wording which, in Noth's view, makes it possible to speak of the *history* of a particular story.

Tradition in the usual sense of the word and tradition in this special sense are of course related to one another: the stories which Israel told about its past were part of their inherited *beliefs*. Nevertheless in evaluating the claim of the tradition-historians of the Pentateuch that it is possible to trace the history of these stories over a long period of oral transmission it is important to realize that the word 'tradition' is being used by them in this special sense. To trace the history of religious ideas or beliefs by studying ancient religious texts, which is the function of the historian of religion, is one thing; to trace the prehistory of religious texts themselves in their pre-literary oral stage is quite another, and requires a quite different technique. (Some German scholars distinguish the two by using different terms for them: *Traditionsgeschichte* for the general study of religious beliefs, and *Überlieferungsgeschichte* for the study of narrative traditions.) It is with the second of these techniques that we are concerned here.

C. *The Study of the Oral Tradition*

In their attempt to trace the history and development of the narrative 'traditions' of the Pentateuch the tradition-historians, following Gunkel's lead, made the following assumptions:

1. The stories are, at least in the main, not fictitious literary compositions invented by the authors of the written Pentateuch but are based on older material which was available to these authors.
2. This material was in oral rather than written form.
3. Most of it had come into existence at an early date in the form of short narratives of limited scope.
4. In transforming this material into a single continuous narrative the Pentateuchal writers were only completing a process which had begun in the oral period and was already well advanced when they took it over.
5. The first, oral, stage of this process was a gradual one covering several centuries.
6. The Pentateuch in its final form provides sufficient clues to make it possible to reconstruct this process in all its stages from the original short stories to its completion.

The task to which the tradition-historians have addressed themselves is thus considerably more difficult to carry out than that attempted by Wellhausen and the documentary critics, and even more hypothetical in character. The documentary critics were working with something concrete and tangible: the text of the Pentateuch as it exists today. Although their 'documents', J, E, D and P, are hypothetical in that they do not now exist separately as literary works and their existence has to be inferred, most of the material which they are supposed by the critics to have comprised is extant in the Pentateuch in a virtually unchanged form. The Documentary Hypothesis is simply an attempt to unravel the extant text: to show that the material is composite and to explain how it came to be arranged in its present form. As has been stated, the documentary critics did not think it possible to penetrate behind the written text to investigate a possible pre-literary stage in its development. The tradition-historians, however, propose to do just that: they believe it to be possible to penetrate back beyond the extant words of the Pentateuch and to discover and identify earlier forms of the material which no longer exist and for which there is no direct evidence. This can only be done on the basis of some even more fundamental assumptions:

1.   That Israel's traditions about its early history originated in circumstances in which the composition of written records is extremely improbable;
2.   That the character and processes of oral tradition and composition as practised by those who first composed and transmitted this early material can be deduced by comparison with the 'oral literature' of other peoples which has been studied by modern folklorists;
3.   That oral traditions of this kind, though subject to a degree of modification in the course of transmission, are capable of relatively faithful reproduction over a long period of time;
4.   That there is reason to suppose that Israel had a tradition of storytelling which could have been the vehicle for the preservation of such traditions;
5.   That it is possible by studying a written text to discover whether it is based on oral composition or not.

In the section which follows, these questions will be considered in turn.

1. *Oral Tradition and the Use of Writing*

Gunkel took for granted the validity of the Documentary Hypothesis, according to which the Pentateuchal traditions were first committed to writing in the ninth or eighth century BC. Later scholars have revised this date: von Rad placed the Yahwist in the tenth century— the period of David and Solomon—and Noth argued for the existence of a single continuous narrative source ('G') which may have been already committed to writing earlier still, in the period which preceded the establishment of a national state under Saul and David. All these scholars took it for granted, however, that the earliest written records of the traditions had been preceded by a lengthy period during which the individual narratives were created, transmitted and developed without the aid of writing.

As is well known, writing was invented and was widely used by the civilized peoples of the ancient Near East well before Israel appeared on the scene. However, it was long believed by Old Testament scholars that at least until their settlement in Palestine the ancestors of the historical Israel were nomadic tribes living apart from the centres of culture and having little contact with them. Consequently it was believed to be out of the question that they could have been acquainted with the art of writing.

However, more recent research has shown that the nomadic theory of Israelite origins does not present an accurate picture of actual social conditions in the ancient Near East. Although there is at the present time no consensus of opinion about the precise nature of Israelite and proto-Israelite society, it is now known that in the ancient Near East generally the kind of social dichotomy once assumed to have existed between urban and agricultural communities on the one hand and pastoral tribes on the other is a misconception based on a false analogy with modern Middle Eastern nomadism, which is a comparatively recent phenomenon.

This newly acquired datum of archaeological and sociological research has led to a reappraisal of what the Pentateuchal narratives, especially those of Genesis, actually say. It is now recognized by many scholars that these stories by no means represent the patriarchs as living a truly nomadic life. Though often depicted as living in tents and as making various extensive journeys—though always with a specific purpose!—they are mainly represented as slave-owning, settled farmers who practised agriculture (Gen. 26.12) as well as owning large flocks and herds, and as having contacts with urban centres. Some recent scholars (Mendenhall, Gottwald) have even argued that the Israelites were not immigrants into Palestine at all, but Canaanite peasants who revolted against the rule of the local city-states and founded their own free society.

Whatever may have been their origin, the probability that the Israelites were from the beginning part and parcel of the civilized world of the ancient Near East greatly weakens the view that they were for a long time incapable of recording their traditions in writing. Writing for literary purposes was familiar to the Canaanites and Phoenicians from an early period, as is shown for example by the Ugaritic tablets (fifteenth to fourteenth century). Moreover the author of the Egyptian story of *Wen-Amon* from the eleventh century BC represents the prince of Byblos as consulting the 'books of the days of his fathers' in which the past relations between Byblos and Egypt were recorded: a recognition by an Egyptian of an established Phoenician practice of recording past events in writing. Further, the alphabetic Proto-Semitic inscriptions written by Semitic workmen in

Sinai indicate that in the middle of the second millennium BC the knowledge of writing was far from being restricted to a small scribal class. This and other evidence which could be cited does not, of course, *prove* that any of the Pentateuchal narratives was in fact written down at such an early date; but it is now difficult to maintain that they *must* have undergone a long period of oral transmission simply on the grounds of a supposed ignorance of writing.

A somewhat different case for oral transmission was put forward by a group of Scandinavian scholars (Nyberg, followed by Birkeland, Nielsen and Engnell). These rejected the entire literary approach to the question of the composition of the Old Testament, including the Documentary Hypothesis: 'The written Old Testament is a creation of the post-exilic community: of what existed earlier undoubtedly only a small part was in written form' (Nyberg, p. 8). According to this theory the period of oral transmission had continued for several centuries longer than even Gunkel had supposed.

This hypothesis was based not on the assumption of Israelite illiteracy but on the view that throughout the ancient Near East and among many other peoples as well, writing played only an insignificant part in the life of the people until comparatively late times, being restricted to a small scribal class and used only for very limited purposes such as the drafting of administrative documents and the preservation of important religious texts and laws. Material like the Pentateuchal narratives did not fall into any of these classes and would have been of no concern to these court or temple scribes. Thus even in a time of relative literacy they could have been preserved only through oral transmission. Only when some major crisis occurred in the national life and there was a danger that these traditions would be lost would they have been committed to writing. Such a crisis in the case of Israel was the disaster of 587 BC and the disruption of normal life which followed. Great emphasis was laid by these scholars on the phenomenal memories of 'Oriental' peoples, who even in much later times have been capable of reciting lengthy compositions without the aid of written texts.

The improbabilities of this theory have been pointed out by Widengren, Mowinckel, van der Ploeg and others and will be dealt with only briefly here. Its estimate of the relative unimportance of writing and of the restricted use made of it in the ancient Near East is greatly exaggerated and was in fact only very sketchily argued by its advocates. Direct evidence of a long period of oral tradition preceding literary texts from that region is very slight, although there is nothing wholly improbable about it; and although many texts are preserved only in relatively late copies, it is not usually possible to determine precisely when they were first written. Moreover, the practice of reciting literary works from memory does not preclude the possibility that such works already existed in written form: the *Qur'an* is a good example of this. Whether the Pentateuchal narratives would have been regarded as worthy of committal to writing at an early stage we have no means of judging: they are unique among extant ancient Near Eastern literature, and if they are indeed of very early origin it would be surprising if they had not acquired considerable status as important religious works at an early stage, since otherwise it would be difficult to account for the very high status which was accorded to them later. The view that they were for a long time regarded as nothing more than folktales is an assumption which requires proof. Comparisons with written material from other periods such as the rabbinic literature are of doubtful value because of their different background: the rabbinic traditions, for example, were first transmitted orally in the midst of a literate society for quite special reasons.

It is therefore legitimate to conclude that the hypothesis of a long period of oral tradition and transmission of the Pentateuchal narratives preceding the earliest written texts, whether valid or not, cannot be established either on the basis of ignorance of writing on the part of the early Israelites or on theories about the restricted use of writing in literate societies. The fact that writing was probably more widespread in Israel than was earlier thought to be the case does not, however, provide proof of an early date for the written Pentateuch: it merely means that its date will have to be established, if at all, on other grounds.

2. *The Use of Foreign Models*

Gunkel's views about the nature of the stories of Genesis were based on the model of the European *Sagen*, which he believed to be typical of pre-literate peoples in general, irrespective of time and place. This notion of an universal pattern of oral narrative has remained a major feature of Pentateuchal studies up to the present time.

This particular model, which was reinforced by the 'epic laws' formulated by Olrik in 1908, remained dominant for a long time, its influence being still discernible in the work of von Rad (1938), Noth (1948) and even later writers. Later on attention became concentrated on comparisons with early Icelandic *saga*, whose affinities with the patriarchal stories were first suggested by Jolles. The influence of Jolles is particularly prominent in the work of Westermann (1964), who interpreted these stories as 'family histories' (*Familiegeschichten*) of the same type as the Icelandic 'family sagas'. Most recently use has been made of other models, especially the Homeric poems and mediaeval epics (believed to have originated orally) and modern 'oral literature' from Yugoslavia, Africa and elsewhere.

This use of models from cultures remote from ancient Israel raises serious questions of methodology.

a. *Sage, saga* and *sagn*

It is first necessary to deal with some *problems of terminology*. The chief of these is a confusion which has arisen between the German word *Sage* and the *saga* of the Scandinavian languages.

German *Sage* (plural *Sagen*) is a broad and not very precisely defined term in popular usage which Gunkel specifically retained in the popular sense. Olrik, whose work will be discussed below, also used it in this loose sense: he identified it with 'folk narrative' (*Volksdichtung*), in which he comprised material of many and various kinds, including both prose and poetry: myths, songs, hero-stories and local legends. He also used the word 'epic' interchangeably with *Sage*: his 'epic laws' were intended, he stated, to define the way in which the 'Volk' universally expressed itself in speech.

More recently the term *Sage* has been used in a narrower sense to denote a popular tale which purports to preserve memories of actual past events, in distinction from the *Märchen* (a term used by the brothers Grimm, usually translated into English by 'fairytales'), which relate marvellous happenings in a world of make-believe and make no such claim. Nevertheless, even with this restriction *Sage* remains a very broad term, and its continued use in Pentateuchal studies is unfortunate, since it tends to conceal important differences between one kind of material and another. The Norwegian and Danish equivalent of it is *sagn*.

In the Scandinavian languages, there is also a word *saga*. Although etymologically *sagn* and *saga* (and also German *Sage*) are related, the

words are completely distinct in meaning. The meaning of *saga* is quite specific: it refers to a class of *literary* (i.e. written) works composed from the thirteenth to the fifteenth centuries AD, which refer *inter alia* to the settlement of Iceland in the tenth to eleventh centuries. As will be indicated below, the question whether the *sagas* are based on oral traditions dating from the events which they describe, and if so to what extent, is disputed. They are thus not only *not* equivalent to the German *Sagen*, but are at any rate in their extant form literary and not oral works.

The common confusion between *Sage* and *saga* is understandable but unfortunate. It occurs most frequently in translations of German and Scandinavian works into English and other languages, but frequently also in original works in English. Attempts to avoid the confusion by translating *Sage* by 'legend' are hardly less confusing, since 'legend' also has other meanings. In common usage legend usually means a story about the past of dubious historical value; while in its proper sense it denotes a (mainly) mediaeval work about the lives of the saints (e.g. *The Golden Legend*). It is best avoided.

In this book the words *Sage* and *saga* will be left untranslated. The Norwegian word *sagn*, since it is the exact equivalent of *Sage*, will not be used.

b. *Olrik's 'epic laws'*
Axel Olrik was not an Old Testament scholar but a Danish folklorist. His researches led him to formulate the hypothesis that the 'folk narratives' of a wide variety of peoples manifest the same formal characteristics: that is, however much the subjects or themes with which they deal may differ, these narratives are constructed on identical lines and use the same devices in their presentation of character and action. They do not attempt to portray everyday life but create a 'world of *Sage*' of their own. The remarkable consistency of their common pattern springs from the fact that 'primitive man' (Olrik's own expression) shares a common mentality whose limited intellectual resources 'restrict the freedom of composition in an entirely different and more rigid way than in our [sc. modern] literature'. Although there are admittedly *some* differences between the *Sage*-forms of different peoples, these are merely 'dialectal variations' of the common pattern.

Olrik treated this subject on several separate occasions. In his early article (published in Danish in 1908 with a German, slightly modified, version in 1909 [ET 1965]) he restricted his examples to

European oral traditions: Norse *saga*, ancient Greek, Scandinavian and Teutonic mythology and heroic tales like the *Chanson de Roland*, though he hinted that his 'laws' were of wider application. In a fuller study published in 1921 in Danish from a manuscript left unfinished at his death he included a chapter on the patriarchal stories of Genesis in which he argued that these also exemplify the epic laws. His study of Genesis had been inspired by reading the third edition of Gunkel's commentary on Genesis, which had in turn been strongly influenced by his own earlier study.

It is unfortunate that Olrik's presentation of his laws is unclear and inconsistent, for this has led to some confusion in the work of scholars—both Old Testament scholars and others—who have attempted to use his work. There is no tabulation or numbering of the laws in any of his treatments of the subject. Some seem to be variant or near-variant forms of others; others appear to be alternatives, special cases, or even exceptions to the general rule. Again, the same law may appear under different names or be differently formulated in different paragraphs. There are also some differences between the 1909 article and the book of 1921, particularly in the number of laws proposed: in the former there are about twelve or thirteen, while in the latter the number has risen to something between fourteen and sixteen; but these do not entirely correspond to items in the former. Altogether Olrik formulated about twenty or twenty-one laws. Such is the confusion on this point that some scholars (e.g. Van Seters, 1975, p. 160) find only ten, while others (e.g. McTurk) enumerate, and work with, twenty! This discrepancy is, however, partly due to the fact that many writers on the subject appear to be familiar only with the article of 1909, which does not represent Olrik's most mature conclusions.

In view of their importance for the present discussion the laws are here presented in their fullest form, but not in the same order as in any of Olrik's own writings. His own presentation lacks any attempt at systematic arrangement or even consistency; here the laws have been grouped under a few general headings. They have also been reworded in the interests of clarity; but Olrik's own names for them are given in brackets.

Olrik's laws

General structural characteristics. An oral narrative

1. has a clear structure and selects for mention only those aspects of real life which directly serve its purpose (*the law of perspicuity or clear arrangement*);

2. has a unity of plot which moves naturally towards a single concluding action, each detail contributing to the dénouement (*the law of [epic] unity of plot*);

3. may, however, exceptionally, narrate two or more episodes if this is essential for the depiction of the principal character(s) (*the law of ideal unity of plot*—this structure is, however, a sign of later development and the fruit of more mature 'reflection');

4. eschews information not directly relevant to the plot (*the law of the logic of oral narrative*);

5. employs the technique of heightening the tension through a series (usually three) of progressively more impressive actions—for example, more difficult tasks, more extraordinary events or deeds (*the law of progression*);

6. proceeds in a straight line with no retrospective references to previous events, and, unless this is strictly required by the plot, without changes of scene (*the law of direct continuity of plot*);

7. lays the greatest emphasis on the concluding member in a series of characters or events (*the law of terminal stress*). (Sometimes there is an *initial* stress on one of the characters, but this is given not to the most important character in terms of the action, but only to the one who is *formally* the most important, e.g. a king);

8. does not plunge immediately into the tensions of the plot, but begins calmly, moving from a static situation to one of excitement (*the law of opening*);

9. equally does not close abruptly when the action has reached its dénouement, but ends with a return to tranquillity (*the law of closing*).

Internal structural characteristics. An oral narrative

10. gives a clear, vivid picture of each episode and presents the characters in actions which are intensely memorable (*the law of plastic lucidity or of tableau-scenes*);

11. uses the device of repetition or near-repetition in order to emphasize the importance of a speech, action or item of information (*the law of repetition*);
12. presents similar events or characters in a way which gives them a common pattern (*the law of patterning*);
13. has a predilection for the number three with regard to characters, objects and successive events (*the law of three*).

Characterization. An oral narrative

14. is primarily concerned with one single character (*the law of concentration on the central character*);
15. has only two main characters, though there may be several minor ones (*the law of two main characters*);
16. puts only two characters into any one scene or episode (*the law of two to a scene*);
17. presents the main character early in the story before introducing the others (*the law of the priority of the main character*);
18. emphasizes the contrasting qualities and actions of the two characters who appear in any scene (*the law of contrast*);
19. does not give a direct description of persons or things but reveals their appearance and character exclusively through actions (*the law of restriction to action*);
20. presents two characters who appear as partners or in similar roles in less impressive terms than would be the case if only one character were involved (*the law of 'twins'*).

It should first be emphasized that all these 'laws' are concerned only with *formal* characteristics: they are not concerned with the themes or contents of the stories, but only with the manner of their telling: that is, with the restrictions laid upon their 'arthurs' by the limitations of the 'primitive' mentality. According to Olrik's view, therefore, the lack of thematic parallels between the stories of different peoples in no way invalidates the universal application of the laws.

A puzzling feature of the laws is the fact that Olrik appears to have mixed together two quite different kinds of criteria without distinguishing between them: for while some of the laws appear to specify certain features which are *essential* to all oral narrative, other features certainly are not. For example, such laws as those of perspicuity or clear arrangement (number 1 in the above scheme), unity of plot (2), the logic of oral narrative (4), direct continuity of plot (6), repetition (11) and two to a scene (16) refer to major characteristics which seem to be essential, while on the other hand those of progression (5) and more particularly of the number three (13) and of twins (20) are by no means applicable to *all* oral narratives: many plots provide no opportunity for the introduction of such features. Presumably in including these Olrik meant no more than that *when* these features occur they are characteristic of the mentality which produces *Sage*. Olrik's jumbling together of two different kinds of criteria in a single category—to which he gave the uncompromising designation 'law' (*Gesetz*)—makes their use as criteria extremely difficult—a difficulty which applies to their use in connection with other literatures besides the Old Testament.

Although Olrik's laws have been systematically applied, despite this difficulty, to some other literatures (e.g. by McTurk in his analysis of the story of Cynewulf and Cyneheard in the Anglo-Saxon *Chronicle* and its possible resemblance to the Icelandic *sagas*), it is remarkable that no really systematic attempt has been made to apply them to the Pentateuchal narratives. As will be seen below, the principal studies of the Pentateuchal narratives from the time of Gunkel onwards have made *sporadic* use of *some* of them in the study of selected narratives —Van Seters in particular summarized them under ten headings (1975, pp. 160-61) and applied them to a group of stories in Genesis—but nothing short of a *full* study of *all* the Pentateuchal narratives on the basis of the laws would be sufficient to establish whether, and to what extent, Olrik's criteria apply to them. It is not possible to undertake that study here: that would require a separate monograph.

The use of Olrik's laws in the study of the Pentateuch

To assess the value of the laws for Pentateuchal study it is necessary to address three questions:

1. Are Olrik's laws valid criteria for the identification of oral tradition (*Sage*)?
2. How should they be applied?
3. How far, if at all, do the Pentateuchal narratives fit these criteria?

1. *Are Olrik's laws valid?* Most Old Testament scholars from Gunkel onwards have assumed that Olrik's laws are universally

accepted by folklorists and not to be questioned; and they have used them to support their view that many (at least) of the Pentateuchal narratives originated as *Sage*. Most recently, however, especially since Van Seters made substantial use of the laws to attack rather than to defend this view, some have expressed doubts about their validity or relevance. The fact is that in the study of folklore and kindred fields during the eighty years since they were first formulated, the 'laws' have suffered varying fortunes; but after a period of relative neglect and criticism there is now a strong tendency to rehabilitate them and to reinstate them as valid criteria for assessing the possibility of the existence of oral sources behind written texts. Indeed, A. Dundes, in his *The Study of Folklore* (1965), published the first English translation of Olrik's 1909 article, and in his introduction to that translation commented that Olrik's findings have 'withstood the criticism of the passing years', and claimed that they 'continue to excite each generation of folklorists' (p. 129). Since then increasing use has been made of them in specialist studies, for example by McTurk (1981) and T. Hunt (*Studia Celtica*, 1973/4, pp. 107-20).

Old Testament scholars are not always well-informed, or even convinced of the necessity to be well-informed, about the current state of affairs: for example, Cazelles, in a review of Van Seters's 1975 book, dismissed the relevance of the 'laws' to the study of Genesis with a reference to 'the criteria of A. Olrik, the application of which we leave Van Seters to discuss with the folklorists' (*VT* 28 [1978], p. 249), while A. de Pury, in his review of the same book, commented: 'This virtual canonization of Olrik's criteria is one of the major weaknesses of Van Seters's work. . . . The twelve pages written by Olrik in 1909 are not, after all, the last word on the question!' (*RB* 85 [1978], p. 605). De Pury was evidently not aware of Olrik's later work, or of the fact that the 1909 article was deemed worthy of an English translation as late as 1965. The question remains, however, whether the laws are *universally* valid. Very little investigation of their applicability to non-European traditions appears to have been carried out with the exception of Pentateuchal studies.

2. *How should they be applied?* The acceptance of Olrik's laws as a valid description of the character of *Sage*—or, at least, of the particular *Sagen* of the European peoples with which he was primarily concerned—does not of itself necessarily justify all the uses to which they have been put. As has already been pointed out, they are not, in spite of Olrik's designation, really 'laws', but rather

indications of features which *may* occur in a *Sage* but do not all necessarily do so in *every Sage*. Although they may be useful, in combination with other criteria, in detecting the presence in written texts of *techniques* which *ultimately* derive from oral composition, the features to which they call attention are too general, and, on the other hand, in some instances too precise, to be used as criteria for the more specific purpose of determining whether a particular story actually originated orally.

Olrik's definition of *Sage* is too broad for a precise analysis; and indeed, some of the 'laws'—for example, those of clear arrangement, progression, openings, closings, concentration on a central character—may be found in almost any kind of narrative literature, including modern novels. The 'laws' are most likely to be of use when applied to large bodies or collections of literature, and when there is a presumption, or at least a strong possibility, that these have an oral origin; and even here, although they may serve to confirm this impression, they are hardly sufficient to prove its correctness by themselves. There is no reason why the conventions and techniques of oral composition should not have been carried over and used in purely written compositions; and if such works were composed by writers in whose time oral tradition was still a living reality, it is quite probable that they should have employed oral techniques (see Culley, 1976, pp. 28-30). Even Olrik himself admitted that *some* written compositions show the influence of *some* of the laws, although he dismissed this phenomenon as exceptional (1921, p. 81).

3. *Do Olrik's laws fit the Pentateuchal narratives?* Gunkel (1901a, especially the 3rd edn) relied heavily on them, using at least fourteen of them—though in different contexts—as criteria for his thesis that the narratives of Genesis are primarily *Sage*: the laws of perspicuity or clear arrangement, epic unity of plot, progression, direct continuity of plot, opening and closing, plastic lucidity, repetition, patterning, concentration on the central character, two main characters, two to a scene, contrast and restriction to action. Olrik himself, in his study of certain selected narratives of Genesis (1921, pp. 128-42), reached a similar conclusion. Gunkel strongly emphasized that future students of Old Testament narrative must make use of these 'universally valid laws'.

However, despite his general contention that 'Genesis is a collection of *Sagen*', Gunkel recognized that not all the narratives in Genesis (leaving aside the 'P' material) do in fact conform to Olrik's laws. This was of course partly to be explained by the modifications undergone by the original *Sagen* in the course of transmission and to the effects of their combination into larger narrative complexes; but Gunkel also admitted that some narratives had lacked the characteristics of *Sage* from the very first. He distinguished between various types of story, ranging from 'very ancient' (*uralte*) *Sagen* to later and more complex (*ausführliche*) ones—e.g. Gen. 24—and finally to highly sophisticated narratives (*Kunstwerke*) such as the Joseph Story, to which he gave the designation *Novelle*. Each type, he maintained, represented a stage of cultural progress: an increased freedom of expression gradually overcame the mental limitations which had given birth to the simple *Sagen*. To these later compositions Olrik's laws did not apply. Nevertheless Gunkel insisted that they also had been composed orally.

If Gunkel was obliged to admit that not all the narratives of Genesis conform to the character of *Sage* as defined by Olrik, even more negative conclusions have been reached recently by Van Seters in his study of the Abraham material (1975). It is important to note that Van Seters fully accepted the validity of Olrik's laws; what he questioned was their applicability to the narratives in question. His conclusion was that only a very few of the Abraham narratives—notably Gen. 12.10-20 and 16.1-12—conform to them. That such very different conclusions can be drawn from the application of the same criteria to the same material is to some extent explained by the difficulty of interpreting the laws themselves. Van Seters's study has been criticized on various grounds; but his application of the laws to the Genesis material still awaits a rebuttal.

There is a further point of importance which needs to be made from the point of view of the assessment of tradition-history. Gunkel, as has been stated above, drew a distinction between 'very old' and 'later' *Sagen*. How old is folklore? Presumably it can be created at any time when there is a living oral tradition; and—although Gunkel himself believed the contrary—oral tradition does not necesarily come to an end with the advent of a literate society. Olrik's laws can give no assistance in determining the *age* of any particular story: Gunkel's assumption of a lineal progression of culture marked by a series of stages in the development of *Sage* into more 'artistic' composition (*Kunstwerk*) is an over-simple view which takes no account of the complexities of actual pre-literate, or indeed, literate, societies. Van Seters, in his discussion of the meagre amount of folklore which he detected in Genesis, pointed out the weakness of such an approach: 'The narrators of the written tradition, whenever they lived, had access to large amounts of folklore, which they could have used in various ways without any of it being of a very primitive character. The application of Olrik's laws may be useful in understanding the sources of a narrator and his mode of composition without saying much about the history of the tradition' (1975, p. 161). And: 'The degree to which the stories reflect any oral tradition may be explained entirely by the use of folkloristic forms and motifs that were accessible to Israelite culture throughout its history and not primarily by the deposit of a preliterate period' (p. 309). If this is true, the conclusion is inevitable that 'The notion, so frequently expressed and most strongly by Noth, that a long and complex tradition-history lies behind the whole of the present literary form is ... completely unfounded' (p. 310).

c. *Jolles and the Icelandic sagas*

A somewhat different kind of comparison between the Pentateuchal narratives and stories from other cultures, and one which has exercised, and continues to exercise, great influence on Old Testament scholarship, was proposed by A. Jolles in a work entitled *Einfache Formen* ('Simple Forms') (1930). By 'simple forms' Jolles meant short forms of speech which arise naturally and anonymously in simple societies which have not yet developed an awareness of the possibility of conscious artistry in the use of words. There were a number of such 'simple forms', both in prose and poetical form. Jolles attempted to distinguish betwen these not primarily on the basis of their external characteristics, but by attempting to penetrate their fundamental 'way of thinking' (*Geistesbeschäftigung*).

Among the narrative types of 'simple form' Jolles distinguished between myth, *Märchen* ('fairytale') and *Sage*. His understanding of *Sage*, however, differed considerably from the current understanding of that term, and was much more restricted in its scope. As with other types of 'simple form', he maintained that *Sage* no longer exists in its pure, original state, and can only be brought to light by a sensitive study of the later, written literature, which has to a large extent obscured its original character. But he believed that it is possible to discover, beneath the surface of the written texts, the 'inner form' or 'spiritual (i.e. intellectual) world' which gave birth to the simple form of *Sage* upon which these later versions were based.

Although Jolles found some examples of stories reflecting this 'spiritual world' in ancient Greek and Germanic sources, he based his reconstruction mainly on the Norse 'family' *sagas*, whose characteristics he set out in considerable detail. These are now preserved in a large collection of later mediaeval texts; but Jolles believed that these are based on a long oral tradition going back to the period which they describe: that of the settlement of Iceland by small groups of immigrants from other parts of Scandinavia in the tenth and eleventh centuries AD.

The Norse *sagas* comprise two or three distinct groups; but Jolles believed that the oldest group, and that which influenced the development of the others, was that of the so-called 'family *sagas*'. In these, the family is the central, and only, concern: there were as yet no national state or institutions, no national politics, and no 'official' history: the individual family was still the basic social unit, living its own self-sufficient, 'autarchical' life with few outside contacts. The individuals whose actions are commemorated in the family *sagas* consequently act entirely in the interests of their families, and the relationships portrayed are always family relationships. It was thus the family which determined the 'way of thinking' manifested by these *sagas*. Jolles listed as their characteristic themes a pride in ancestors, family possessions and rights of inheritance, family loyalties and blood revenge; but also family hatreds and feuds, wife-stealing, adultery and incest. These tales had been preserved and transmitted orally from one generation to another for several centuries by later groups who believed them to be the histories of their own lineal ancestors. So the 'family story' was identical with the tribal history. It was preserved because it was thought to epitomize the characteristics, loyalties and concerns which the tribe thought to be essentially its own and which its members strove to emulate and maintain, while taking warning from departures from these norms which were also recorded in the *sagas*. Because even before their committal to writing the *sagas* had been already adapted to serve as models and warnings for later generations, their *original* form can no longer be reconstructed in detail: only traces of the original 'way of thinking' can be discerned. Eventually the *sagas* acquired a consciously aesthetic or artistic, and literary, character.

Jolles's influence on Pentateuchal scholarship can be traced to the two pages (87-88) in which, himself not a biblical scholar, he singled out the patriarchal stories of Genesis as similar in kind to the Norse and other *sagas*. These also, he maintained, belong to a type of literature in which 'a whole people is conceived as a family and conceives itself as such'. Many of the same themes and concerns appear: for example, 'the offering of a son as the most terrible test imaginable' to a father (an allusion to Abraham's 'sacrifice' of Isaac and Agamemnon's sacrifice of Iphigenia); the prominence of the paternal blessing, which 'retains its power through the generations'; a 'god of the fathers' (an allusion to Alt); loyalty between brothers, but also envy and quarrels between brothers and other family members; and a cast of characters virtually confined to the immediate family: fathers, mothers, sons, daughters, brothers and sisters. The genealogies in Genesis, he argued, also point in the same direction: they represent the Israelite people as lineally descended from the 'heroes' Abraham, Isaac and Jacob through twelve brothers, serving to confirm the notion of the tribe as identical with the family, and also that of the importance of family inheritance. Jolles also suggested that the difference in character and interests between the stories of Genesis and the national and political 'histories' centred on the family of David (in 2 Samuel and 1 Kings) corresponds to that between the Icelandic 'family *sagas* and the Icelandic "kings" *sagas*', which he believed to be of later origin, and to reflect a more highly organized way of life.

Jolles's theory has been used in a variety of ways by Old Testament scholars. His influence is clearly discernible in the work of the two most important tradition-historians of the Pentateuch, von Rad and Noth. Noth, specifically acknowledging his indebtedness to Jolles, asserted that the Icelandic sagas provide the best model for understanding the 'way of thinking' manifested by the Pentateuchal stories, and concluded that the latter, like the former, are based on oral traditions handed down from a period of tribalism preceding the formation of a national state (1948, p. 47 and note 152; ET p. 47 and note 152). Von Rad also (1956, p. 23, note 1; ET p. 33, n. * and also in later editions) quoted Jolles in support of the distinction between *Sage* and historical writing in Israel which he had made earlier in his work on the beginnings of historical writing in Israel (1944). However, neither of these scholars paid attention to the implications of Jolles's theory for the question of the possible historical content of the original stories, of which they took a very negative view.

This question was raised and fully discussed by Westermann (1964, 1981). He was interested in the question whether the 'way of life' portrayed in the patriarchal stories corresponds in any respect to historical reality. On the one hand he was dissatisfied with the negative views of Gunkel and his followers von Rad and Noth, who had given scant consideration to this question; but he was equally unable to accept the over-confident positive appraisal of the historical value of the stories made by Albright and his school, who claimed that archaeological data confirmed their opinion. He held that the patriarchal stories are typical 'family stories' of the type described by Jolles: that is, that although they are not to be regarded as historical records, they nevertheless preserve, despite later editing, a true picture of an actual, particular, and precisely definable society in which the self-sufficient, 'autarchical' and intimate family had constituted the entire 'world' of its members.

One of the consequences of Westermann's views, if they were to be accepted, would be that the use of the term *Sage* as a blanket term comprising the Pentateuchal narratives as a whole would have to be abandoned; and in fact Westermann recommended that the term should be avoided as too vague to be other than confusing. His precise definition of the patriarchal stories in the strict sense intended by Jolles puts them in an entirely different category from the rest of the Pentateuchal narratives: clearly the Exodus complex of stories in Exod. 1–15 and the stories of the sojourn in the wilderness in Exodus and Numbers (not to mention the early chapters of Genesis) would have to be treated on an entirely different basis from them, since they obviously do not have the characteristics of 'family stories' in Jolles's sense: they are concerned not with intimate family life and relationships but with the relationship between a single leader (not the 'father') and an undifferentiated mass of his followers. This reflects a different 'way of thinking' from that with which Jolles was concerned, and its study requires a new 'model', the search for which has barely begun. But the abandonment of the concept of *Sage* in its over-broad sense as applicable to the Pentateuchal narratives as a whole strikes at the root of the work of tradition-historians such as von Rad and Noth.

The extent of the influence of Jolles on Pentateuchal scholarship up to the present time may be measured by the references to his work in recent Introductions to the Old Testament, for example in the latest editions of Eissfeldt's (1976) and Kaiser's (1978), and in that of Rendtorff (1983). Koch also (pp. 171-75; ET pp. 151-55) relied heavily on his theory in his categorization of the *Sagen* of Genesis.

Koch and Rendtorff appear to regard the insights of Jolles as complementary to those of Olrik and Gunkel. For them, Jolles's attempt to define precisely the 'way of thinking' of the authors of the *sagas* in terms of the family and its concerns makes it possible to refine Gunkel's analysis of the patriarchal stories and so to describe a particular stage in the prehistory of Israel. But, as Van Seters has pointed out, 'Jolles and Olrik have two quite different bodies of material in mind' (p. 137). Whereas Gunkel, following Olrik and followed in his turn implicitly by von Rad, Noth and others, had explicitly used the word '*Sage*' 'in no other sense than is attributed to it in common usage' (1901, 3rd edn. p. VIII)—that is, as including in its scope *any* kind of orally transmitted story purporting to relate to the events of a past age—, Jolles had deplored this vague use of the term. What he was concerned with was one particular kind of story which he found best exemplified in the Icelandic *sagas*. It was also to be found elsewhere, in *some* oral traditions of *some* other peoples which had passed through a comparable stage of social and cultural development, and also a comparable experience, to that of the Icelandic settlers, but not by any means in *all* oral narratives.

Is the confidence placed by so many Old Testament scholars in the theory of Jolles justified? Not according to Van Seters: he asserted, first, that Jolles's views on the specific character of *Sage* are 'highly unconventional' and were therefore 'rejected from the start', and second, that his work is widely regarded by the specialists as a 'complete distortion of the character and development of Icelandic saga', which 'many authorities regard . . . as primarily literary works with only a limited amount of oral tradition behind them', composed for the most part in the thirteenth century (pp. 135-36). In fact the situation is more complex than Van Seters suggests; the reprinting of Jolles's book in 1958, almost thirty years after its original publication, indicates that his views have by no means been totally discarded.

The truth is that modern folklorists are seriously divided in their views on these questions. On the one hand G. Turville-Petre expressed a majority opinion when he asserted that 'The existence of (oral) sagas in twelfth century Iceland has not yet been proved, and even if they existed, it will never be possible to show what they were like. . . . The sagas which we know are not in oral form, and . . . their usually polished style is the outcome of generations of training in literary composition' (p. v.), and that 'It would not be correct to say that the family sagas were summaries of oral tales' (p. 223). But on the other hand, McTurk, writing in 1981, defended 'the assumption that the sagas were largely oral in origin', citing other recent authorities as an indication that this view is once more gaining ground (pp. 86, 113-15). The question is clearly one whose solution lies beyond the scope of this book; but in view of the fact that Jolles's views are, to say the least, by no means universally accepted by folklorists, the value of his comparison of the patriarchal narratives with the Icelandic *sagas* must remain questionable. Further, the inability of the specialists in the study of the *sagas* to agree on the question of their oral origin has a wider significance, for it suggests that if after a long period of intensive investigation no agreed and reliable *criteria* have emerged for the detection of oral sources behind the Icelandic *sagas*, this may well be equally true of attempts to perform the same kind of operation with regard to other bodies of literature. Old Testament form—and tradition-critics, who in general are far less skilled in these matters, may well be living in a fools' paradise.

In addition to these considerations, Van Seters has pointed out a further objection to the use of Jolles's model for the characterization of the patriarchal narratives: that the term 'family stories' is far too vague, and conceals very great differences between the way of life supposed to be reflected in the *sagas* and that reflected in Genesis. He points out with justification—and this is true of *all* those Old Testament scholars who have used Jolles's model—that 'Westermann did not attempt actually to describe a particular example of an Icelandic saga and then compare it with the stories in Genesis'. He adds: 'If he had, the inappropriateness of the comparison would have been self-evident' (1983, pp. 223-24). This failure to make a detailed comparison goes back to Jolles himself: he thought it possible to describe the 'way of thinking' (*Geistesbeschäftigung*) reflected in the *sagas* in an extremely abstract way which somehow transcended their actual contents. Such a comparison—of which a full treatment is obviously not possible here, but which should certainly be undertaken—would indeed reveal that the differences between the *sagas*, which 'are not small episodic units, but very complex literary works that often run to several hundred pages' (Van Seters, 1975, p. 137) and the patriarchal stories are much greater than has been generally supposed: for example, the *sagas* are mainly of an extremely violent and tragic character with conflicts and confrontations leading to the violent death of the heroic champions.

Such events are of their very substance. The family disputes in the fundamentally peaceable stories of Genesis cannot in any way be compared with this. (Petsch already in 1932 questioned the appropriateness of Jolles's description of these *sagas* as 'family stories'.)

The methodological fault lies, both with Jolles and with Westermann and other Old Testament scholars, in an excessive tendency to abstraction. A comment by R.R. Wilson, made in connection with the pitfalls into which Old Testament scholars may fall in the use not of Icelandic *sagas* but of examples of *modern* folklore for comparative purposes is relevant here: 'When the oral literatures of different societies are compared, a number of similar genres can be discerned, but these genres are parallel only at a fairly high level of abstraction. . . . As a result biblical scholars have had difficulty finding detailed cross-cultural parallels that help to interpret the specific literary forms of the Old Testament' (p. 55).

Finally, whatever may have been the nature of the society supposedly portrayed in the original Icelandic oral *sagas*, there remains the question whether the 'autarchical', self-sufficient, isolated family life supposed by Jolles and Westermann to have been led by the Hebrew patriarchs ever existed in reality. This question has recently been raised by Blum (p. 502). He pointed out that no evidence has been produced for the existence of such a very special form of society. Westermann (1981, p. 90) refers vaguely to some 'reports from the Old Babylonian period, in which nomads from the west, first as individuals and in families, then in tribes, penetrated into the cultivated land and finally came to obtain a share in the kingship'. But since he gives no indication of the identity of these 'reports', it is not possible to assess his interpretation of the 'family' stage in this process, which might provide a plausible analogy to the way of life of the Hebrew patriarchs. It is difficult to avoid the conclusion that the 'autarchical' society of the patriarchs has simply been read into the stories of Genesis through over-reliance on the Icelandic model proposed by Jolles. And, as Blum pointed out, if this argumentation is faulty, there is no reason why the patriarchal traditions should be particularly ancient, and so no need to suppose a lengthy period of oral transmission of them.

d. *'Oral literature' in the modern world*
Perhaps the most significant new development with potential

relevance for the understanding of Old Testament narratives and especially those of the Pentateuch since the time of Gunkel and Olrik (and Jolles) is the immense progress made in anthropology and the study of modern folklore. The accumulation by field anthropologists of vast quantities of examples of 'oral literature' from many parts of the world, still continuing apace, research into the characteristics of this material in local and regional studies in its sociological and anthropological contexts, and, further, comparative studies leading to conclusions about the nature of the phenomenon of 'oral literature' in general have, despite differences of emphasis on many points of detail, led to a broad consensus of scholarly opinion on the subject.

The term 'oral literature' is a broad one. It refers to the practice among non-literate communities—or communities still mainly unaffected, in their customs and way of life, by the use of writing—of communicating traditional songs, poems, stories, epics etc. by means of public recital or 'performance'. Concerning this phenomenon, as practised in many parts of the modern world, there is general agreement on a number of points, including the following:

1. 'Performance' in this sense is not something of which any member of the community is capable, but is restricted to qualified persons generally recognized as such. There is an extended period of training which must be undergone under an older and experienced 'performer'.

2. The 'performer' is not simply a transmitter of forms of words fixed by tradition. He is free to vary the form and words of the traditional material, and is thus to a considerable extent a creator or 'author'. His skill in varying his material to produce new effects is one of the features most appreciated by his audience. The degree of freedom which he may exercise is, however, to some extent limited by the occasion and the nature of the material. There is always a combination of stability or continuity and of variety in an oral 'performance'.

3. The actual form and wording of any 'performance' depend on a variety of factors, especially on the setting, the occasion and the audience.

4. 'Audience participation' is expected and is a normal feature of a 'performance'. The comments and interpolations made by the audience may materially affect the form of words used.

5. There is therefore not only improvisation to fit the occasion—sometimes including allusions to recent events and situations familiar to both performer and audience—but also *instant* improvisation. There is therefore no one 'authentic version' of a work. In a sense, each performance is a separate 'literary' creation.

6. The effect created by the performance depends to a large extent on intonation, pauses, differences of pitch and other auditory signals, and also on facial expression, gesture, bodily stance, etc. Much oral literature is sung or recited with instrumental accompaniment.

7. The performance is built up from a traditional 'skeleton' (in the case of narratives, plot) combined with other traditional themes.

8. The performer relies to a large extent for his composition on the use of ready-made stock phrases, words and short 'scenes' or imagery. This is particularly noticeable in poetry, where metre both limits the forms of expression and at the same time permits the rapid 'slotting in' of prefabricated lines, half-lines etc. of a fixed length.

9. The growth of general literacy eventually kills oral literature. But the process is a gradual and complex one. Both oral and written literature can exist side by side.

10. A genuine oral work which has been committed to writing is (evidently) simply the record of a single 'performance', that is, of one out of innumerable different versions which have been performed. It should also be recognized that the very process of recording by dictation, which was presumably the ancient method and is still sometimes used today, can affect the 'performer' by slowing him down and in other obvious ways, and so result in a text which differs from what he would have said or sung in a 'free' oral performance.

Although the above conclusions seem relatively assured, recent writers have stressed that the study of modern 'oral literature' is still in its infancy. Not only does the continuous stream of new information and examples necessitate the continual modification of older theories; it has also been maintained—for example, by one of the most authoritative writers on the subject, Ruth Finnegan, in *Oral Literature in Africa*—that some important aspects of the subject have hitherto been neglected, and hasty conclusions, especially of a comparative kind, drawn. It is significant for our present purpose that she makes this comment with regard to *narrative* oral literature in particular:

> Detailed studies in depth of the literary and social significance of the various stories in any one society are notably lacking. It is time more attention was focused on these aspects, and less on the comparative classification of stories, the tracing of the history of their plots, or the enumeration, however impressive, of the quantities of texts that have so far been collected (p. 330).

Some of the earlier 'scientific' studies of modern oral literature took it for granted that the knowledge gained about its practice in *contemporary* non-literate societies could be directly applied as a means of testing the oral origins of *ancient* literature. For example, the Chadwicks in their comprehensive account of oral literature included a substantial section on the Old Testament in which they concluded that early Hebrew literature derived 'in large part' from oral tradition, and that 'saga . . . forms the largest and most important element in the earliest Hebrew records' (vol. II, p. 629). The views of Gunkel were thus held to be confirmed by modern folklore studies. Few folklorists, however, have pursued this subject in any detail, and indeed until recently few Old Testament scholars and commentators have taken modern folklore studies into account: they have tacitly assumed that Gunkel's concept of *Sage* and of its applicability to the narratives of Genesis may still be taken as broadly correct. However, other ancient and mediaeval works have been subjected to investigations of this kind, notably *Beowulf* and the *Chanson de Roland*, and above all the *Iliad* and the *Odyssey*. With regard to Homer, it is now generally accepted, as a result of Milman Parry's study of oral poetry in modern Yugoslavia, that the Homeric poems were originally orally composed, though the extent to which the analogy with modern oral composition can be legitimately taken remains a matter of dispute (see Kirk, 1962, pp. 59ff. and A. Parry 1971, pp. xxxviii ff.).

For a number of reasons Homer may be a special case. How far the criteria used in Homeric studies are valid for testing the oral origins of other kinds of ancient literary texts is a question which needs careful examination. At first sight it would appear that, whatever similarities may be found between two such literatures—of form, theme or style, or of social, cultural or 'spiritual' background—, the gap between the modern world (whether in Africa, Europe or elsewhere) and the ancient Semitic world is so great that these similarities must be superficial and coincidental, and therefore useless for the establishment of a real analogy which would justify the use of one 'literature' to illuminate the other. The use of such analogies presupposes the validity of some general theory of human cultural development: either the evolutionism, now generally discredited, of Frazer and his school, according to which there are 'unilinear and parallel stages of social and cultural evolution through which all societies must pass' (Finnegan, p. 35) or diffusionism, according to which cultural traits have spread geographically throughout the world—a view which is equally unprovable, especially with regard to non-literate cultures which have neither written records nor a scientific interest in cultural origins, and in itself highly improbable when set up as a general and universal theory (see Finnegan, pp. 34-41, 317-30).

If, despite these reservations, a convincing parallel is to be drawn between Old Testament narrative literature and modern oral narrative literature, it is essential that certain conditions should be fulfilled. First, it has to be shown that the study of *modern* oral literature is sufficiently advanced and commands a sufficient consensus of opinion among the specialists, to provide a full and reliable picture of its character, whether in general terms, or, if this is not possible, with regard to some particular area of the world. Secondly, it must be shown that the *Old Testament* provides a viable body of texts of a generally comparable character to the modern examples with which it is to be compared. Thirdly, Old Testament scholars must familiarize themselves with folklore studies and be prepared to undertake the serious detailed work of comparison of every relevant aspect of the subject, avoiding vague generalizations. These three points will now be considered in turn, bearing in mind that the burden of proof rests upon those who maintain that such a comparison *is* possible. In what follows, use will be made of studies by anthropologists and folklorists and by Old Testament scholars whose work is informed by a knowledge of those studies.

1. With regard to the first point, that of the existence of an adequate body of reliable information about the character of modern oral literature, it is particularly unfortunate that most of the work has been done on poetry rather than on prose narratives, concerning which Van Seters remarked: 'folklorists are agreed that the prose

narrative forms are the least likely to be preserved in any fixed manner' (1975, p. 158). With regard to Africa, Finnegan devoted a large section of her chapter on prose narratives to a castigation of the inadequacy of earlier studies (pp. 315-34). Although vast amounts of material have been published, the emphasis has been on quantity rather than on quality of research. Much has been inaccurately or inadequately recorded, often merely in the form of plot summaries. Presuppositions drawn from general cultural theories such as those mentioned above, and limitation of discussion to such matters as typology of plot and motifs and on strict (and premature) classification of genres, together with false assumptions about the fixity and antiquity of oral narrative, have resulted in the neglect of such important matters as the question of the 'performers'' originality, the part played by the audiences, and the social and cultural background. Although Finnegan herself attempted to remedy this neglect to some extent and to point the way to more fruitful future research, it is clear from her remarks that much more detailed research needs to be done: her comments are in fact, as she herself remarks, of necessity largely 'destructive' criticism.

Other commentators (e.g. Culley, 1963 and Wilson) have indicated that this state of affairs is not confined to African studies. In other fields, too, most of the work has been confined to *poetic* oral literature. Yet, as Wilson remarked, 'Particularly in the Pentateuch and the Deuteronomistic History . . . the present written narratives seem far removed from the largely poetic oral epics that have been studied by folklorists'. Yet some Old Testament scholars (e.g. Gunn) have made extensive use of works such as that of Lord, which is exclusively concerned with poetical works, in their discussions of prose 'oral composition', without giving due regard to the obvious fact that the techniques of composition in the two types of literature are of necessity very different. It is true that some Old Testament scholars (e.g. Albright) have tried to prove that the narratives of the Pentateuch are prose versions of a lost Hebrew epic poem; but this proposal has very little to support it, and has been generally rejected. Even if it were correct, it would merely complicate the problem of composition and would tell us nothing about the composition of the actual prose text which we possess.

On various aspects of the study of oral *prose* literature of modern non-literate societies which at first sight may appear to offer analogies with Old Testament narrative there is generally no agreed opinion among folklorists. Finnegan, for example, castigated those who make 'confident assertions about the great age of certain stories' without producing evidence for this. Prose 'performers' exhibit an originality at each telling of their tales equal to that shown by 'performers' of poetry: consequently, 'Contrary to the assumptions of many writers, the likelihood of stories having been handed down from generation to generation in a word-perfect form is in practice very remote'. She was also sceptical about the value of the study of *motifs* supposedly common to many cultures, a form of study which reached its apogee in the massive six-volume *Motif-index of Folk Literature* of Stith Thompson. Some Old Testament scholars have detected the presence of such motifs in a variety of Old Testament narratives, and have claimed that this proves that they originated in 'oral composition'. Such an approach, however, places too much emphasis on individual elements in a story at the expense of the story as a whole, and also assigns too little importance to its *distinctive* elements (Finnegan, pp. 320 ff.).

A further common practice of folklorists which has recently been questioned is that of genre-criticism: the classification of the oral prose narratives of an individual culture and their comparison with the supposed genres detected in other cultures in order to demonstrate common cultural and literary features. In Old Testament studies this kind of comparative study goes back to Gunkel, and has ever since played an important role in form-critical and traditio-historical analyses. It is now suggested, however, that in the study of some oral literatures such classification is premature, that the rigid distinction between genres is often artificial, and that the narrative genres of one culture have too hastily been equated with those of others with which in fact they have little in common. On this last point Wilson, as noted above in another connection, comments that the genres thus equated are often 'parallel only at a fairly high level of abstraction', and that consequently 'biblical scholars have had difficulty finding detailed cross-cultural parallels that help to interpret the specific literary forms of the Old Testament'.

Recently, too, stress has increasingly been laid, in contrast to earlier optimistic studies, on the limits of what can be achieved by the study of oral literature. Finnegan is totally sceptical, for example, about attempts to trace the history of the development of particular African stories: 'Even if the basic plot did, in a given case, turn out really to date back centuries or millennia . . . this would be only a very minor element in the finished work of art produced in the actual telling. The verbal elaboration, the drama of the performance itself, everything in fact which makes it a truly *aesthetic* product comes from the contemporary teller and his audience and not from the remote past' (p. 319). Long agreed: noting that prose narratives, being 'relatively unfixed in structure', are more affected by change than poetry, he concluded that attempts—such as are frequently made in Old Testament as well as in folklore studies—to reconstruct earlier versions of stories may be misleading because the data are simply not available (pp. 192, 198; cf. also Wilson, p. 54).

The validity of the concept of a fixed relationship between *Sitz im Leben* and genre or *Gattung*, so dear to Old Testament scholars, has also come to be regarded as dubious in the light of observation of 'performances' of modern oral prose (and other) literature. *Gattung* is a variable, not a fixed, feature of oral performance: the performance of a particular narrative or poem takes its character on each occasion from the setting in which it is performed, and in doing so frequently changes completely what has been hitherto regarded as its fixed *Gattung*. Attempts to find a single *Sitz im Leben* 'now seem artificial and contrived'. Conversely, 'A genre of oral literature need not be tied exclusively to a single setting' (Long, pp. 192, 197).

2. With regard to the second requisite for the making of a significant parallel between modern oral literature and Old Testament narrative, that of the adequacy of the Old Testament material as a point of comparison, there are two questions to be considered: the *quantity* of the Old Testament material available and the possibility that for various reasons the Old Testament narratives have *a special character* which makes them simply a literary anomaly and so not susceptible of such comparison.

A number of recent scholars writing on this subject have pointed out the small amount of Old Testament material available in comparison with the vast amount of modern oral literature which has been collected and is available for study. Although the students of the latter may sometimes feel themselves to be overwhelmed by their material and the immense labour involved in sifting, classifying, and eventually assessing it, quantity is, in itself, not merely a useful means of checking any theories which may be put forward, but is even an essential prerequisite for the carrying out of such research. The slapdash procedures and over-hasty conclusions characteristic of so much earlier study of the subject from the time of the Grimm brothers onwards were due not only to the lack of refined and sophisticated methods, but equally to the patchiness and inadequacy of the material available. Only through the possession of a large number of examples of various kinds is it possible to obtain anything approaching a true and full picture of the process and products of oral composition and performance. In general it may be said that, when properly used, the greater the quantity the more reliable the results; and that when the number of examples available is really small, accurate conclusions are an impossibility. On the other hand, despite Finnegan's warning of the danger of too great a concentration on collecting examples to the neglect of analysis, the continuing flood of data still flowing in is likely to lead to a constant improvement in the understanding of oral literature and of the societies in which it arises and is practised.

In the Old Testament, the number of distinguishable individual stories which might be compared with modern oral narratives is very small indeed, even if the net is spread very wide to include texts from the former prophets, the prophetical books and elsewhere which have in the past been generally considered to be written literature from the beginning. The area in which this limitation has been most obvious is that of variants, doublets or parallel accounts of the same or closely similar incidents. In the Old Testament, most of these supposed variants occur only in pairs or at the most in threes; and there are only a handful of such groups. A great deal of discussion has taken place concerning the relationship between these variant versions, particularly Gen. 12.10-20 and its parallels and other stories about Abraham, and certain narratives concerning Moses; but no agreement has been reached. In many of the recent discussions of these passages the possibility of variant *oral* traditions has been to the fore. Yet, if even the folklorists, with a mass of information available to them about different versions and different 'performances', and with the possibility of comparing each of these 'sets' with many others from the same culture, have not yet succeeded in reaching agreed conclusions about the patterns of oral tradition and transmission, it seems highly unlikely that Old Testament scholars will be successful in reaching conclusions about their limited material which would enable them to make useful comparisons with the oral literature of other cultures, especially in view of the fact that the Old Testament material comes to them in a form which has undergone a probably very complicated process of redactional modification since it was first committed to writing.

The question about the *special character* of Old Testament narrative is more difficult to answer. It is clear that in general comparisons are useless unless there is some possiblity of 'comparing like with like'. To give an example, despite Dryden's clever satire *Absolem and Achitophel*, the existence of some similar features between events in the reign of David as described in 2 Samuel and court intrigues in the reign of Charles II does not justify the conclusion that the two types of literature are fundamentally similar. Certainly prose narratives purporting to relate the past history of particular peoples or communities are to be found in the repertoire of oral literature in some parts of the world, for example in Africa (Finnegan, pp. 367-73), although it is significant that, at any rate in the legends and narratives of the kingdoms of Western Sudan, 'there is a tradition of Arabic culture and of written historical chronicles in either Arabic or local languages . . . which has affected oral literary forms' (p. 372). Recent students of Old Testament narrative such as Culley and Wilson are generally sceptical about the usefulness of comparing the Old Testament with modern oral narrative material, maintaining that the latter, as 'folktales' (admittedly an imprecise term) 'are certainly different from the kind of historical legend found in the Bible' (Culley, 1976, p. 17) or that 'Research has shown that Israelite literature has more unique features than Gunkel supposed, and for this reason folklorists have been able to supply very few examples of genres that closely resemble those found in the Bible' (Wilson, p. 55). It also appears that the collection and study of this type of modern oral literature have not always been of a high quality: Finnegan comments, with regard to African narratives, that 'the evidence . . . hardly sustains the generally accepted view of the great importance of this form as a specialized literary type in non-Islamic Africa. In many cases these narratives appear only as elements in other narrations, or they appear as elicited or pieced-together recordings by foreign collectors rather than as spontaneous art forms. Altogether much more research needs to be done on the indigenous contexts, tone, and classifications of 'historical narratives' before we can make assertions about them'.

A particular argument which has been put forward in favour of the uniqueness of the Old Testament narratives concerns their supposedly 'sacred' character. This opinion needs to be examined carefully. On the one hand the line between 'sacred' and (presumably) 'secular' is a somewhat imprecise one, and there are certainly some examples of modern oral narratives about the past, especially those which border on myth (also a term difficult to define), which qualify for the designation 'sacred' as much as those of the Old Testament. On the other hand, the 'sacred' character of some at least of the Old Testament narratives, especially of some of the patriarchal stories in Genesis, is derived from their present form and from their present position in the final redaction of the biblical books as we have them now, and may not have been a characteristic of earlier versions, whether written or oral. This particular argument in favour of their 'uniqueness' is not, therefore, very impressive. Nevertheless there does appear to be insufficient evidence available at present to permit the drawing of firm conclusions about the oral origins of Old Testament narratives on the basis of a comparison with the examples of modern 'historical' oral prose literature which have been collected.

3. Given the problems and uncertainties outlined in the above paragraphs, it is hardly surprising that the third condition for a fruitful comparison between modern oral prose literature and Old Testament narrative literature has not been fulfilled: there has been no attempt to compare the two except in a very general way. Nothing has been attempted which is comparable with the way in which poetical material has been used. This may well be because the prose material is not, at any rate in our present state of knowledge, comparable. The attempt—for example, by Gunn in his study of *The Story of King David* (1978)—to compare Old Testament prose texts with modern *poetical* oral literature is an indication of the problem. Thanks to the discovery of the Yugoslavian oral poets and to the more formulaic nature of oral poetry, poetry is a genre in which it has been possible to obtain fairly assured results, which have been effectively used in the elucidation of the processes of composition not only of the Homeric and other epics, but also of Old Testament poetical literature such as the Psalms (e.g. in the work of Culley). But the attempt to utilize this knowledge of modern *poetical* oral literature to elucidate the mode of composition of Old Testament *prose* narrative, which is obviously of an entirely different character, is a sign of desperation. The composition of prose narrative, whether oral or written, poses quite different problems from that of poetry,

and is necessarily carried out in an entirely different way. Further, the metrical character of poetry gives it a relatively fixed shape which makes it far easier to memorize than prose, and thus makes accurate transmission much less of a problem.

The above considerations, then, show that comparison with oral literature, real or supposed, of other cultures—whether of European *Sagen*, Icelandic *saga*, or modern oral literature—with Old Testament narratives has failed to produce substantial proof that the Pentateuchal stories are based on oral traditions. However, the study of modern oral literature *may* possibly be of use in just one respect: the knowledge gained from field studies about the nature of oral transmission may help us to decide whether it is reasonable to suppose that the Pentateuchal narratives, *supposing them to be based on oral traditions*, are likely to have been handed down faithfully and accurately over a long period of time. The accuracy and faithfulness of oral transmission have already to some extent been discussed above; but some further exploration of the question is needed. In addition, the *internal* evidence for oral transmission provided by the Old Testament itself will be examined: it will be asked, first, whether the Old Testament provides enough information about the nature and customs of Israelite society to make a theory of extended oral tradition plausible, and secondly, whether it is possible from internal evidence to determine whether a particular text is based on oral composition.

3. *Oral Tradition: Fixed or Fluid?*

Before 'scientific' field studies of the practice of oral literature in Africa, Yugoslavia and elsewhere began to make an impact on Old Testament scholarship it was common to argue that in non-literate societies the oral transmission of traditions was almost as reliable as the scribal process of copying the written word. Human memories in these societies were held to be far more accurate and retentive than is the case in the modern world. Martin Noth in his work on the Pentateuchal traditions evidently assumed that this was so when he wrote that 'The decisive steps on the way to the formation of the Pentateuch were taken during the preliterary stage, and literary fixations only gave final form to the material which in its essentials was already given' (1948, pp. 1-2; ET pp. 1-2). In other words, the period immediately preceding the committal of the Pentateuchal tradition to writing was one in which the tradition, still in an oral form, was fixed and so transmitted from one generation to another.

Yet before that oral fixation Noth envisaged a long period during which the traditions were not yet fixed but were constantly developing. This is the assumption which lies behind the whole of his Pentateuchal studies. In other words, he envisaged two stages of oral transmission of these traditions: an extremely fluid one followed by a more or less completely fixed one. He was not alone in this opinion: Mowinckel (1946, pp. 26-36) held the same opinion, and Ahlström (p. 70) quoted Mowinckel's opinion with approval.

In his study of the Homeric poems, G.S. Kirk (1962, pp. 95-98) went a stage further: using material gleaned from field studies of modern Yugoslavian oral poets by Parry and others, and applying them to Homer, he sketched the 'life-cycle of an oral tradition', distinguishing no less than four stages: originative, creative, reproductive and degenerate. This may seem to be an unnecessarily elaborate and somewhat speculative scheme; but in essence it is very similar to that of Mowinckel and Ahlström: the most significant division within Kirk's 'life-cycle' is that which marks the end of the 'creative' stage and the beginning of the 'reproductive' one.

But can this rigid scheme of a chronological sequence of fluid ('creative') and fixed ('reproductive') stages be justified? In order to accept such a view it would seem to be necessary to postulate some event or change of circumstances of a radical nature to explain why the 'performers' of a poem or prose narrative should have ceased to think of themselves as creative artists and to have adopted the role of mere transmitters of a fixed tradition. In the case of the Homeric poems, according to Kirk, this new factor was the appearance of the 'monumental singer', the great poet who possessed literary abilities which far exceeded those of the common run of 'creative' singers, and created a work which the 'reproductive' singers who followed him recognized as a work of genius and used as their model, reproducing it in a 'not too mutilated' form. In the case of the Pentateuchal traditions as their history is understood by Noth, the new factor was not the appearance of an individual literary genius but the coming into existence on the soil of Palestine of an entity which could call itself 'Israel' and which needed a comprehensive and authoritative account of what it now conceived to be its *common* tradition.

Both Kirk's and Noth's reconstructions are necessarily hypothetical.

The only verifiable *facts* which we possess concerning oral tradition and its transmission are those which are based on observation of the living traditions of modern non-literate societies; and these suggest a more flexible model. As has already been indicated, it is clear from those observations that in oral performance there is always a combination of the fixed and the innovative: the performers conceive themselves, on the one hand, to be reproducing the traditional forms and material which they have learned from their predecessors or teachers, and to a large extent they are in fact doing so; but, on the other hand, each performance is also to some extent a new literary creation. This combination of conservatism with flexibility and innovation is now generally recognized as a fact by scholars concerned with the Old Testament material as oral literature. But the *proportions* in which traditional and innovative elements occur in any given performance vary greatly according to a variety of circumstances.

Is it possible to define the circumstances in which oral transmission is most likely to be a faithful reproduction of ancient traditions? The most important factors here, apart from the actual circumstances of a particular performance—of which we can know nothing—are the nature of the material transmitted and the purpose of its preservation. Various criteria of this kind have been proposed. Matter thought to be essential to social order and the well-being of the community as a whole clearly needs precise formulation: this would be the case especially with *laws*. Similarly in the field of *education*, where memorization always played an important role, relatively fixed 'oral texts' are to be expected. In matters concerning the *cult*, the accurate transmission of cultic regulations would be of paramount importance. In line with this type of argument, some scholars (e.g. Engnell) have argued that the *narrative* material in the Pentateuch would also have been faithfully and accurately transmitted because it would have been regarded as 'sacred'. But the concept of 'sacredness' is a vague one. Does 'sacred' mean 'cultic'? If so, there is certainly a case for maintaining that the Pentateuchal narratives may have been regarded as (relatively) unalterable; but the view of Alt, von Rad, Noth and their followers that many of these narratives were composed for and recited on cultic occasions is pure hypothesis, and by no means generally accepted. Moreover, recent study of the *prophetical* material in the Old Testament suggests that the words of the prophets, despite their status as the words of God himself, were not regarded as inviolable but were subjected to substantial alteration.

The categories of Old Testament material legal, educational and cultic, which, as suggested above, are especially likely to have been carefully and accurately preserved in oral transmission were, it may be presumed, transmitted under the supervision and control of definable classes of person: priests and teachers. But in the case of the Pentateuchal narratives, as will be shown below, we possess no information whatever about the circles in which they may have been transmitted, or the purposes for which they were preserved from one generation to the next. Many of them have little about them which could be called 'sacred', and may well, as has often been suggested, have been told mainly for entertainment. If indeed their origin *is* oral, Gunkel's designation of them as *Sagen* may not be so wide of the mark. But precisely because we have no information about the manner of their transmission it is impossible to draw any conclusions about their antiquity, their history, the faithfulness or otherwise of their transmission, or indeed whether they originated as oral compositions at all.

4. *Storytellers and Audiences in the Old Testament*

There can be no doubt that the ancient Israelites, like other peoples, told stories. The narrative books are filled with stories of many kinds, often told in a very lively manner which suggests long practice. Yet very few of these stories are set in contexts which provide information about the circumstances and occasions of their telling, or about the storytellers and their audiences. Whatever their origins, the stories have been anonymously recorded in writing and are simply 'there'. There is, rather strangely, no word in the Hebrew of the Old Testament equivalent to 'story' in the sense of a simple tale. Words like *dābār*, 'saying, report', *māšāl*, 'proverb, saying, parable', *midrāš*, 'didactic story, commentary' (very rare, and only in Chronicles), *tōlēdōt* (usually 'genealogy', very occasionally 'history, account', e.g. Gen. 37.2) are all either too general or denote some special kind of communication. There is no word at all corresponding to 'narrator' or 'storyteller'.

There are, it is true, scenes in the narrative books of the Old Testament in the course of which stories are told: where someone makes a report, or gives an account, to another person about something which has occurred. But these are not events of the remote past like those of the Pentateuch: they are practical reports, each made with a specific purpose, of very recent events, usually events witnessed by the speaker himself. For example, Abraham's servant reports to Laban the circumstances which have brought him to Aram-naharaim to seek Rebekah's hand in marriage for Isaac (Gen. 24.34-49); the Amalekite, hoping for a reward, describes the death of Saul (2 Sam. 1.6-10); Pharaoh's butler and baker, and Pharaoh himself recount to Joseph their dreams, hoping for an interpretation of them (Gen. 40.9-11, 16-17; 41.17-24). Even Moses' recapitulation in Deut. 1-10 of the nation's forty years' wandering in the wilderness is not an account of remote events but is presented as a reminder to 'all Israel' of events within their own experience (the narrative is in the first person plural) and as a warning to them. There are also a few examples of fictional stories told in order to provoke a particular reaction on the part of the hearer: for example, the stories told to David by Nathan (2 Sam. 12.1-4) and by the wise woman of Tekoa (2 Sam. 14.5-7).

Other examples of 'the story within a story' could be given. But such narratives tell us nothing about a regular practice of telling stories about past events of an earlier period, nor do they point to any kind of oral transmission of narratives. Each is a story told on a particular occasion for a particular purpose about an event or events which were either of very recent occurrence or entirely fictional. There is no evidence here that storytelling was practised regularly before assembled audiences on special occasions as a form of entertainment; indeed, in the two clear examples of purely verbal diversions on such occasions which we have, the visit of the Queen of Sheba to Solomon (1 Kgs 10.1-3) and Samson's wedding feast (Judg. 14.10-18), the time was passed not in storytelling but in propounding *riddles*. Since one of these occasions was a ceremonial visit to a royal court and the other a bucolic wedding, we may surmise that this custom was practised at all levels of society. Other forms of entertainment at parties included instrumental music and singing (Amos 6.4-5).

There is in fact no evidence at all in the Old Testament to support either of Gunkel's suggestions for a *Sitz im Leben* of the '*Sage*'—the winter evenings when the family gathered to while away the long hours, or the visit of the itinerant, 'professional' storyteller. This silence does not, of course, constitute proof that either of these practices was unknown in ancient Israel; but it ought to warn us that these are entirely inferential hypotheses based on analogies from other cultures.

Gunkel, however, made a third suggestion: that some of the *Sagen* in Genesis may have originated in the replies given to children who asked their fathers about the reasons for certain customs observed by the family. The passages in question are Exod. 12.26-27; 13.8-10, 14-16; Deut. 6.20-25; Jos. 4.6-7, 21-24. (It should be noted that Gunkel was unable to find any such passages in Genesis; nor do any of the answers given to the questions refer to incidents in Genesis: Gunkel, who did not elaborate his suggestion at any length, simply surmised that such stories as those concerning Sodom and Bethel *might* have arisen as answers to questions asked when contemplating the Dead Sea or standing on the heights of Bethel!).

The questions asked in Exod. 12.26 and 13.14-15 (and by implication in Exod. 13.8) concern the reasons for performing certain religious rites: the Passover and the sacrifice of the firstborn of cattle; that in Deut. 6.20 concerns the reason for the laws which Yahweh has imposed on the people; those in Jos. 4 concern the significance of the twelve stones set up by Joshua after the miraculous crossing of the Jordan. The answers given to the questions vary considerably in content but all refer to events recorded in the Pentateuch or the book of Joshua: the slaughter of the Egyptian firstborn and the 'passing over' of the Israelites (Exod. 12.27); the Exodus from Egypt (Exod. 13.8); the Exodus and the slaughter of the Egyptian firstborn (Exod. 13.14-15); the slavery in Egypt, the Exodus, the performance of 'signs and wonders' and the gift of the land (Deut. 6.20); and the crossing of the Jordan on dry land with a reference to the earlier crossing of the Red Sea (Jos. 4.6, 21).

None of these parental replies can be called 'stories'. They have rather (to use a phrase which later acquired a special significance in the work of von Rad) a 'credal' character: they refer in the fewest possible words and in a somewhat formulaic manner to an event or a series of events which were clearly of vital importance to Israel's faith and which were to be transmitted as such from one generation to the next. These passages undoubtedly testify to a custom of oral transmission of particular forms of words, and at any rate in some cases to some kind of connection between them and the cult; but they are not *narratives*. It is of course possible that they may have subsequently been turned into narratives by the addition of further detail, as it is equally possible that they may be summaries of narratives which already existed; but they do not in themselves witness to a practice of the oral transmission of narrative.

It was, however, also Gunkel who set in motion a somewhat different approach to the Pentateuchal narratives: relying partly on the passages just mentioned, he identified a class of *Sage* in Genesis—and elsewhere in the Pentateuch and Joshua—'whose purpose is to explain the regulations for worship'. These narratives go beyond the simple answering of children's questions. They comprise stories which are intended to explain not only the reasons for particular religious rites, but also aetiological stories which account for and establish the legitimacy of particular sanctuaries such as Bethel, Shechem and Beersheba by describing how they were founded in ancient times as the result of a theophany vouchsafed to a holy man or patriarch at these places. 'Foundation stories' of this kind are a phenomenon well known in the ancient world outside Israel.

Gunkel's notion was taken up and elaborated on a massive scale by later scholars. First Pedersen (1926, 1934) proposed the theory that the whole of Exodus 1–15 is not an amalgam of documentary 'sources' as it was generally supposed to be, but a 'Passover legend'— a continuous account of Yahweh's defeat of Egypt and rescue of his people which grew gradually through the centuries as it was continuously transmitted, but which was from the first recited at the feast of Passover, whose foundation, and the reasons for it, are stated in chapter 12. Its purpose was to legitimize the celebration. Although this pioneering theory was accepted by a few scholars including Engnell, it had serious faults, and was virtually demolished in 1951 by Mowinckel, who among other arguments (he was above all concerned to defend the Documentary Hypothesis with regard to these chapters) pointed out that much of the material included in them is in no way related to the main theme postulated by Pedersen and cannot be accounted for by a theory of the gradual growth of an oral tradition.

Gunkel's notion of a connection between Pentateuchal narrative material and particular sanctuaries was, however, taken up in a somewhat different way and with greater scholarly agreement by a succession of scholars, especially Alt, von Rad, Noth and Westermann. These all, as has been remarked earlier, accepted Gunkel's view of oral tradition without question: Alt stated simply that in the study of the patriarchal stories 'We are dependent on a collection of *Sagen* which were transmitted orally for a long time before they were put into literary form' (1929, p. 1; ET p. 3), but then went further than Gunkel in tying these *Sagen* as a whole to particular sanctuaries: 'The part played by Abraham, Isaac and Jacob in the tradition of the Israelite *Sagen* is principally due to their receiving a revelation from a god and founding his cult' (p. 48; ET p. 47); 'The places in Palestine where the *Sagen* are enacted are almost always sanctuaries, and as a rule the *Sagen* themselves are concerned with theophanies and rites carried out at these places' (p. 50; ET p. 49).

This is a very comprehensive claim which even to the superficial reader of Genesis must seem to be, at the least, overstated. But von Rad carried Alt's view a stage further with his theory of a 'little creed' (exemplified in Deut. 26 and other passages) which was the result of the bringing together—at the sanctuary of Gilgal—of the various traditions of the groups which constituted the newly formed 'Israel' (except for the Sinai tradition, which originated at Shechem) into a single common tradition. Noth, accepting von Rad's basic thesis, elaborated it still further.

It should be noted that in all these elaborations of the notion of the role played by the sanctuaries in the transmission of the Pentateuchal narratives none of these scholars made any advance on Gunkel's vague notion of the actual mechanics of the transmission of the material. Not a word is said in the Old Testament about the way in which *narratives* (as distinct from laws) might have been used in the worship practised at these sanctuaries, or about functionaries who might have been the agents of the transmission. Van Seters's conclusion after discussing these various views (1975, pp. 139-48) is fully justified: 'Gunkel, Alt, von Rad, Noth and Westermann . . . have not established the form of the stories, their function, the identity of the bearers of these traditions, or the process by which they might have arrived at their extant shape' (p. 148). This is true even of the only story which 'looks like a reference to the founding of a sanctuary', the story of Jacob at Bethel (p. 141). The 'cultic storyteller', like the other storytellers of ancient Israel, together with his audience, remains a shadowy hypothesis.

5. *Oral and Written Composition: the Question of Criteria*

It has been assumed by many scholars that it is possible to tell whether or not a prose text was composed and transmitted orally before it was committed to writing. Recently, however, this assumption has been seriously questioned.

Gunkel's view that 'Genesis is a collection of *Sagen*' was for a long time so influential that scholars like Noth built elaborate and far-reaching hypotheses on it without questioning his assumption that its stories are in fact of oral origin and not simply literary fiction. Those scholars who did address themselves to the question of the criteria for the detection of 'oral tradition' did not go beyond vague generalizations. Nielsen, for example, simply stated that the formal characteristics of oral composition are 'a monotonous style, recurrent expressions, a fluent, paratactical style' (i.e. a preference for co-ordination rather than subordination), 'a certain rhythm and euphony . . . and anacolutha' (i.e. instances of grammatical inconsequence) (1950, p. 36). He offered no proof of the correctness of this statement, though he and others also cited Olrik's 'epic laws' as criteria.

The only really substantial argument put forward as proof of oral composition of Old Testament narratives was in connection with 'doublets'. This argument goes back to Gunkel, who noted the fact that many European *Sagen* are found in variant forms which they have assumed in the course of diffused oral transmission (1910, pp. LXV-LXVII). He took it for granted that an analogous process is the only possible explanation of the doublets in Genesis. He then proceeded to argue further that since the other *Sagen* in Genesis of which only *one* version is preserved are of the same general character, they too must have been orally composed and transmitted. He took no account of other possible explanations of doublets such as the dependence of one *written* version on another. His conclusions were accepted without further reflection by many later scholars.

It is important to observe that Gunkel's explanation of the *origin* of the doublets does not by itself account for the *preservation* of both versions in the final work. This was held to be accounted for by the Documentary Hypothesis: each document had incorporated a different version of these stories, and it was the redactors who retained both versions because they did not feel at liberty to eliminate either. But if the Documentary Hypothesis is rejected, some other explanation of the duplication is required.

Several recent scholars have recognized that the question of doublets is a crucial one when criteria are being sought for the detection of oral composition of Old Testament narratives. An alternative to the theory of oral variants preserved through the machinery of the documentary process is to suppose that a *writer*— whether a creative writer or an 'improver'—deliberately chose to tell a story twice, or to add a new version of it to the old one, for some literary or theological purpose of his own.

It is not difficult to imagine what such a purpose might have been: indeed, there are more than one possibility. It is generally agreed by those who have studied these passages—documentary critics, form-critics, traditio-historical critics, advocates as well as opponents of the theory of oral composition—that the different versions of duplicated stories (e.g. Gen. 12.10-20; 20; 26) are not on the same level but express different theologies and ethical points of view. This suggested to Sandmel (1961) an analogy with the practice familiar from the rabbinic literature of 'improving' a (written) story by rewriting it in a new way for theological reasons, yet at the same time retaining its earlier version out of a 'reluctance to expunge' a text already hallowed by time and devotion.

Others have found a purely literary (in the sense of aesthetic) reason for such duplication: Alter, for example, maintained that 'duplicated stories' in the Old Testament are due to the common convention of using 'type-scenes' in order to bind a work together and give it shape and direction (pp. 49-51), while Berlin compared the use of this device to that used in the making of a film, in which a rounded picture may be obtained by depicting an event from several different angles. Repeated incidents may also serve for emphasis: thus the threefold deliverance of a patriarch (Abraham or Isaac) from a similar situation (as in Gen. 12.10-20 and parallels) serves to emphasize God's salvific purpose in protecting the recipients of his promises and their descendants.

The criteria for determining whether doublets are the result of oral transmission or of purely literary activity have been discussed in detail by Van Seters (1975). In the case of the doublets in the Abraham stories he demonstrated that *one version presupposes the other*: that is, that the author of one version was acquainted with the other in something like its present form. For example, there are features in Gen. 20—the story of Abraham's sojourn in Gerar-- which are not self-explanatory but presuppose the author's—and the reader's—acquaintance with the earlier story of Abraham's sojourn in Egypt in Gen. 12.10-20. An example of this is Abraham's telling the king of Gerar that Sarah is his sister, a piece of misleading information which results in the king's taking her into his harem (20.2). No explanation is given here of this strange statement: an acquaintance with Gen. 12.11-13 is apparently presupposed, where a reason is given for Abraham's action in similar circumstances on a previous occasion. At the same time, Van Seters argued, the reason for the creation of the new version (chapter 20) is quite clear: its author had new and theological points which he wanted to make. But because the earlier version of the story was familiar, he did not need to reproduce it in all its details.

Van Seters's conclusion is that version A of this story (12.10-20) is based on an oral folktale, since it obeys Olrik's 'epic laws'. The author of version B (ch. 20) knew version A in its written form and composed his new version of it as a purely literary creation: version B had no direct oral origins at all. In fact, as our earlier discussion of folklore and Olrik's 'laws' has shown, there is no reason to suppose that *either* version necessarily had an oral origin; but this does not affect Van Seters's point that the variants in question are not the result of independent variant oral versions, but that one version is dependent on the other, and that that dependence is of a literary rather than an oral character.

Theoretically it is no doubt possible that this procedure of creating an 'improved' version of the story could have taken place in the course of *oral* transmission: Van Seters's criterion of the dependence of one version on the other does not actually *prove* that it was a purely literary process. But if it is argued that 'duplication' *did* take place at an oral stage, it becomes necessary to formulate a complex theory of the development of oral transmission which is purely speculative and impossible to control by means of any concrete information which we possess. We should have to assume a degree of theological and ethical sophistication in the deliberate remodelling of oral tradition which is more appropriate to a later, scribal age; and we should also have to devise explanations of the circumstances which led to *both* of the oral versions being preserved. If, on the other hand, we suppose—to take Van Seters's example—that version B was the result of a written, literary process, it is far easier to find explanations for it. Moreover, our speculations—for such they are always bound to be—will then rest on firmer ground in that they will be concerned with the biblical *text* which we actually possess. At the least, it is clear that we are not obliged to introduce a theory of oral transmission in order to account for the doublets in the Pentateuchal narratives.

A different kind of investigation of the criteria for oral transmission was carried out by Ringgren (1949). He made a detailed comparison, not of doublets in the Gunkelian sense (i.e., stories which are parallel but not textually identical) but of those texts—few in number—which actually *appear twice* in the Old Testament: texts which *are* clearly intended to be identical in every way, but which nevertheless have small textual variants which may be presumed to be due to errors, e.g. Psalm 18 and 2 Sam. 22; Isa. 2.2-4 and Mic. 4.1-3; Isa. 37.22-35 and 2 Kgs 19.21-34. Ringgren's purpose was to discover whether these minor variants are likely to have been caused in the process of copying written texts or in the process of oral transmission: in other words, whether the fault was that of the eye, or of the ear or the memory. He concluded that in some, though not in all, instances the error was aural: in Psalm 18 especially, the divergences from 2 Sam. 22 are not typical of scribal error (a subject on which a great deal of information is available) but are best explained as due to 'slips of memory, or the like', and thus point to oral transmission of some kind.

Ringgren was aware that this conclusion—which he presented very tentatively—did not necessarily prove that these texts had been composed orally: there were other possible explanations for these oral (or aural) slips. The fact is that the processes of oral and written transmission are not to be thought of as necessarily mutually exclusive or chronologically distinct. As was the case with some other traditions such as that of Islam, oral transmission frequently continues even after a text has been committed to writing, and the two modes of transmission influence one another. This opens up a whole range of alternative possibilities. For example, a text which had been written from the start might have been imperfectly memorized and then later recommitted to writing from memory with the errors incorporated, so creating a version which differed slightly from the original; or the copying of a written text might have been carried out by dictation rather than by a single copyist transcribing it directly from the original. These and other possible processes would result in oral (or aural) mistakes which would have nothing to do with oral *composition* or (in the usual meaning of the phrase) 'oral transmission' at all.

It should also be noted that most of the examples available in the

Old Testament and studied by Ringgren are poetry, not prose; that none of them is a narrative; and that their number is so small as to make generalization extremely hazardous. When all these considerations are taken together, it must be concluded that Ringgren's study, though extremely interesting and useful, has not proved the oral composition or transmission of Old Testament narratives.

There is now a growing recognition of the fact that in the case of prose narrative no reliable criteria have been discovered for the detection of oral composition. Thus Culley (1963) already showed some caution in discussing the question: while maintaining that 'The method of oral composition produces characteristics which are different from the characteristics of literature composed by writing', and that 'In theory, we should be able to isolate those characteristics and upon analysis tell whether a text has come out of oral tradition where oral composition was practised or has come from a literary tradition', he admitted that 'So far this sort of analysis has been best undertaken in the field of oral narrative poetry' (p. 122). In 1976 he struck a more negative note: 'I feel that it is premature to suggest that we can define the nature and characteristics of oral and scribal tradition with sufficient clarity to be able to identify with a great deal of confidence those segments of the Abraham stories which lie close to oral tradition and those which are the result of literary composition' (pp. 28-29). Other recent scholars (e.g. Ahlström, p. 72 and Knight, p. 392) have also stressed the uncertainty of the criteria so far employed and our ignorance of the oral techniques employed in ancient times.

Other scholars have questioned whether one can speak of an 'oral style' at all when studying ancient literature. They argue that ancient writers would naturally have continued to employ in their literary works the same 'oral' style which had been the norm in earlier, preliterate times. Ahlström pertinently posed the question: 'Why should the style of composition change when it comes to writing?' (p. 71)—a question which has not yet been answered. Culley (1976, p. 66) further pointed out that a distinctive prose style takes time to develop: the closer a writer lived to the 'oral' period of literature, the more likely he would be to retain 'oral' features in his written work.

A further point of great importance has been made by Ruth Finnegan in a general discussion of 'oral' and 'written' literature: she there pointed out some significant differences between literary practice and the conception of 'literature' in the ancient world compared with the modern, especially the often forgotten fact that ancient literature was intended to be read aloud:

> The relationship between oral and written literature . . . is a difference of degree and not of kind. . . . The literature of the classical world . . . laid far more stress on the oral aspect than does more recent literature. . . . The presence of writing can coexist with an emphasis on the significance of performance as one of the main means of the effective transmission of a literary work. . . . Throughout much of antiquity even written works were normally read aloud rather than silently, and one means of transmitting and, as it were, 'publishing' a literary composition was to deliver it aloud to a group of friends (p. 18).

Mutatis mutandis, this would have been equally true of the ancient Semitic world, including Israel.

In the case of written literature which was not only intended to be read aloud as a means of 'publication' but was also intended, as many of the Pentateuchal narratives may well have been, to be memorized and thus to become 'oral literature' in a secondary sense, it is also likely, as Ahlström pointed out, that a writer would quite deliberately employ mnemonic and similar 'aural' devices to assist accurate memorization and transmission.

A further general point of a somewhat different kind may be made. It concerns the role of the scribe or recorder who first committed oral texts to writing. It has been argued by Lord and others on the basis of experience in the recording of modern Yugoslavian oral poetry that the very circumstance of the taking down of an oral 'performance'— at least before the advent of mechanical means of recording speech— inhibits the spontaneity of the singer and so materially changes the style and words of the 'text'. In view of this, Knight commented that 'the obvious consequence is that traditio-historical research becomes basically invalid. How can one reconstruct the history of a tradition if the recording stage itself becomes an impenetrable barrier?' (pp. 390-91). This comment is presumably relevant to oral prose as well as to poetic texts, and would be valid even if it could be assumed that stories such as those in the Pentateuch have been preserved exactly as they were taken down from (or by) an oral 'performer'. If it is granted that later redaction of the original recording has taken place, the likelihood of 'oral' features (if such were identifiable) having been preserved becomes even more remote.

Finally, the effect of the recent *literary (aesthetic) approach to Old Testament narrative* on theories of oral composition should be noted. Those scholars who pursue this form of study are concerned to bring to light the artistic qualities not only of the individual, short narrative units which the form-critics have universally regarded as having originated as independent units orally composed and orally and separately transmitted, but of very large tracts of narrative: Silberman, for example, regarded the patriarchal stories of Genesis, including the story of Joseph, as a single work of literary art; and Alter also worked with very large units in his detailed study. This way of looking at the narrative works of the Old Testament marks the most revolutionary change in the study of these books for a very long time; and if some of its practitioners tend, as is usually the case with revolutionary movements, to overstate their case and discover signs of literary skill where others may fail to find them, there can be little doubt that the new method has thrown new light on the composition of the narrative literature of the Old Testament, most of all perhaps on the book of Genesis.

Scholars who have reflected on the wider implications of the new 'literary criticism' (e.g. Berlin and Silberman) have concentrated mainly on its implications for the Documentary Hypothesis: the new-found literary unity of large tracts of Pentateuchal narrative is obviously hardly compatible with a theory of literary 'documents' combined by redactors. But the implications for *form*-criticism, and so ultimately for theories of oral composition, are no less far-reaching: for the methods used by the form-critics to distinguish one *unit* from another are basically the same as those employed by the documentary critics to separate one *document* from another. Berlin and Silberman between them have listed many of the criteria used explicitly or implicitly by the form-critics; they can ultimately be reduced to two: 1. the negative one of inconsistency between one unit and another and 2. the positive one of the ability of a unit to stand on its own.

1. These scholars have pointed out that the literary phenomena labelled 'inconsistencies' by both documentary and form-critics are in fact often identical with devices used in modern fiction which are regarded by literary critics as signs of artistic skill: they include the repetition of words or phrases, the retelling of incidents from different points of view, the complex interweaving of plots and sub-

plots, retardations to create suspense, and even long digressions: 'What would *Tristram Shandy* be without its digressions?', asked Silberman. Berlin argued that in failing to appreciate these devices and in interpreting them as indications of subsequent 'seams' and 'joins' between disparate stories, the form-critics no less than the documentary critics have shown a deplorable insensitivity to the 'poetics' of biblical narrative.

2. Since the time of Gunkel and Olrik the form-critics have identified as independent units of tradition (*Sagen*) narratives which when detached from their present contexts make satisfactory stories, each possessing such characteristics as a clear beginning and end, a clear and unitary plot with a satisfactory structure moving towards a crisis and then away from the crisis to a satisfactory solution, and each requiring no external information for its full comprehension. But, as Berlin pointed out (pp. 122 ff.), such self-containedness by no means proves that a story was originally independent. The fact that it *can* be read as a separate and independent story does not mean that it *must* be so read. Literary authors both ancient and modern have commonly chosen to divide their works into separate chapters, each with its own clearly marked beginning, ending and plot; and this is usually taken to be an indication of literary skill. In some early works of European fiction this way of writing is particularly common. *Tom Jones*, for example, consists to a large extent of quite unconnected incidents which, like many stories in Genesis, are linked together by no more than the name of the principal character, and make no reference to previous incidents. On the other hand, the patriarchal stories *are* in fact frequently linked together—by references to God's promises and previous dealings with the patriarch who is the principal character, or with his father or grandfather. These links are usually regarded by both documentary and form-critics as later additions to the 'original' story; but since the excision is often made on the basis of the principle that the story *must* originally have been independent and self-contained, there is a circular argument here.

It could, of course, be argued that, even if the new literary critics have successfully demonstrated that large tracts of the Pentateuch are polished literary works rather than the products of the stringing together of a number of originally independent short units by redactors, the literary artists who produced these masterpieces may have done so in an oral medium rather than at their desks as writers. It is true that oral prose narrative is not always brief and not always simple. But the oral option is far less probable than the written one, since, as has been shown above, there is no longer an antecedent *presupposition* in favour of oral composition of the Pentateuchal narratives. Examples of literary works comparable to the biblical narratives as a whole (e.g. Herodotus's *Histories*) *exist*, while evidence of the oral composition of such complex prose narrative works does not. Moreover, and more significantly, the new literary critics have shown the weakness of the *criteria* employed by the form-critics for the detection of short originally independent narrative units in the Pentateuch.

D. *Traditio-Historical Methods: Some Examples*

The above considerations neither prove nor disprove the presence of oral tradition behind the narratives of the Pentateuch. However, they suggest very strongly that the oral hypothesis cannot simply be presupposed and treated as an assured basis for the construction of traditio-historical theories, and that what has often been taken to be proof of a long process of oral transmission is equally explicable in terms of literary style. This does not mean that none of the Pentateuch is based on oral tales; but the tradition-historians have claimed to know more about these tales than can be proved. They assume that the core of the Pentateuchal narrative is much older than its written record and reaches back into very early times. If this is so, the proof of it will have to be found elsewhere than in the results of the study of oral literature.

Unlike the Documentary Hypothesis, which despite minor variations presents itself substantially as a single, easily definable theory, the traditio-historical theories regarding the Pentateuch are too diverse to be described under a single head. In principle, each needs a separate assessment. Since this task is beyond the scope of the present study (for a full account up to 1972 see Knight), it must suffice to examine selected examples of this approach.

1. *Martin Noth*

Although he frequently warned his readers about the provisional nature of his undertaking and also occasionally admitted that he was unable to account for this or that particular detail, Noth's work on the Pentateuchal traditions gives the impression of complete confidence in the traditio-historical approach as a means of reconstructing the entire process of the development of these traditions from their earliest beginnings to their first committal to writing. His *Überlieferungsgeschichte des Pentateuch* is the most complete acount of this process ever undertaken: it leaves virtually nothing unaccounted for.

Noth defined his aim as follows: 'The chief task is . . . to determine the basic themes from which the great corpus of the transmitted Pentateuch developed, to uncover their roots, to investigate how they were filled out with individual traditions, to seek out the connections between them, and to assess their significance' (1948, p. 3; ET p. 3). He was in fact proposing to put into effect the programme envisaged by von Rad, who, himself following Gunkel, had written that the Pentateuch belongs to a type of literature 'of which we may expect to recognize the early stages, the "*Sitz im Leben*", and the subsequent development to the point at which it reached the greatly extended form in which it now lies before us' (1938, pp. 10-11; ET p. 3). This was a task more ambitious than any similar task undertaken with respect to any ancient work of history.

Noth's two *primary assumptions* were 1. that an oral tradition lies behind the bulk of the Pentateuchal narratives; and 2. that adequate techniques exist for getting behind the written text to find substantial traces of the origin and development of that tradition before it came to be used as source-material by the biblical writers. It is precisely these assumptions that have been questioned in the previous section of this book. It is also important to notice that Noth made a number of other questionable assumptions.

He accepted, in its main lines, the *Documentary Hypothesis*. He accepted, and built upon, von Rad's hypothesis of the '*little creed*'. His own hypotheses of the *amphictyony* and the *Deuteronomistic History*, both of which he had developed earlier, were closely related to his traditio-historical reconstruction. He also based some of his more detailed traditio-historical conclusions on particular *reconstructions of historical events*: for example, his explanation of the combination of east and west Jordanian elements in the complex of stories about Jacob rests on the hypothesis of a migration to the east of the Jordan by groups of people settled in the west, who took their traditions about Jacob with them and merged them with traditions which they found or developed in their new surroundings. Or again, a complicated explanation of the story of the treaty between Jacob and Laban (Gen. 31.44-54) is said to be founded on what he called the 'historical fact' (a rare admission for him) of a boundary treaty between Ephraimites and Aramaeans. Even more important for his reconstruction was his view that 'the Pentateuchal tradition which came to be the common Israelite epic was that formed by the particular memories and traditions of the central Palestinian tribes and reflective of their point of view' (p. 61; ET p. 57). Such historical judgments, which may well be correct, are hypotheses rather than established facts. To a large degree Noth's historical and traditio-historical views stand or fall together.

In his views on *the nature of oral tradition* Noth was heavily dependent on the views of earlier scholars such as Gunkel, Gressmann and Jolles. He assumed with them that the genres and patterns of oral transmission found among quite different peoples have common characteristics which make it possible to use conclusions formed in one field of investigation to make assertions about another. For example, he cited Jolles in support of his statement that 'the vigorous growth of a saga-tradition . . . is usually found' in a tribal rather than in a centralized society: 'The Icelandic sagas of the tenth and eleventh centuries AD constitute the most important example open to historical investigation of a saga-formation in this sense' (p. 47, n. 152; ET pp. 44, n. 152).

Other assumptions made by Noth show his dependence on Gunkel. He assumed as a general principle that the earliest narrative traditions are short and concise, and used this as the basis for distinguishing the original elements from which later and more elaborate complexes of tradition have been constructed. For example, in the case of the Jacob traditions, in which 'the basic traditio-historical material is overlaid especially heavily with generous accretions from later times' (p. 86; ET p. 80) he took it for granted that numerous short, concise narratives must somehow lie behind the present text, which is the result of 'the collection of innumerable details into one complex composition' (p. 96; ET p. 88). This notion, that brevity is a sign of antiquity, was widely held in Noth's time, but has now been shown to be erroneous.

The assumption that it is possible to distinguish between earlier and later traditions is fundamental to Noth's thesis: his entire work proceeds on this basis, with regard both to the origins of individual narratives and to the reconstruction of the successive stages by which the main themes were filled out to form the completed 'all-Israelite'

Pentateuchal tradition. One of the criteria which Noth employed for this purpose is that of *style*; but, as had been the case with Gunkel, his use of this criterion was too general to be convincing. For example, he asserted that the narratives in Genesis associated with Hebron and Mamre 'do not belong to the original material of the Abraham tradition' because 'they exhibit the later, discursive *Sagen*-style' (pp. 120-21; ET pp. 109-10). Similarly, Gen. 24 is said to be 'traditio-historically . . . late, as is evidenced by its quite discursive style' (pp. 217-18; ET p. 199). Even if it were the case that the art of narration developed along fixed lines from the simple and concise to the 'discursive', the dangers of subjectivism attendant upon the use of the criterion of style are very apparent: for example, on certain of the stories of the people's murmuring in the wilderness, Noth simply commented—without giving any reason—'In any case (*jedenfalls*) they do not *give the impression*' (my italics) 'of being original, popular traditions' (p. 138; ET p. 125). There are many other examples in his work of such subjectivism.

A further assumption which plays an important role in Noth's arguments is that *stories may change their protagonists* in the course of oral transmission; and that in particular well-known figures tend to attract to themselves stories with which they had originally had no connection. There can be no doubt that such a thing is possible, but Noth makes it an almost universal principle; indeed, without it his entire thesis would collapse: his view that the five traditional 'themes' of the Pentateuch were originally unconnected depends completely on his ability to prove that Moses, who is the leading figure in every part of the Pentateuch except the book of Genesis, originally had no connection at all with any of the stories told about him, but was subsequently 'inserted' into them.

Some of the arguments employed by Noth to substantiate this thesis were extremely forced. For example, he used the episode (Exod. 5.6-19) in which the anonymous 'foremen' of the people negotiate with Pharaoh in Moses' absence, together with the shadowy figures of the 'elders' (3.16, 18; 4.29), to exclude Moses from the entire 'theme' of 'guidance out of Egypt': either of these groups, he claimed, was 'quite adequate in this theme as the spokesmen of the Israelites before Moses appeared in the tradition in the position of leadership. Consequently, it seems to me to be indisputable that the theme "guidance out of Egypt" cannot lay claim to the figure of Moses as having an original connection with it' (pp. 179-80; ET p. 163).

Again, Moses is excluded by Noth from the Sinai theme on the grounds that in the story of the making of the covenant (Exod. 24.1, 2, 9-11) there are 'too many' persons present. He therefore eliminated successively Aaron, Nadab and Elihu *and* Moses from the 'original' account, leaving only the unnamed seventy elders, simply on the grounds that 'It is hardly likely that from the beginning' all these people 'were joined with and united with Moses in this story' (p. 178; ET p. 162). Olrik's law of 'two to a scene' may have lain behind this remark (if seventy elders can be thought of as equivalent to a single person); but the reason for excluding Moses, who is ostensibly the leader, rather than the others seems to be simply that, as the only prominent figure in the whole Sinai theme as it now stands, it may be assumed *a priori* that he cannot originally have had anything to do with it. It is on the basis of assumptions of this kind that Moses has been excluded by Noth from every one of the 'original' traditions of the Pentateuch.

If Noth placed no reliance on the names of leading personalities in the stories as indications of their authenticity, the opposite was the case with *place-names*. Earliest traditions, he maintained, arise in particular places, whose names—for example, Bethel or Shechem—authenticate them. This principle is, however, a particularly elusive one, since elsewhere Noth admitted that stories originally connected with one place could 'wander' and eventually be transferred to another (as in the case of the stories about Lot, pp. 167-71; ET pp. 151-56). His use of this criterion, the so-called principle of *Ortsgebundenheit* or 'attachment to a particular place', seems to lack consistency.

A particular form of this principle is Noth's emphasis on the importance of 'grave traditions', that is, traditions which state the location of the grave of an important figure and which may be supposed to have arisen from a custom of visiting and venerating the hallowed spot. Noth twice stated categorically that 'a grave tradition usually gives the most reliable indication of the original provenance of a particular figure of tradition' (p. 186; ET pp. 169-70; cf. p. 121; ET p. 110). For this assertion he gave no reason and quoted no authority. But in fact he was inconsistent in his application of this dictum.

In his treatment of the locus of the 'original' traditions about Abraham and Isaac, the former of whom has, he said, only a 'later' attestation of a grave-tradition (P) while the latter has none at all, he stated that an exception must be made to his rule: 'in the case of the "patriarchs" who received a divine revelation and promise, the holy place of the traditional encounter with God, but not the grave site, belonged to the basic material of the tradition' (p. 121; ET p. 110). This looks like special pleading; and it is quite inconsistent with the way in which Noth dealt with the search for the 'original' tradition about Moses. For Moses, who was, according to all the Pentateuchal sources, pre-eminently a person who received divine revelations at a number of named places, was presumably on a par with the patriarchs in this respect; yet, dismissing all the accounts of these revelations as secondary, Noth insisted that the statement about Moses's burial and grave site in Deut. 34.6 is 'the most original element of the Moses tradition still preserved' (p. 186; ET p. 169), despite the fact that, like that of Abraham, it occurs only in a very late source (P).

The arbitrary nature of this conclusion is compounded by the fact that this text states that the precise location of the grave is unknown—a fact which removes all possibility that we have here an authentic tradition based on a custom of visiting the grave which had persisted up to the time when the tradition was recorded. Noth's attempts to overcome these difficulties are extremely forced.

It may be added that Noth's acceptance of Moses' grave tradition as historically reliable despite its attestation only in a later source is all the more surprising in view of his rejection of the notice about Miriam's death and burial in Num. 20.1, which is also attributed to P: here he stated simply and without further explanation that it is not possible to 'give any weight' to this notice as 'P did not apparently pass on an older tradition here' (p. 200; ET pp. 182-83).

The overriding importance of the role played by the *cult* in the creation, preservation and development of the Pentateuchal traditions is yet another of Noth's assumptions—one which he took over from earlier studies, notably those of Alt and von Rad. Apart from the theme of 'guidance in the wilderness', which he regarded as 'not a very important or really independent theme' (p. 62; ET p. 58), all 'the great Pentateuchal themes arose on the soil of the cultic life as the contents of confessions of faith which used to be recited in more or less fixed forms on particular, recurring occasions' (p. 207; ET p. 190). In the case of the patriarchal narratives, the smaller units out of which the 'theme' was composed also for the most part had had cultic origins, having arisen as accounts of divine revelations to the patriarchs and then, after the settlement in Palestine, been brought into association with local Canaanite cults of which the individual patriarchs came to be regarded as founders. Finally, with the development of the amphictyony, it was again in a cultic setting that these 'themes' became linked together in the all-Israelite confession of the 'little creed'. It was only with the 'narrative elaboration of the great cultically rooted Pentateuchal themes' which culminated in 'G' that 'the Pentateuchal narrative in its detailed exposition abandoned the cultic sphere, in which the origins determinative of the whole were rooted' and 'passed from the mouth of the priests or the worshipping community into the mouth of the popular narrator' (pp. 214-15; ET p. 197). (It should be noted that this final development, from priest to popular narrator, does not correspond to what is known of oral traditions elsewhere, and appears to have been regarded by Noth as unique to Israel.)

We have seen in a previous section of this book that the notion of cultic recital of narrative traditions is purely speculative and that there is no positive evidence to support it. So great, however, was Noth's confidence in the theory of cultic origins for the Pentateuchal narrative material that he did not hesitate to build theories of cultic history on its basis. For example, on the meagre foundation of a story in Num. 25.1-5 about Israel's apostasy in participating in Moabite rites in the worship of the god Baal-Peor, together with a single verse (Num. 23.28) in which the seer Balaam is associated with Peor and a few biblical verses which point to the existence of two different traditions about Balaam, one favourable and the other unfavourable, he constructed a picture of a famous 'boundary sanctuary' which was originally highly esteemed by various neighbouring peoples, including Israelites, who gathered there to worship Baal-Peor, but which was deemed idolatrous at a later stage of the Pentateuchal tradition (pp. 80-86; ET pp. 74-79).

However, as in the case of the 'grave-traditions', Noth was very arbitrary in his use of evidence. For in the case of Kadesh, whose importance as a cult-centre with strong Mosaic connections had been strongly urged by E. Meyer (*Die Israeliten und ihre Nachbarstämme*, 1906) and other scholars, Noth sweepingly dismissed all such evidence: 'neither in the Pentateuchal narrative itself nor anywhere else in the Old Testament is there a "Kadesh tradition", and even less a tradition about a cult of Kadesh' (p. 181; ET p. 164). Since the information about Baal-Peor seems, to say the least, hardly more substantial than that about Kadesh, where the Israelites are said to have stayed 'many days' (Deut. 1.46), which is identified with Meribah (Num. 27.14; Deut. 32.51), and round which, as in the case of Baal-Peor, many stories gathered (for Noth elsewhere a sign of a practice of 'cultic recital'), it is difficult to avoid the conclusion that he was illogically selective in the application of his view about the importance of the cult as the original locus of narrative traditions. In the case of Kadesh the reason for this is not far to seek. The discussion of Kadesh (pp. 180-82; ET pp. 164-66) occurs in a chapter concerned with the originality of Moses in the Pentateuchal traditions; and an admission that there was some truth in the hypotheses of a 'Kadesh tradition' would seriously have jeopardized Noth's attempt to prove that Moses originally had no place in the theme 'guidance in the wilderness'.

In his attempt to distinguish the various elements of tradition and to determine how and in what chronological sequence these had been brought together, Noth took over from the documentary critics the *literary* criterion of contradictions and applied it to his traditio-historical investigation of the earlier *oral* tradition. In principle, this criterion is a valid one, but one which must be used with caution, since, as has already been pointed out, it is difficult to be certain that what seems to be inconsistent and incompatible to the modern mind might not have been similarly adjudged by an ancient narrator.

In fact, Noth's use of this criterion was frequently extremely subjective. An illustration of this subjectivity is his attempt to prove that the various Pentateuchal 'themes' were originally unconnected. For example, he claimed to have found a fundamental discrepancy between the theme 'guidance out of Egypt' and the theme 'guidance into the arable land' (i.e. Exodus and Settlement) on the grounds that, while the former theme presupposes the arrival of the Israelites in Palestine from the west, the latter, even in its truncated form in the final chapters of Numbers, presupposes an invasion from the east. He concluded that these two bodies of tradition must have arisen among two quite different groups.

In the Pentateuch in its present form these two themes are linked by the account of Israel's wandering in the wilderness (Noth's 'guidance in the wilderness'), in the course of which several explanations are offered for the detour in question, among others the difficulty of defeating or overcoming the hostility of the inhabitants of southern Canaan and other neighbouring peoples. The change of route is even signalled in Num. 14.25, which Noth attributed to J. But he dismissed all this as having had no original place in the traditions. The theme 'guidance in the wilderness', he asserted, is a quite secondary one, 'not very important or really independent', since it 'presupposes in every instance the themes "guidance out of Egypt" and "guidance into the promised land"'! It 'probably . . . arose simply from a narrative impulse to tell something concrete about the further fortunes of the Israelite tribes after the "guidance out of Egypt"' (pp. 62-63; ET pp. 58-59). As for the notice in Num. 14.25, it is dismissed as 'inadequate and ambiguous'. In a similar fashion, Noth found reasons for concluding that *all* the themes of the Pentateuch were originally independent of one another. It is difficult to avoid the impression that the evidence has been manipulated to make it fit a preconceived hypothesis.

The treatment of Exod. 5, already referred to in another connection, provides a further example of Noth's use of the criterion of inconsistencies. It may readily be admitted that with the exception of the probably intrusive verse 4, neither Moses nor Aaron appears in this story (verses 3-19), and that Noth was correct in saying that 'Moses recedes completely into the background, and the Israelite foremen negotiate on their own with Pharaoh, while Moses, as it surprisingly turns out in verse 20, waits outside!' (p. 76; ET p. 71). But his conclusion is an extremely sweeping one: 'Manifestly in Exod. 5.3-19 we come upon the petrefaction of a stage in the history of the traditions when the figure of Moses had not yet found its way into the theme "guidance out of Egypt"'. That is to say, this one scene in which Moses does not appear in the course of the negotiations with Pharaoh is regarded by Noth as sufficiently inconsistent with the remainder of the account of the negotiations to justify a major traditio-historical hypothesis concerning his original place in the entire Exodus theme. It may be admitted that this chapter has undergone some kind of modification, whether of a literary or traditio-historical kind, and it is probable that Moses and Aaron did not originally appear in the story. So far the use of the criterion of discrepancy is a valid one; but the further conclusion that the story belongs to a pre-Moses stage of the tradition goes far beyond the evidence. A story in which the foremen had negotiated with Pharaoh as the normal recipients of his orders about the building operations before Moses and Aaron appeared on the scene is not in any way incompatible with Moses' later assumption of the role of negotiator. Noth has constructed an imposing edifice on very slender foundations.

An even clearer example of his subjective use of this criterion is provided by his treatment of the story of Jacob. In order to support his theory that the Jacob-Esau and Jacob-Laban stories were traditio-historically combined by means of the motif of Jacob's flight from Esau, he argued (pp. 95-97; ET pp. 88-89) that 'several traces' of earlier versions of these stories have been preserved in the present text which were quite independent of one another. These indications are, first, Rebekah's promise to Jacob to call him back when Esau's anger had subsided (Gen. 27.45), to which no further reference is made, and second, the statement in 29.14 that Jacob stayed with Laban 'one month', when in fact he remained many years. But in fact there are no discrepancies here at all. The story in its present form by no means requires that Rebekah's words should have been recalled when Jacob decided to prolong his stay; and the remark that he stayed with Laban one month, interpreted in its context, does not carry the implication of an immediate departure after the month had elapsed: its natural meaning is that he had stayed one month when Laban proposed that his position should be regularized by his being paid a wage for assisting in the work of the household. These verses, then, do not constitute contradictions arising from modifications made to the story of Jacob at either an oral or a literary stage. Whether the Jacob-Esau and Jacob-Laban stories in fact originated separately is another matter. It is Noth's arguments which are unacceptable.

Much of Noth's detailed reconstruction of the Pentateuchal traditions was obtained by *piling one speculation upon another*. A good example of this procedure is his treatment of the stories involving Abraham and Lot (pp. 167-70; ET pp. 151-54). Noth's purpose here was to show that the connection between the two figures was not made until a comparatively late stage in the development of the theme 'promise to the patriarchs'.

The initial reason for holding this view was given in the somewhat sweeping assertion that 'The uncle-nephew relationship hardly represents an original element in folk narrative, since it is not in itself an essential kinship relation'. It thus became necessary to explain by what process this relationship had found a place in the tradition. This led Noth to weave a complex web of speculations, of which the most surprising feature is the attribution of a major role to an entirely minor character, Lot's father Haran, about whom nothing whatever is said in the biblical text apart from the mention of his name in genealogical notices in Gen. 11.26-31. It was therefore pure speculation when Noth asserted: 'Evidently (*offenbar*) Haran, who stood to Abraham in the simple relation of brother and to Lot in that of father, once had an important significance in these contexts into which his son Lot subsequently succeeded. In the final form of the tradition, however, he has completely receded into the background, to play only a completely subordinate role as a connecting link between Abraham and Lot.' When one looks for evidence to support this assertion, one finds nothing but further speculation based on the name 'Haran'.

Noth connected the name Haran with the place-name Beth-Haran. This place is mentioned only once in the Old Testament (Num. 32.36), and may in fact be a corruption of Beth-Haram (Josh. 13.27). But, on the grounds that it is stated to have been located near the Dead Sea and so not far from the location of the stories about Lot, Noth assumed that it must have been in some way associated with the man Haran. Originally, however, he asserted, the Haran of Beth-Haran was a god: it was 'the local deity worshipped in Beth-Haran', which could be translated 'temple of Haran'. The connection of the place with the *man* Haran was secondary, due to a misinterpretation of the name Beth-Haran by the local inhabitants as meaning 'Haran's house', that is, the dwelling-place of the *man* Haran. This is a most unlikely supposition in view of the fact that 'Beth' followed by the name of a deity was a familiar form of place-names.

The next step in this process was taken, according to Noth, when Haran, in view of the proximity of his house to Sodom and Gomorrah, came to be regarded as a notably pious man who was the sole survivor of the catastrophe which had destroyed those cities. Subsequently it came to be further supposed that he was the brother of another notable pious man who had lived at Hebron and who later came to be identified with Abraham. But there was another figure associated with the region: Lot, whose associations were with nearby Zoar (Gen. 19.30-38). It was, then, Noth claimed, 'quite easy' to connect this figure with Haran by making Lot the son of Haran and so the nephew of Abraham. Finally, 'since the story of Lot contained more concrete details than the story of Haran, Lot came to be the more popular narrative figure . . . and also soon attracted to himself the entire narrative content' of the story of the destruction of Sodom and Gomorrah.

Noth admitted that this reconstruction of an extremely complicated series of stages in the development of this part of the patriarchal traditions—all of which, it must be remembered, were completed before any of them was committed to writing—was only tentative. But it well illustrates the methods which he employed on a larger scale. There is not a single feature of this series of speculations which is supported by concrete evidence, from the mysterious rise and fall of a 'Haran tradition' to the supposition of an otherwise unattested— and surely quite unnecessary—deity Haran. But each supposition is made to serve as the basis for another.

In general, Noth's work is marked by an extreme scepticism about the antiquity of particular traditions. Occasionally, however, he argued *in favour* of an early date in a way that almost seems perverse. An example of this is his treatment of Moses' marriage.

Noth asserted that the tradition of Moses' marriage to a foreign woman—not necessarily the daughter of the Midianite priest Jethro—'is so little separable from his person that here at last we actually hit upon an original Moses tradition. ... Here we may assume with good reason that we have an original historical datum' (p. 184; ET p. 168).

The grounds on which Noth made this—for him—very positive statement are difficult to discover. At first it seems that it has something to do with the story told in Exod. 18 of the visit of Jethro to Moses and the Israelites at the 'mountain of God'. On this Noth commented that Moses' marriage relationship 'is so firmly rooted in this narrative . . . that the story is inconceivable without this motif'. But then we learn that the motif has probably 'been blended only secondarily with the tradition of the meeting with the Midianites' (p. 186; ET p. 169); so Noth's conclusion that Moses' foreign marriage was a historical fact can presumably not be derived from Exod. 18. In fact he only put forward in its favour a single piece of evidence: the fact that the Old Testament has preserved three quite different and apparently independent traditions about Moses' having had a foreign wife, the other two being the statements that he married a Cushite (Num. 12.1) and that his father-in-law was a Kenite (Judg. 1.16; 4.11). He concluded from this: 'That the marriage of Moses to a foreign woman . . . goes back to an historical fact is shown by its appearance in no less than three mutually independent versions. . . . Now, it is certainly not likely that Moses had three different foreign wives. Rather, we obviously have here in three different narrative versions the same original element of tradition . . . which is thus made all the more reliable' (p. 185; ET pp. 168-69). This is his only argument on the point, apart from the rather cryptic remark that the foreign marriage is not 'separable from his person'.

That Noth should have regarded the 'triple attestation' of Moses' foreign marriage as proof of its historicity is surprising. For the fact that in each case the nationality of the wife differs demands a more convincing explanation than is provided by the somewhat lame remark that 'obviously the narrators no longer knew the specific extraction of Moses' foreign wife'. That they did not know it throws doubt on the view that we have a triple attestation of a single 'original' element of tradition. Other explanations of the variations are possible. Moreover it may be doubted whether such forgetfulness is probable in such a case; and if the original nationality of the wife *had* been forgotten, we might expect the tradition to have referred simply to 'a foreign wife'.

Be that as it may, it is surprising that Noth should have insisted so strongly that the tradition of the foreign wife is proven. If a tendency to assign historical status to the tradition were a characteristic of Noth's general approach to the material, this insistence would not appear remarkable; but this is so far from being the case that it stands out as a curiosity.

It is instructive to compare his treatment of this feature with—for example—his attempt to show that Moses had no connection with the events of the oppression in Egypt, the Plagues, or the Exodus (the theme of 'guidance out of Egypt', pp. 178-80; ET pp. 162-63). Here, the birth and abandonment of the child Moses having been dismissed—in agreement with many other scholars—as secondary, Noth held the flight to Midian and the encounter with God at the mountain to be merely 'an anticipatory elaboration of Exod. 18.1-12', and the stories of the Plagues and the Passover to be later developments of the tradition, and concluded that in this theme 'nothing specific remains for Moses . . . other than what self-evidently had to be said about him once he was on the point of becoming *the* leader of the Israelites from Egypt on'. The name Moses he admitted to be Egyptian, but he argued that it could be accounted for in other ways than by supposing him ever to have been in Egypt. He admitted that 'in the narration of this theme we find no other single leader who perhaps could have been replaced by Moses in the tradition', but astonishingly asserted, as has already been observed, that the anonymous 'elders' of chapters 3 and 4, or the 'foremen' of chapter 5, whose role in the present text is extremely minor, 'fully sufficed in this theme as the spokesmen of the Israelites before Moses stepped into the position of leadership in the tradition'. In his treatment of these chapters, as in his treatment of many others, Noth displayed a reductionist and sceptical attitude towards the traditions which, apparently as a matter of principle, allowed speculation—e.g. that the 'elders' were once much more important than now appears in the text—to take precedence over the statements in the text—e.g. that the departure of the Israelites from Egypt was made possible by a single determined leader—even when the latter would seem to have the greater plausibility. The fact that in Moses' foreign marriage he chose to find a kernel of historical truth and a sign of an early tradition suggests a subjective rather than a scientific approach on his part to traditio-historical study.

It has been argued by some scholars in defence of Noth's traditio-historical work that his presuppositions and methods ought not to be criticized individually in isolation: to do so is to fail to do justice to their cumulative strength when they are considered as a whole. B.W. Anderson, for example, listed six criteria by which Noth judged narratives to be early or secondary, and commented that they 'work hand in hand and mutually reinforce one another. It is facile to point out weaknesses in any one of these clues when it is taken by itself' (Introduction to Noth, 1948, ET, p. xv). There is no doubt some truth in this. But Noth's methods of work were not confined to the making of judgments about what is 'early' and what is 'secondary'. What are perhaps the most dubious features of his approach to the Pentateuchal traditions are of a much more general and all-pervasive character: on the one hand a sceptical approach to the material so thoroughgoing that a figure so prominent in so much of the material as that of Moses can be almost totally 'dissolved', and, on the other, an undue propensity to pile hypothesis upon hypothesis and so to construct a whole 'tradition-history' out of the flimsiest of 'clues'.

2. *Engnell, Nielsen and Carlson*

The Scandinavian scholars Engnell and Nielsen sometimes gave the impression in their writings that traditio-historical criticism as they understood it was something quite unique and radically different from German traditio-historical criticism. In fact they were heavily indebted to the work of Gunkel, von Rad and Noth, with whose fundamental ideas on the subject they agreed.

It is unfortunate that these Scandinavian scholars have produced very little study of the method as it applies to the Pentateuch. Engnell, in his few short contributions to the subject, confined himself almost entirely to attacking the Documentary Hypothesis and to theorizing in a general way about his 'new' method. During the twenty years between 1945 (the date of the publication of the first volume of his Introduction to the Old Testament) and his death in 1964 he published no detailed study of the Pentateuchal narratives at all: only some parts of the projected second volume of the Introduction, which was to deal with the individual books of the Old Testament, were written, and these have never been published. Even if they had, it appears that they would not have amounted to a detailed study of the texts.

Neither has Nielsen treated the subject in detail. The only examples of his use of the traditio-historical method which are relevant to Pentateuchal studies are ten pages on Gen. 6–9 in his general work *Oral Tradition* (1954), almost entirely devoted to a criticism of the documentary analysis of those chapters, parts of his 'traditio-critical' study *Shechem* (1955), a work which is mainly concerned with the history of religious ideas and partly with non-Pentateuchal texts, and his study of the Decalogue (*The Ten Commandments in Perspective*) (1965), which is not a narrative text. Apart from these few works, only *David the Chosen King* by R.A. Carlson, a pupil and close disciple of Engnell—a study not of the Pentateuch but of 2 Samuel—gives some idea of what a full study of the Pentateuchal traditions by Engnell or Nielsen might have been like.

The two main features of Engnell's and Nielsen's approach to Pentateuchal traditio-historical criticism which were original were their belief that this kind of criticism is an *alternative* to the Documentary Hypothesis rather than complementary to it, and their scepticism about the possibility of tracing the history of the traditions in detail.

In contrast to Noth, Engnell and Nielsen rejected the Documentary Hypothesis in its entirety. This rejection was due partly to their conviction—already discussed above—that the use of writing for all but a few specialized purposes was a late innovation, and partly to their perception of serious weaknesses in the hypothesis itself. Their criticism of what Engnell called the 'book view' of modern biblical scholars with its failure to understand the mentality of the ancient Semitic world and their high regard for the reliability of oral tradition also played a part in the development of their views. Thus in their attack on the Documentary Hypothesis these scholars played an important and perhaps even decisive role; but in their general view of the development of the Pentateuchal traditions they did not differ markedly from Noth, except that they believed that the traditio-historical method made documentary theories unnecessary and irrelevant.

A second major difference from Noth was that, although they agreed with him that the Pentateuchal traditions had undergone a long and complicated process of development before their committal to writing, these scholars were extremely sceptical about the possibility of discovering anything about the details of this process. Indeed, Engnell's failure to produce concrete examples of the application of his 'traditio-historical method' may well have been due to a basic doubt about its practicability: having prescribed the method with apparent confidence, he drew back from the task itself. This seems clear from his two programmatic essays on the subject, published towards the end of his life in 1960 and 1962 (ET 1969). In both he began with some very positive statements about the task and the methods to be employed:

> The traditio-historical method is an *analytical* method, aimed at a working out *so far as possible* of tradition works, tradition complexes, and separate tradition unities, as well as all possible strands with an oral tradition. . . . Hand in hand with the analysis must also go the *synthesis*, the interpretation of the smaller units in relation to their context, since the mere distinguishing of the separate literary units does not in any way solve the problem of tradition (1960, p. 22; cf. 1969, pp. 4-5).

But in each essay he then immediately went on to stress the extreme difficulty of carrying out these tasks:

> When we have to do with a consistent oral tradition it is most often so, that the fusion and uniformation of the different traditions has been carried out so thoroughly already at the oral stage, that the analytical task of discerning the unities and of following the growing of tradition proves to be extremely difficult, so that only

more or less hypothetical results can be reached (1960, p. 23; cf. 1969, p. 6).

Several scholars (e.g. Ringgren, 1966, p. 646; Knight, p. 272; McKane, p. 194) have interpreted Engnell's various remarks on this subject as meaning that a proper 'history of Pentateuchal traditions' such as was attempted by Noth cannot be carried out. If that is so, Engnell's 'tradition-history', as Ringgren remarked, is not a *history* at all. Nielsen himself now agrees with this judgment and has recently, many years after Engnell's death, expressed it in a survey of the history of the traditio-historical study of the Pentateuch (1984):

> Here Ringgren's observations are quite correct, that Engnell's version of tradition history consists in stopping short at [he means not attempting to go back behind] the finished literary product . . . Emphasis on the finished literary product, the composition as it stands, as the primary datum of research, runs the risk of neglecting the "historical" in tradition history, a point many of Engnell's critics have also stressed. This ultimately leads to the study of redaction history, compositional technique, and structuralism (p. 17).

Carlson's work, whose subtitle is 'A Traditio-Historical Approach to the Second Book of Samuel', well exemplifies Nielsen's remarks quoted above. This work follows Engnell's approach so closely that it may legitimately be used, *faute de mieux*, as at least an indication of the lines on which Engnell might have proceeded if he had in fact undertaken a detailed analysis of the Pentateuchal narratives.

In his preliminary remarks, Carlson clearly stated his position: 'We shall use the term "traditio-historical" in its *analytical* sense, as introduced by Engnell' and as 'an analytical alternative to literary criticism' (i.e., documentary criticism) (pp. 10, 11). Traditio-historical analysis, he asserted, is concerned with 'following and describing certain aspects of the history of the various types of material in the Old Testament, from formation to final redaction' (p. 11).

But the possibility of carrying out this programme seems to have been as remote for Carlson as it was for Engnell, since the final redaction forms an impenetrable barrier. Carlson remarked that in the course of his preliminary studies he 'came to realize the great importance of the *final* stage [my italics] in the process of tradition which is known as "redactional history" (*Redaktionsgeschichte*)' (p. 22). The Deuteronomists, who in Carlson's view were responsible for the final text of 2 Samuel, have imposed their theological stamp on the traditions so thoroughly as to obliterate their earlier form. In addition, they—the Deuteronomists—have themselves made use of the same compositional techniques as those which had been used in the earlier stages of oral transmission, with the result that it is now impossible to distinguish their compositional work from what had been done in those earlier stages: 'The use made by the D-group of compositional framework and various patterns in the associative interweaving of the material shows the extent to which the Deuteronomic process is dependent on the techniques of oral transmission' (p. 36), a point which has been made earlier in this work. Consequently 'The task of reconstructing a pre-Deuteronomic cycle of tradition in 1-2 Samuel is so complicated as to be impossible' (p. 43). This fact did not, however, prevent Carlson from coming to the curious conclusion, strongly reminiscent of Engnell's own confusion, that 'the legitimacy of Engnell's demand for a traditio-historical analysis of the texts is thus established' (p. 44)!

What form this 'traditio-historical analysis' could possibly take in view of Carlson's previous statements is not apparent. At any rate, Carlson's book is wholly concerned, in its analysis of the texts, with the Deuteronomistic editors of 2 Samuel and the compositional techniques which they applied to the traditional material as it was available to them at its final stage. That these traditions had a long and complicated earlier history is recognized, but almost nothing is said in the book about this history. Carlson's study is a perfect illustration, *mutatis mutandis*, of Engnell's understanding of 'tradition-history' in which there is, and indeed can be, no history of the traditions attempted at all. (Cf. the comments of Knight, p. 399, Veijola, p. 45, and the review of Carlson's book in *Revue Biblique* 71 [1964], especially p. 619.)

It can only be concluded that, although Engnell (and, by implication, Carlson) agreed with Noth and his followers on the *general* point that a long and complicated history lies behind the narrative texts of the Pentateuch, their extreme scepticism about the possibility of discovering anything about it is in effect a total rejection of Noth's major presupposition, on which his 'history of Pentateuchal traditions' rests, that such a reconstruction is not only possible but can actually be carried out in considerable detail. In this sense, Engnell and Carlson must be reckoned as opponents rather than supporters of the method of traditio-historical analysis.

3. *Georg Fohrer*

D.A. Knight in his survey of Old Testament traditio-historical research wrote of von Rad and Noth: 'Their theses and methods have been determinative and even paradigmatic for the studies that have come in their wake'. Indeed, for many scholars, especially in Germany, this kind of approach became, together with literary (documentary) criticism, form criticism and the new-styled 'redaction criticism' (formerly regarded as an integral part of literary criticism) simply one of the essential disciplines to be applied as a matter of course to every Pentateuchal text. The only doubtful question was in what order these processes were to be applied to the text, and in particular whether documentary criticism should precede the others or not.

If Noth's method was a sound one, it might be expected that its use would lead to rather similar results when different scholars applied it to the same texts. In fact this was far from being the case. It is important to discover the reasons for this: whether, for example, the differing results are due to different historical or religio-historical presuppositions, or whether the method itself is lacking in precision, permitting a variety of interpretations of the same material. Some light may be thrown on these questions by comparing Noth's work with that of Georg Fohrer.

Fohrer described the principles and methods of traditio-historical criticism as he understood them in the Introduction to his *Überlieferung und Geschichte des Exodus* (1964), his *Einleitung in das Alte Testament* (1965) and the composite volume *Exegese des Alten Testaments* (1973, pp. 118-36). The first-named of these publications is a detailed study of Exod. 1–15 in which he used traditio-historical techniques in combination with literary-critical ones. He has thus provided a major example of his use of the method as well as general accounts of his own understanding of its character and function.

The aim of traditio-historical study was no less comprehensive for Fohrer than for Noth: 'Traditio-historical study deals with the prehistory of the books of the Old Testament and examines the gradual accumulation of traditions until their written form'. It 'not only inquires how the textual units achieved their final form but also seeks to trace the entire process by which the units came into being' (1965, ET p. 20). In his work on Exod. 1–15 Fohrer claimed to have achieved this aim: he believed that he had identified both the 'ancient cores of tradition' and the material which was added to these in the oral stage; he had shown how the 'original, independent tradition-complexes' were formed, and so on until the composition of the first comprehensive narrative; he had also succeeded in assigning at least relative dates to these stages of composition. His confidence in his analysis was so great that he drew up detailed tables in which the successive stages of oral as well as written composition are set out (1964, pp. 118-19; 1965, pp. 130-31).

The methods employed by Fohrer to achieve these objectives were very similar to those employed by Noth. His historical and religio-historical presuppositions, however, were quite different. In the introduction to his study of Exod. 1–15 he announced his intention to examine these chapters afresh in order to discover the truth about the historical role of Moses. He made it clear that he did not share Noth's scepticism. Accordingly he set out to re-examine critically Noth's view that the different Pentateuchal 'themes' were originally unconnected with one another, and also that Moses did not originally appear in any of them.

Much of Fohrer's study, as might be expected, is in effect a dialogue with Noth. His arguments cannot be presented here in detail; one example may suffice as an example of the way in which the same texts were interpreted quite differently by the two scholars. Noth, under the influence of his presupposition that the 'themes' were originally unconnected, maintained that the story of Moses' encounter with God at the 'mountain of God' in Exod. 3.1-12 is a late insertion into the Exodus theme ('guidance out of Egypt') intended to 'foreshadow' the later encounter with Midianites, also at the 'mountain of God', and so create a secondary link with the theme 'guidance in the wilderness' and possibly also with the Sinai theme. Fohrer, on the other hand, argued that Exod. 3 is inextricably linked with, and quite essential to, the Exodus story:

> All the essential elements of tradition are linked together inseparably and from the beginning: Moses's stay in Midian, the revelation at the mountain of God or Sinai, the deliverance promised there, the commissioning of Moses to announce or carry out this deliverance and the allusion to the making of the covenant which was to follow. Exodus and Sinai traditions form a single tradition-complex (pp. 52-53).

Fohrer's conviction that the 'themes' belong together is as decisive as Noth's conviction that they do not. The difference between the two scholars is due to their presuppositions and not to their traditio-historical method, which is the same. Whether one reads Noth's or Fohrer's detailed discussions, one is struck with the frequency of statements such as that this or that text can or cannot be 'original' or 'ancient' or 'not originally connected', often made without adequate substantiation. Fohrer in fact went further than Noth in admitting quite frankly that religio-historical presuppositions ultimately control his literary and traditio-historical analyses. For him, Noth's virtual elimination of Moses as a religious leader *must* be wrong on religio-historical grounds, and therefore any argument which supports this view must be faulty:

> One cannot put a hypothesis of *traditio-historical manipulations* in the place of such *religio-historical facts* [my italics] and relationships, any more than the origin of Israel's belief in Yahweh can properly be traced back to the 'agglomeration of traditions'. . . . There is no religion which originated in this way. In all cases where religio-historical study makes it possible to grasp the origin and beginnings of a religion, that religion is seen to be grounded not in an anonymous collective and its traditions, but in the experiences of a single person: it is the work of a founder (1964, p. 53).

In such circumstances there seems to be no objective way of choosing between one scholarly reconstruction and another. If the results are so much dominated by the presuppositions which are brought to the task rather than by the rigour of the method, the method itself cannot but be called into question.

4. *R. Rendtorff*

Rendtorff's views about the history of the Pentateuchal traditions have already been discussed in some detail (pp. 94-95, 98-105, 109-10, 119-20 above). In some respects his ideas remain remarkably close to those of Gunkel and his followers including von Rad and Noth. He defines *Sage* in much the same way as Gunkel, seeing it as having originated in the circle of the family, and even reiterating Gunkel's speculations about the gatherings at which these traditional tales will originally have been told—though the *Sitz im Leben* is now 'before the city gate' rather than round the fire on winter evenings— and also Gunkel's further speculation that they were subsequently disseminated by 'professional narrators'.

Gunkel's detailed work was, of course, confined to Genesis; and Rendtorff pointed out that the other books of the Pentateuch differ from Genesis in being concerned with a whole people rather than individuals, and also that it is much more difficult to identify individual *Sagen* in them, since their original structure has to a large extent been lost; moreover, in Exod. 1–15 in particular there is very little evidence of their existence. Nevertheless Rendtorff remains very dependent on the view first put forward by Gunkel that the Pentateuchal narratives developed and grew by a continuous process in which smaller units were gradually and progressively combined to form larger ones. Where he differs radically from his traditio-historical predecessors (with the exception of Nielsen and Engnell) is in his total rejection of the Documentary Hypothesis as incompatible with a traditio-historical understanding of the process of growth.

In his monograph of 1977 Rendtorff made no higher claim for his own reconstruction than that it is a 'sketch' which needs to be tested further. It is perhaps significant that the title of this work is 'The traditio-historical *problem* of the Pentateuch'—a contrast with Noth's '*history* of Pentateuchal traditions'. Be that as it may, he put forward his thesis with a degree of hesitancy which sometimes amounts to inconsistency. Thus although in some places he asserted categorically that the various 'larger units' all constitute *independent* units (pp. 26-27, 71-75), he referred in other places only to the '*relative* self-containedness of the Sinai pericope' (p. 25) and the *high degree* of independence and self-containedness' of the 'larger units' as a whole, each of which 'presents itself as a *more or less* self-contained unit' (p. 28; italics mine).

In his article on Moses as the founder of a religion (1975b) Rendtorff expressed these hesitations even more clearly. There he criticized Noth's absolutism about the total independence of his 'themes': referring to an article by Herrmann on this subject, he wrote: 'In his fundamental criticism of Noth's methodological proposal to split the Pentateuch into five *Hauptthemen* I agree with Herrmann. This is all right as a working hypothesis, but Noth has absolutized it. To do this, as Herrmann says, is to suppose the existence of quite different spheres of life (*Lebenskreise*)' (p. 158; cf. pp. 165-70). He also opposed Noth's exclusion of Moses from the Exodus and Sinai themes: Noth, he wrote, did not 'test thoroughly enough' the involvement (*Verankerung*) of Moses with those 'themes' (p. 157). This is a crucial matter, since if Moses was involved from the very beginning in both it is difficult to see how these two traditions could have originally existed in total independence of one another.

These inconsistencies in Rendtorff's work would seem to betray some lack of confidence in his own methods of investigation. The article on Moses, and in particular Rendtorff's references there to the implications of Noth's views for Israel's early history, may suggest that Rendtorff saw in Noth's radical historical scepticism the logical consequence of his own reasoning, and was therefore reluctant to pursue his methodology too far.

In his theory of a Pentateuch put together as a comprehensive written work only at a relatively late stage, Rendtorff aligned himself with Engnell and Nielsen; but in his view that it is possible to reconstruct in some detail the earlier development of the traditions which it contains he parted company with those scholars and showed his dependence on Noth—except that, unlike Noth, he was very cautious about assigning even approximate dates to the various stages and made no attempt to co-ordinate these with a hypothetical reconstruction of the history of the Israelite tribes. It is also important to notice that he made little reference to oral tradition as such. The question of the point at which *oral* transmission gave place to written seems to be for him essentially unimportant.

Another important point of difference from Noth is that, perhaps because he does not distinguish bwetwen oral and written transmission, Rendtorff has completely avoided Noth's characteristically speculative mode of traditio-historical reconstruction and, in his attempt to establish his theory of the role of the 'larger units', quite simply uses *the methods of literary criticism* (in the Wellhausenian sense). Having accepted what are essentially the main conclusions reached by Gunkel about the growth of these traditions, he has sought confirmation of them and attempted to add precision to them by the use of literary-critical arguments.

Accepting the widely held view that the patriarchal traditions are held together by the theme of the divine promises made to the patriarchs, Rendtorff followed Westermann (1964) in his view that an analysis of the different types of promise (of blessing, progeny, land, blessing conferred on the nations of the world, etc.) and of the integration or lack of integration of the various promise-speeches into their respective narrative contexts provides clues to the formation of the patriarchal stories as a whole. In general, he held that promises which form an integral part of a story are older than those which are only loosely attached to a story or which stand on their own. The latter bear the marks of the work of 'editors' who have bound the stories together, first into separate groups and then into a single whole, using them to express their own different 'theologies'.

Thus Rendtorff saw the development of the patriarchal 'unit' as very complex, beginning with the separate work of editors of different parts of the material who connected the original *Sagen* together and put their stamp on it, and ending with the work of the editor of the whole 'larger unit', who was of course himself followed by the (probably Deuteronomic) editor of the whole Pentateuch. This *literary-critical* analysis was thus held to confirm earlier *traditio-historical* conclusions.

Regardless of whether Rendtorff was thinking here of oral or written composition, this is purely literary criticism which assumes a precision of language, a concern for minuteness of detail and a practice, at each stage of the process, of exactness of transmission which are in fact unknown to 'oral' performance. In this respect, then, Rendtorff is not a tradition-historian at all in the sense in which the term is usually understood. The process which he assumed in his discussion of the promises in Genesis could only have taken place with regard to a written text; and this brings us back again to early pre-Pentateuchal 'documents', even though these are not the comprehensive, continuous documents of the Documentary Hypothesis.

One of the most crucial features of Rendtorff's thesis is his claim to be able to distinguish the work of the various 'editors' of the 'larger units' from that of the *final* editor of the Pentateuch. He identified the latter in a series of eight texts which link the 'larger units' together into a whole: Gen. 50.24; Exod. 13.5, 11; 32.13; 33.1-3a; Num. 11.12; 14.23; 32.11. These all have a common feature peculiar to them which, he maintained, betrays their particular 'theology': they all refer to an oath sworn to the fathers to give them the land. This combination of the divine oath with the promise of the land occurs regularly in the book of Deuteronomy, but nowhere else in Genesis-Numbers. Its first occurrence in Gen. 50.24 marks the link between the first two 'larger units', and the other occurrences stand in equally crucial positions.

That the similarity of expression to that of Deuteronomy proves that these passages are the product of a Deuteronomic editor cannot be regarded as certain: the author of Deuteronomy may simply have made use of a terminology derived from some other tradition from which the author of these passages in Genesis–Numbers also derived it: it takes more than a single coincidence of expression to establish the presence of a Deuteronomic theology. The passages are too short to permit this question to be checked. But, once again, it should be noted that this argument is a literary-critical one similar to those of the documentary critics, and indeed a very fragile one: there is really nothing to distinguish the editors of the 'larger units' from those of the 'comprehensive edition' except a single terminological coincidence.

In his article on Gen. 28.10-22 (1982) Rendtorff provided a detailed example of his understanding of the way in which particular passages were built up. He distinguished no less than five major elements, as well as some minor ones, in these thirteen verses: verse 10 binds the episode to its present context; verses 11-13a$^\alpha$, 16-19a constitute a unified cult-aetiology of Bethel; 19b is probably a later explanatory gloss attached to this; verses 13aβ-15 are a divine speech inserted into the cult-aetiology, which in its present form serves to bind it together both with the rest of the Jacob-story and also with the whole 'larger unit' of the patriarchal stories; and verses 20-22 are neither a narrative nor a fragment of one, but an originally independent speech made by Jacob on the occasion of a vow which he made when he set up a *maṣṣebah*: this has subsequently undergone a complicated development, having been brought into connection with the question of the payment of tithes at the sanctuary at Bethel (verse 22b), and then even later given a theological 'accent' in verse 21b.

There is virtually nothing in this entire argument which differs in method from that of, say, Wellhausen's *Composition des Hexateuchs*. Rendtorff did not wish to deny this: 'The analysis has shown that many of the observations which led to the source-division which has been customary up to now are absolutely correct'. But, he maintained, these methods have been misused: for example, while agreeing with Fohrer (1973, pp. 196-97) that the passage in its present form is a theological statement intended to connect Jacob with the promise of land and progeny, he remarked: 'But it has now been shown that this is in no way an indication of the presence of different "sources" in this text, but that it rather reveals a theological editing and interpretation which brings the text into the larger context of the Jacob story and of the patriarchal stories' (p. 519). It is difficult to avoid the impression that Rendtorff was not examining this passage objectively as he claimed, but that he merely substituted his own set of presuppositions for the earlier 'documentary' ones.

To sum up: Rendtorff is a tradition-historian only in the limited sense that he accepts, in general terms, the views of Gunkel and his followers about the way in which the 'larger unit' of the patriarchal stories (and, by implication, to some extent the other 'larger units') was formed: from *Einzelsage* to larger collections, culminating in the separate Abraham, Isaac and Jacob stories. The methods which he uses to support these views are, however, those of literary criticism. Unfortunately these methods are not appropriate to those earliest stages: if the early development of the material took place at an *oral* stage, it must be said that this is not the way in which oral transmission does in fact take place; if, on the contrary, it occurred through the written word and a process of editing and redaction of written works, Rendtorff has merely replaced the comparatively simple Documentary Hypothesis which postulated only a small number of written sources and redactors with a bewildering multiplicity of sources and redactors. To ignore the question whether oral or written transmission is envisaged does not solve the problem. It must be concluded that if he is a tradition-historian Rendtorff has not advanced the use of the traditio-historical method, and that if he is a literary critic he has merely replaced one documentary hypothesis with another and more complicated one.

5. *E. Blum*

Recently, E. Blum, a pupil of Rendtorff, has published an immensely detailed (564 page) study of the composition of the 'patriarchal history' in which he has attempted to fill out Rendtorff's analysis in a verse-by-verse (and sometimes phrase-by-phrase) investigation of the whole of Gen. 12–50 along similar lines to Rendtorff's study of Gen. 28.10-22, at the same time postulating an increased number of stages of composition and also making some new observations. The confidence with which he has carried out this task is reminiscent— although of course the methods used are quite different—of Noth's major work on the Pentateuchal traditions.

In many respects Blum's presuppositions and methods are derived from Rendtorff. Like him, he is not concerned to differentiate between oral and written composition and takes little interest in this question. He also follows him in his use of literary criticism as his main tool: his chief criteria for distinguishing one stratum or 'edition' from another are the presence or absence of cross-references, links between different passages and differences of outlook and theology. Again, in agreement with Rendtorff, much of the work is devoted to an attempt to demonstrate that these methods do not lead to a documentary hypothesis in the classical sense but to an entirely different kind of hypothesis of originally independent 'histories': the 'Jakobgeschichte' and the 'Abrahamgeschichte', later combined into the 'Vätergeschichte' or Patriarchal History, the latter corresponding to Rendtorff's 'larger unit' of the patriarchal stories. Again like Rendtorff Blum argues that this last was first combined with the rest of what is now the Pentateuch in a Deuteronomic (or Deuterono-mistic) edition to which the 'P' material was added at a still later date.

According to Blum, the early narratives, some of which had already undergone a first stage of conflation, were taken up during the period of the monarchy and formed in a series of stages into two 'histories': the 'history of Jacob' (in the northern kingdom in the reign of Jeroboam I) and the 'history of Abraham' (in Judah). Between 722 and 587 these were combined in Judah into a first edition of the whole 'patriarchal history' (Vg^1). Subsequently, during the Babylonian Exile, this was expanded into a second edition (Vg^2). In the late sixth century, Vg^2 was combined with the other separate 'histories' which had come into existence, to form a Deuteronomistic Pentateuch. Each of these stages can thus be dated, approximately and in some cases exactly, by the particular circumstances, interests and requirements of different periods and areas which are reflected by the various additions, editorial links and comments made by the editor-narrators.

Blum's study, while deriving its inspiration from Rendtorff and in many respects a continuation of his work, differs from his in four important respects:

1. In contrast to Rendtorff's caution in this matter, Blum believes it to be possible to assign the different stages of the process to particular points in Israel's history.
2. He attempts to detect the various stages of composition much more precisely than Rendtorff appears to have thought possible, especially in the distinction which he makes between Vg^1 and Vg^2.
3. He assigns a much greater role to *authors*. Thus although he

believes some of the Jacob-Esau stories to have been composed (before their combination with those concerning Jacob and Laban) from much smaller units or *Sagen*, he considers the Jacob-Laban stories to be a *Novelle* like the Joseph story: a consciously created single narrative whose component parts never existed as short *Sagen* but are deliberately created *scenes* within a unified composition. None of these 'scenes' is capable of existing on its own. This method of composition is also to be seen in some of the Abraham stories.

4. He rejects the assumption, made by Gunkel, Noth and others, that the stories in Genesis are necessarily early. He begins his study with the early monarchy and does not attempt to go back beyond that period for their origin. In other words, he does not presuppose or argue for a long period of transmission linking the stories with the lives of the characters presented in the stories, or with any other earlier period. He also, significantly, maintains that the nomadic colouring which sometimes appears in them is not a genuine historical reminiscence but merely a way of portraying what was believed by their authors to be how such remote ancestors would have lived.

Blum stresses even more clearly than Rendtorff the inability of traditio-historical methods (in the sense in which they were understood and practised by Gunkel and those who followed him) to account for the composition of the Pentateuch (or at least of Genesis). Rendtorff still paid lip-service to the notions of his traditio-historical predecesors about *Sage*, its transmission and development; but he found it impossible to follow Noth in his theories about how such 'traditions' had become combined with one another and transformed in some hypothetical state when they were still couched in forms and language of which there is no direct evidence in the *text* which we actually possess; his insistence on *literary* methods sprang from his realization that it is only a strict examination of the details of this text—our only source of information—that can lead to theories which are more than vague speculations.

Blum has taken this conviction a step further—almost to its logical conclusion. He believes that we can know nothing of any 'traditions' older than the period of the existence of Israel as a nation-state because before that time there is no knowledge of historical events or circumstances to which they can be attached. There is therefore no reason to assume that there was any long period of oral transmission previous to that. But in reaching this conclusion Blum has abandoned any pretence to be a 'tradition-historian' in the former sense of that phrase. Whether his or Rendtorff's hypotheses and arguments about the way in which the Pentateuch came into existence are acceptable or whether they, like both Noth and the documentary critics, have gone beyond the evidence available is another matter; but it is a matter which is not the concern of 'tradition-history' except in a quite new sense. Blum disclaims the idea that his is yet another 'documentary hypothesis'; but this is only a question of terminology. The distance between him and the new 'literary' critics such as Van Seters is not as great as might be supposed.

6. *Summary and Conclusions*

A number of attempts to throw light on the history of the composition of the narrative material in the Pentateuch by the use of traditio-historical methods, either in conjunction with or as an alternative to the Documentary Hypothesis, have now been considered. In contrast with the latter, however, it is clear that no agreed results have emerged. Although the influence of Martin Noth—and, through him, of Gunkel—has been dominant, other quite different notes have been sounded.

Among the tradition-historians who have taken the Documentary Hypothesis as their point of departure, *Noth* constructed the most comprehensive and impressive hypothesis. His work was, however, dominated by historical, traditio-historical and religio-historical assumptions, and also by a fundamental scepticism about the possibility that any historical facts might lie on the surface of the text: his reconstruction of the *tradition*-history of the Pentateuch therefore had to be made to conform to his hypothetical reconstruction of the origins and early *history of Israel*, which consisted entirely of 'reading between the lines' and almost never—sometimes, it would seem, as a matter of principle—took any 'historical' statement at its face value. He was, however, preoccupied with the question of history, and so found it necessary to weave a web of hypothetical tradition-histories out of sometimes very slight and even dubious evidence, and to pile one hypothesis upon another.

Fohrer in general employed the same methods—both literary-critical (in his acceptance, with his own modifications, of the Documentary Hypothesis) and tradition-historical—but often reached quite different conclusions on the basis of the same textual evidence. This was mainly due to the fact that his attitude towards the possible historical value of the text was more positive than that of Noth, and to his different religio-historical views in general. The difference between Fohrer's results and those of Noth shows the degree of subjectivity which characterizes much traditio-historical work.

Engnell and *Nielsen* were the first tradition-historians to reject the Documentary Hypothesis in its entirety and to approach the question of the history of the Pentateuchal traditions (before their final committal to writing at a late stage) entirely in terms of oral tradition. Much of their work was devoted to pointing out the weakness of the Documentary Hypothesis and to attacking the 'book view' of the literary critics as a modern European viewpoint entirely inappropriate for the proper understanding of ancient literature including the Old Testament. Unfortunately these scholars carried out very little detailed study of the texts; but it is clear both from their general statements about the discipline in general and especially from the analogous work of *Carlson* on 2 Samuel that, despite their reference to their work as 'tradition— history', they were extremely sceptical about the possibility of reconstructing the stages of the development of the oral tradition, and were therefore, at least by implication, opponents rather than supporters of tradition-criticism as exemplified in the detailed work of Noth and his followers.

Rendtorff, although he was at one with Engnell and Nielsen in his total rejection of the Documentary Hypothesis, did not see the history of the Pentateuchal traditions simply in terms of oral transmission: indeed, he appears to regard the distinction between oral and written tradition as of little importance. Thus in his elaborate reconstruction of the patriarchal 'larger unit' it is not clear whether or not he considers the process of its composition to have taken place under the conditions of purely oral transmission, though his acceptance of Gunkel's views about *Sage* in his Introduction suggests that he believes that at the beginning of the process there *was* an oral stage. However this may be, his scheme of the growth of the Pentateuchal traditions by way of originally independent 'larger units' put together by 'editors' and then in turn themselves combined at a late stage into a single comprehensive 'edition' was worked out by means of purely *literary-critical* methods.

The originality of Rendtorff's understanding of the process lies in its independence of the classical documents: he considers that it was only their inability to free themselves from the influence of Wellhausen which prevented von Rad and Noth from seeing that the independent growth of the 'larger units' is in fact incompatible with these documents. Yet because the ways in which he supposes this development to have taken place are in fact characteristic of writers and not of oral 'performers', his study has assumed the appearance of a new *documentary* hypothesis. It is to the theory of documents running right through the Pentateuch that Rendtorff objects: not to written sources as such.

Finally in the work of *Blum*, who in his study of the patriarchal 'histories' has applied Rendtorff's literary-critical methods to the minutest points of detail in a manner quite reminiscent of Wellhausen himself, the wheel has come full circle. Rendtorff and his followers cannot be said to provide support for the method of traditio-historical criticism as that phrase has been understood up till now.

E. *Concluding Assessment*

In the preceding pages an attempt has been made to assess the validity of traditio-historical approaches to the problem of the composition of the Pentateuchal narratives, first by a consideration of their assumptions and methods in general and secondly by a closer inspection of the practical application of these approaches by certain representative scholars. The main conclusions which have been drawn from this investigation are as follows:

1. *The use of writing.* The argument that a large part of the Pentateuchal narratives must have been formed, transmitted and developed orally from very ancient times because writing was not used for such purposes in the ancient Near East until a late period (in the case of Israel, until the sixth century BC) has been shown to be fallacious: it is based partly on a selective use of evidence and partly on a confusion between true oral tradition and the practice within other cultures of the oral recital of texts which already existed in written form, such as the *Qur'an*. Further, the notion that early Israel in particular was a 'primitive' nomadic people to whom the art of writing must have been unknown has been shown, as a result of recent study, to be misconceived. It may also be remarked that there is a circular

argument here: it is assumed *a priori* that the Pentateuchal narratives in question are very ancient, and this assumption is used to prove that they cannot have existed in writing at such an early date.

2. *Foreign models*. Attempts to establish the originally oral nature of the Pentateuchal material and its oral transmission over a long period of time on the basis of analogies drawn from the practice of oral tradition among other peoples and in different periods have, despite their acceptance by a large number of Old Testament scholars, been shown to lack cogency in several respects:

a. *Olrik's so-called 'epic laws'*, which continue to be used by some folklorists and students of comparative literature though their validity is questioned by others, are in fact by no means fully exemplified in the Pentateuchal narratives, and also present difficulties of interpretation and application. Perhaps for these reasons they have never been systematically and rigorously applied to the whole body of Pentateuchal narrative material. Even if their applicability to this material were to be conceded, they would not prove the *antiquity* of those traditions; but such is far from being the case: since the techniques which they enumerate could be, and probably were, used by *writers* as well as by oral narrators, the 'laws' cannot be used to prove the oral origin of any particular text.

b. Comparison with *the Icelandic 'family sagas'*, whose affinity, as 'oral literature', with the patriarchal stories was first suggested by Jolles and assumed by Noth, Koch, Westermann and others, has been shown to be misleading. It is now generally held by specialists in Norse literature that these literary *sagas*, composed in the fourteenth and fifteenth centuries, cannot be shown to be based on oral traditions going back to the much earlier period whose history and way of life they purport to depict, but are probably purely literary compositions. But even if their oral origins were to be conceded, it has now been recognized (*pace* Westermann) that there is little resemblance between the wild and violent 'family life' depicted in the *sagas* and the peaceful lives of the Hebrew patriarchs. There is therefore little resemblance between the two bodies of literature either in form or substance.

c. The use of analogies from *modern 'oral literature'* has also been shown to be beset with difficulties, and in fact remarkably little serious comparison of this kind has been carried out. This is partly due to the fact that, as Ruth Finnegan in particular has made clear, the study of the mass of 'oral literature' which has been collected is itself still in its infancy, and few firm conclusions, or even agreed methods of study, have yet been established. On the Old Testament side the pursuit of this kind of study is hampered by a general ignorance of modern folklore studies and of anthropology on the part of Old Testament scholars, by the extreme paucity of Old Testament material available for study in a field where abundance and variety of material are essential, and by the difficulty of finding examples of modern oral literature which are really comparable with the Old Testament narratives. Most of the comparisons which have been attempted have been between Old Testament *prose* texts and modern oral *poetic* texts—a somewhat futile undertaking, as the processes of composition, transmission and development of oral prose and of poetry are in fact very different.

The study of modern oral literature has, nevertheless, produced a few conclusions which make it very improbable that comparison with the narratives of the Pentateuch can yield positive results for the Old Testament historian of traditions. For example, according to Ruth Finnegan, genre (or *Gattung*) and *Sitz im Leben*, the twin pillars of the Gunkelian hypothesis, are flexible, ill defined and interchangeable in oral narrative literature; and it is even debatable whether any attempt at classification of narrative genres is a realistic or helpful procedure. Furthermore, there is no evidence that any of the stories which have been studied is of great antiquity, and there is no way of tracing their earlier history.

The conclusion seems inevitable, that what cannot be achieved by the student of a living tradition, who is able to observe actual narrative 'performances' in their proper settings and often also to question both performers and audiences about what is going on, is unlikely to be possible for the student of *ancient* narratives who possesses only a written text, itself composed in antiquity. That attempts to shed light on the tradition-history of the Pentateuchal narratives by comparing them with modern oral narratives can be successful seems improbable.

3. *The fluidity of oral tradition.* The study of modern oral literature has also cast very serious doubts upon the hypothesis that many of the Pentateuchal narratives were transmitted over a period of several centuries and still survived in a recognizable form when they were first committed to writing, so that the various 'original' *Sagen*, together with their subsequent oral modifications, can still be perceived through the written text that has come down to us. Observation of modern oral

narrative 'performances' has shown that the freedom of the narrator or 'performer' to change and adapt his narratives to fit the circumstances in which he finds himself makes it improbable that they could be preserved in a recognizable form for very long: the modifications in the telling occur not merely from one generation of narrators to the next but from performance to performance. Moreover, what is actually recorded when such a narrative is committed to writing is merely one of the possible versions; and in addition, the very act of recording tends to produce something different from what would have been produced by an 'unfettered' performance. The counter-argument that the 'sacred' character of the Pentateuchal narratives puts them in a separate category in this respect—a view, incidentally, which would increase the difficulty of finding modern examples for comparison—is somewhat dubious in the absence of any proof that they were in fact recited in the context of a 'sacral' institution of some sort, and in view also of the fact that many of them do not appear to possess any intrinsically 'sacred' character at all. Oral tradition thus has an element of continuity, but it has no fixity: fluidity is its major characteristic.

4. *Storytellers in the Old Testament.* It has been pointed out that there is no evidence in the Old Testament for the existence of a class of professional storytellers in ancient Israel. Since such a professional class is an essential feature of the narrative traditions of modern non-literate societies and is also attested in the case of ancient societies which are known to have had a tradition of oral literature, this silence is significant. Without an institution of this kind it is difficult to see how a continuous and enduring oral tradition could have been maintained.

5. *Oral and written composition.* It has been shown that no satisfactory techniques have yet been developed for detecting the origins of written narratives from evidence provided by the texts themselves. Doublets or variant versions of the same story are not necessarily the written deposits of oral variants: the connection between the two versions may be a purely literary one, one version being a deliberately composed 'revised version' of the other. The inclusion of both in the same literary work may be due to purely artistic or theological reasons, such as a desire to emphasize a point or to present a character in a particular way, for example as doubly (or triply) blessed or afflicted.

With regard to stylistic characteristics, oral narrators and writers may and do frequently use the same techniques; and this is particularly true of the ancient world, where books were intended to be read aloud rather than silently, a fact which, especially when the reading was before an audience, made oral techniques desirable and even necessary, since the work was heard rather than communicated through the eye. Finally, the self-contained nature of a particular unit of narrative is not necessarily an indication of an originally independent and isolated existence (as with Gunkel's *Einzelsagen*): it may be an indication of a deliberate and skilful division of a literary work into 'chapters' or 'scenes' which do not necessarily need connecting links (we may compare the episodic character of many early European novels, in which the only connecting link between the episodes is the identity of the main character).

Doubts about the possibility of tracing the Pentateuchal narrative traditions to their sources and of reconstructing the history of their development before their committal to writing have been reinforced by the study of *the work of representative tradition-historians* in Section D above. The fact that scholars like Noth and Fohrer have reached quite different conclusions on important aspects of the tradition-history owing to their different historical, religio-historical and other presuppositions serves to underline the high degree of subjectivism and conjecture involved in what is ostensibly a 'scientific' method. There is a tendency, especially in the work of Noth and those who have followed him most closely, to select one explanation of the evidence out of a number of possible ones without giving a satisfactory reason, to elevate this into a hypothesis, and then, on the basis of this hypothesis, to erect another.

It is no doubt for this reason that Engnell, Nielsen and their followers, despite their claim that the 'traditio-historical method' is the only valid approach to the question of the composition of the Pentateuch, expressed extreme caution about the possibility of tracing the stages of the development of the pre-literary material; that Rendtorff, again in spite of the title of his major work, 'The Traditio-Historical Problem of the Pentateuch', refused to speculate about a hypothetical oral stage of tradition and reverted to the application of *literary*-critical methods to the texts; and that Blum in his 'The Composition of the Abraham-Story', noting the literary and archaeological arguments of Van Seters and T.L. Thompson, scouts the idea of 'pre-Israelite' traditions in the Pentateuch and sees the Pentateuchal narrative tradition as having had its origins in the period of the early monarchy at the beginning of the first millennium BC.

PART III: AN ALTERNATIVE APPROACH

A. *A Single Author for the Pentateuch?*

If neither the Documentary Hypothesis nor the traditio-historical method, whether separately or in combination, provides a reliable and convincing approach to the question of the composition of the Pentateuch, we must ask whether there remains any possibility of getting behind the final text to discern the origins of the material which it contains and the process which led to its compilation. That it did not spring entirely from the mind of a single writer is evident: it is in some sense a history, compiled from a variety of sources of information.

It should not be supposed that the two main hypotheses discussed above are the only possible ones. During the last few years several attempts have been made to explore new avenues of Pentateuchal research.

1. *Single Authorship or Growth by Accretion?* A number of recent scholars (Wagner, Winnett, Rendtorff, Schmid, Mayes), though differing from one another in important respects, have reached the common conclusion that until the period of the Exile at the earliest there was no 'Pentateuch': in other words, whatever the earlier stages through which the materials now contained in the Pentateuch may have passed, the first *comprehensive* work, covering the whole period from the beginning to Moses, was composed not earlier than the sixth century BC.

Before the implications of this new consensus are explored, one alternative hypothesis deserves mention. This is the theory of Sandmel, already mentioned on several occasions. Sandmel suggested that the Pentateuch grew gradually under the influence of a 'haggadic tendency': that is, it belongs to a type of literature which 'grew by accretion'. In other words, it has no single 'author', nor is it a compilation made by combining the work of a series of consecutive authors: there never was a deliberate act by which an author or 'general editor' formed and carried out a plan to compose a comprehensive 'Pentateuch'. Rather, the Pentateuch grew, right up to the penning of the final word, by the constant 'correction' and expansion of a constantly growing mass of literature which had begun as a collection of 'comparatively naïve materials' through the addition, one after the other, of new versions of earlier stories, together with newly invented ones, without the expunging of the old ones. The inevitable result of this process was the kind of work which the Pentateuch clearly is: a mass of literary, theological and other inconsistencies.

Sandmel's theory thus supposes a total lack of comprehensive planning in the composition of the Pentateuch. Its main strength is the analogy which it adduces with the growth of another literary corpus: the Jewish midrash. It also has the advantage of offering an explanation of the numerous inconsistencies and repetitions which are undoubtedly present in the text. Its principal weakness is that it offers no explanation of the unity of plan and central theme which, despite these inconsistencies, are evident in the completed work. It denies the existence of any positive, rational motive governing its composition as a whole. Moreover, the analogy which Sandmel adduces between the (haggadic) midrash and the Pentateuch is not entirely satisfactory: even if haggadic *methods* may account to some extent for the recasting and duplication of some of the Pentateuchal stories, the resulting *literary works* are quite different in kind. Midrash Rabba on Genesis, for example, the rabbinic work particularly cited by Sandmel, is not an original, independent work like the Pentateuch but a *commentary*. Sandmel's proposal, therefore, which is in fact a new version of the Supplement Hypothesis but without an original solid narrative corpus to be supplemented, is unable to account for the final shape of the Pentateuch. It is rather the opposite approach of seeking to discover whether, despite many inconsistencies, the Pentateuch *as a whole* bears the marks of a single distinctive purpose which offers the best hope of arriving at the truth of the matter. This approach, which postulates a *single authorship* for the Pentateuch, is in some respects a new version of the Fragment Hypothesis.

2. *A Deuteronomistic Pentateuch?* One way of defining the purpose and character of the Pentateuch which has found favour in recent

years is to see it as an expression of the theological standpoint of Deuteronomy or of the Deuteronomistic History. In this view we see a total reversal of the earlier critical consensus of opinion. For both the documentary critics and the tradition-historians it had been common ground that the book of Deuteronomy (virtually the same as D) stood apart from the rest of the Pentateuch as an alien block of material. Noth's hypothesis of a Deuteronomistic History (which included Deuteronomy) as a work compiled in totally different circles from those which shaped the books from Genesis to Numbers and possessing its own characteristic theology reinforced the position of the documentary critics on this question; and Noth was simply expressing what was still a general consensus of opinion when he wrote: 'there is no sign of Deuteronomistic editing in Genesis-Numbers' (1943, p. 13; ET p. 13). The recent statements of Schmid that the main narrative of Genesis-Numbers 'belongs to the environment of the Deuteronomic-Deuteronomistic... literary activity' (p. 167) and of Rendtorff that the first comprehensive edition of the Pentateuch was 'marked with a Deuteronomic stamp' (1977, p. 170) thus present a challenge to all previous views about the nature and purpose of the Pentateuch.

This new opinion was largely inspired by the publication of Perlitt's *Bundestheologie im Alten Testament* (1969), in which it was argued that 'covenant theology', that is, the notion that Israel was bound to Yahweh by a *bᵉrît* or covenant, did not exist in Israel in early times but was an invention of the Deuteronomists in the seventh or sixth century BC. Perlitt's view has been and remains hotly disputed; but his attempt to show that the whole 'Sinai pericope' which speaks of a covenant established on the mountain betrays a Deuteronomic theology had the effect of drawing attention to the possibility that this Deuteronomic theology might also pervade Genesis-Numbers as a whole.

Schmid examined various parts of Genesis-Numbers in that light. He sought to show that in the accounts of Moses' call (Exod. 3–4), the stories of the plagues, the crossing of the Sea, the wanderings in the wilderness and the promises to the patriarchs there are persistent elements of both Deuteronomic thought and language. He argued that these books express a fully developed theology which presents these events in terms of a Deuteronomic interpretation of classical prophecy, and also in terms of a Deuteronomic theology of God's redeeming activity schematized in such typical patterns as distress/

appeal for help/divine intervention/faith and trust, which are especially characteristic of the Deuteronomistic History. In other words, according to Schmid, the whole of Genesis-Numbers is a systematic expression of Deuteronomic theology: a theology far more highly developed than anything which would have been possible in any of the pre-exilic periods previously proposed for the Yahwist. Schmid's principal Pentateuchal narrative is thus the work of a 'late Yahwist' who was a Deuteronomist.

Rendtorff put forward, though with some hesitation, an even more radical suggestion, in which he has been followed by Mayes: he claimed to have found evidence which suggests that Genesis-Numbers never existed as an independent work: rather, it was deliberately composed as an introduction to an already existing Deuteronomistic History (1977, pp. 166-69). This would account not only for its 'Deuteronomic stamp' but also for its abrupt conclusion, lacking, as it does, a proper account of Israel's settlement in Palestine: it was never intended to stand on its own. In support of this thesis, which he did not work out in detail, Rendtorff pointed to a number of features in Genesis-Numbers which are reminiscent of the Deuteronomistic Historian's methods of composition or which look like deliberate devices intended to link the two works together. For example, he noted that Exod. 1.6, 8 record the death of Joseph and his generation in precisely the same way as that in which Judg. 2.8, 10 record the death of Joshua and *his* generation. Both passages, he suggested, are intended to mark out the conclusions of major sections in a long historical work. Again, Num. 27.12-23 appears to be a deliberate reference forward to the account of the death of Moses in Deut. 34. Further, the final chapters of Numbers (32–35) contain an unusually large number of 'Deuteronomistic' elements which help to make a smooth transition to Deuteronomy. Finally, Rendtorff adduced his own scheme of 'larger units' in Genesis—Numbers joined by an editor as similar to the way in which the Deuteronomistic History itself was composed by the combination of substantial bodies of pre-existent material. He admitted, however, that further investigation would be necessary to test his thesis.

Recent study by these and other scholars seems to have succeeded in showing that 'Deuteronomic' influence in Genesis–Numbers is more extensive than was previously supposed. But whether the evidence is sufficient to sustain the hypothesis of a Deuteronomic *edition* of the whole of these books is doubtful. It is not sufficient, with Schmid, to point to substantial sections which are strongly reminiscent of Deuteronomic language and ideas, or, with Rendtorff, to detect a number of editorial linking passages between sections which have a Deuteronomic flavour: indeed, Rendtorff's claim to be able to distinguish clearly between earlier editorial linkages between *smaller* parts of the material and those of the comprehensive redactor of the material as a whole must be regarded with some reserve. It is notoriously difficult to determine the theological character or the religio-historical provenance of passages of such brevity; and Rendtorff himself admitted that the evidence in some cases does not wholly support his views. Moreover, the extent to which it is possible to distinguish Deuteronomic language from the ordinary prose style of roughly the same period is a matter of dispute; and, as Rendtorff himself stated, the word 'Deuteronomic' itself, from the theological point of view, is not very precise, and covers a development of thought which lasted for about two centuries. To prove that the Pentateuch as we have it is basically a Deuteronomic work it would be necessary to demonstrate that the material which it contains has been arranged and edited in its entirety in accordance with a comprehensive and consistent plan and has a structure which is wholly in accordance with a Deuteronomic theology; and this neither Schmid nor Rendtorff has succeeded in doing.

But in order to account for the apparent incompleteness of Genesis-Numbers it may not be necessary to prove that it is a 'Deuteronomic' compilation. It is equally possible that it was composed as a complement to the Deuteronomistic History in a looser and less strictly theological sense: that it is the work of an *historian* whose intention was to provide—not necessarily under the influence of any one 'theology'—an account of the origins of the world and of Israel that would supplement the Deuteronomistic History so that both works together would tell the whole story from the beginning to the fall of the Israelite kingdoms. What might the motivation of such a writer have been? One answer to this question has been given by Van Seters.

3. *A National Historian?*

a. *The Pentateuch and the early Greek historians.* Van Seters (1983) broke new ground in his attempt to set the Pentateuch (and the other historical books of the Old Testament) in the context of the literary traditions of the ancient world. He started from the now widely held view of Albrektson that ancient Israel was not, as had previously been supposed, unique in its concept of history: its belief that historical events are divinely controlled was basically similar to that of neighbouring peoples. Nevertheless none of the Near Eastern peoples achieved historiography in any sense comparable with that found in the historical books of the Old Testament. But ancient Greece was an exception. It is with the historical works of the fifth century Greek historian Herodotus and his immediate predecessors and contemporaries that Van Seters found a remarkable counterpart in the Old Testament.

Van Seters attributed the failure of earlier scholars to compare these two literatures to a lack of communication between biblical and classical studies; and in this he was, in a sense, correct. A comparison of the Pentateuch with the works of the Greek historians would have seemed particularly unprofitable, because the main Pentateuchal source, J, was believed to have been written several centuries before the earliest Greek historical works. But if, as Van Seters and others now maintain, the date of the 'Yahwist' is to be brought down to the sixth century BC, his work would be almost contemporary with them.

Van Seters's comparison does not, however, depend on a hypothesis of direct contact between Greece and Israel at that time, or even on the possibility of some common cultural or literary influence on both: he admitted that such contacts were probably few; and although he tentatively suggested that the Phoenicians, to whom both Greece and Israel owed the alphabet, might have mediated some cultural influences from the Aegean world to both peoples, he did not press this point. Rather, he simply indicated that there are in fact some close and remarkable similarities between the Greek histories and the almost contemporary Old Testament historical works, and posed the question: 'Why should early Hebrew prose have been different?' (p. 37). In this way he challenged established positions both of the source-critical and traditio-historical kind, and invited a new appraisal of the character of the the historical books of the Old Testament unencumbered by preconceived notions.

Of the only two early Greek historians whose works have been preserved intact (the other is Thucydides), it is Herodotus who provides substantial points of comparison with the Pentateuch. Like both the Pentateuch and the Deuteronomistic History, Herodotus's *Histories* was compiled with the use of various sources which the historian organized, though with many long digressions, into a single chronologically ordered narrative. His narrative units are joined by connecting links; but he did not attempt to produce uniformity of style or smoothness of transition from one unit to another.

So, like the historical books of the Old Testament, Herodotus's work set out to be an account of the past. It differs from the Pentateuch and resembles the Deuteronomistic History in that its subject is not the origins of the world and the early history of mankind, but more recent history. However, some of Herodotus's predecessors and contemporaries, whose works are preserved in fairly substantial fragments, wrote prose histories much more closely comparable in contents with the Pentateuch, giving accounts of myths and heroic legends. An example of such works is that of the fifth century historian Hellanicus, who composed a history of Athens from the remote past to his own day, actually creating a fully-fledged 'Athenian tradition' complete with myths, legends, etymologies, genealogies and aetiologies much in the manner of the Pentateuch, and relating them to the origins of the Athenian institutions of his own day. Unfortunately this work is preserved only in a fragmentary form.

It was once thought that Herodotus and other Greek historians incorporated extensive written sources into their work; but this is now thought to be improbable. Plagiarism was frowned upon and would have been easily detected. Nor on the other hand is there any reason to suppose that their work is the result of a lengthy traditio-historical process. These authors have been rightly seen to be creative writers of books which were essentially their own.

Herodotus, whose *Histories* are fortunately completely preserved, undoubtedly did make use of *some* written sources, as he himself admitted; but he attributed far more of his material to oral information obtained in the course of his extensive travels. These claims have, however, been questioned. Some scholars believe that they are fictitious: that Herodotus was simply attempting to bolster his reputation as an authority on a wide variety of matters by claiming to possess 'inside information'. That much of his material was invented by himself is in fact generally agreed, although opinions differ about the extent of this invention. Moreover, although many of his stories are couched in the typical forms of popular narrative, it is regarded as probable that the forms as well as the contents of some of them are his own imitations of these genres. Many of these correspond closely to the genres found in the Pentateuch.

Van Seters emphasized the fact that Herodotus made no attempt to achieve uniformity of style. The individual units, which are of many different kinds, are merely connected by 'parataxis': that is, the narrative 'is made up of larger or smaller units strung together in a loosely connected chain' (p. 37). This method of composition is also characteristic of the Pentateuch, as Gunkel had already noted in the case of Genesis. The links between the units in Herodotus consist of connecting phrases often of an extremely simple character, e.g. 'After this. . .'. However, presumably to avoid monotony, Herodotus did not confine himself to a single formula but used a variety of such connecting phrases—a phenomenon which is usually taken by Pentateuchal critics to indicate the activity of successive redactors. He also used more wide-ranging compositional techniques which serve to bind the whole work, or individual major sections of it, into a unity. Such techniques are familiar from Pentateuchal studies: they include repetitions or near-repetitions of incidents occurring in different parts of the work, the presentation of events or sequences of events in such a way as to bring out analogies between them, and various structural patterns such as advice given and subsequently acted upon or warnings (by oracles or dreams) later fulfilled. Genealogies also serve as compositional devices.

As to the purpose of Herodotus's *Histories* no simple answer can be given. It is a many-sided work, full of long digressions not very closely connected with its ostensible purpose, which is to describe the causes and the course of the wars between the Greeks and the Persians which resulted in the rescue of the Greeks of Ionia from Persian rule. Entertainment and an imaginative account of the past, as well as the provision of information about a great variety of phenomena, were clearly also important aims; but reflections about profound aspects of human existence such as the role of the gods in human affairs, human pride and ambition, the retribution which follows arrogance, the nature of society and the state, and the role of law are also important themes.

Beyond this, however, Herodotus clearly thought it important to record a vital period in the history of his own nation: not in a narrowly nationalistic way, but nevertheless in a way which would encourage Greek ethnic pride and self-respect, and also account for the conditions of the present by investigating their historical causes. Such a purpose, which was closely connected with a sense of 'national' (i.e., Hellenic) identity, was of course not confined to

Herodotus but is common to many ancient historians as well as to modern ones.

Van Seters's purpose in comparing the works of the early Greek historians with the historical books of the Old Testament was not to prove that the latter are in every way similar to the former. The differences between them are as obvious as the similarities. One point of difference which might seem to be an obvious one is, however, less real than it might appear to be: the 'religious' character of the Hebrew histories compared with the supposedly 'secular' one of the Greek ones. Greek notions of religion were different from Hebrew ones; but in their descriptions of the origins of various cultic sites, and in their concern to show how human affairs are affected by the gods, the Greek historians show themselves to be as much concerned in their own way with 'religion' as are the authors of the Pentateuch and the Deuteronomistic History. Given the differences between the character, history and circumstances of the Greek and Jewish peoples of the sixth and fifth centuries BC, it is hardly to be expected that the two literatures should correspond in every way.

Nevertheless, both in literary form and to some extent in general purpose these literatures have much in common. As far as literary form is concerned, many of the stylistic and compositional features which are generally taken, in the case of the Pentateuch, to be signs of traditional composition or plurality of authorship are found in Herodotus to be attributable to a single author who varied his style and compositional techniques for purely literary purposes. And as far as authorial intention is concerned, there is a real sense in which Herodotus and the Pentateuch, as well as the Deuteronomistic History, can be described as 'national' histories intended to help their readers to find their national identities. If both the Documentary Hypothesis and the traditio-historical assumption are rejected, there appears to be no reason why, as is now becoming more and more accepted by recent scholars, the Pentateuch should not also be the work of a single author.

Van Seters, Schmid, Rendtorff and others have given substantial reasons for believing that the earliest 'Pentateuch'—whether it be attributed to 'late J' or to a Deuteronomist—is a late composition. All of these except Van Seters combine this view with the traditio-historical approach. But they all agree that there are very strong reasons for associating the composition of the Pentateuch with the circumstances of the Jewish people in the period of the Exile. It was then, more than at any other time, that the Jews needed to be able to look back at their origins and past history, to learn its lessons, and to understand and grasp their identity as a people, and the principles for which they stood. There is a close analogy here with the early Greek historians, who also wrote histories of their own people for the edification of their own contemporaries, recording the past in an imaginative way which would give them an understanding of their origins, a sense of their identity, and a pride in their achievements.

b. *A 'priestly' writer?* Despite his characterization of the Yahwist as an author and historian, Van Seters remains a 'documentary' critic of the Wellhausenian school: indeed, he has gone out of his way to praise Wellhausen, and in his most recent article (1983) asserted that 'It is time to return to the basic method of literary and historical criticism used by Wellhausen' (p. 170). Although he differs from the Documentary Hypothesis in that he rejects the scheme of parallel sources combined by a series of redactors in favour of one which envisages a series of expanded editions, his 'Yahwist' still represents an intermediate, albeit decisive, stage in a process of composition which comprises first two consecutive 'pre-Yahwist' sources, then the 'Yahwist', and finally P (with some further 'post-priestly' additions). In other words, for him the Pentateuch in its *final* form is, after all, *not* the work of a single historian.

Van Seters's hypothesis of 'pre-J' sources does not seriously conflict with the idea of a single authorship: his 'pre-J' material is not extensive, and may be regarded simply as one among other sources which underwent a previous revision before it was incorporated into the whole. But his presupposition of a final author-redactor P is somewhat surprising: this retention of a major feature of the Documentary Hypothesis (even though for him P is a redaction rather than a wholly independent source) appears to be in conflict with his main thesis. Other recent Pentateuchal critics, however, are aware that the sixth century date now proposed for the main Pentateuchal work (whether it is attributed to the 'Yahwist' or not) puts a question mark against the traditional notion of P either as a comprehensive 'document' or as a final comprehensive edition of the Pentateuch. Rendtorff was quite positive about this; Schmid did not discuss the question in detail, but contented himself with pointing out that his theory of a 'late Yahwist' 'may result in new views with regard to the assessment of the Priestly work' (1976, p. 169; cf. 1981, p. 379).

Van Seters's view that the 'Yahwist''s work cannot have included P is based principally on two considerations: 1. that P has the characteristics of *post*-exilic theology and practice; and 2. that these characteristics are different from and incompatible with those of the Yahwist's work. Both of these considerations are based on the assumption that we possess a clear notion both of the scope and content and also of the date of P. But this is very far from being the case.

The post-exilic—or even exilic—date of P is now far from secure. It has long been recognized that the legislative sections contain a great deal of pre-exilic material. Recently Haran (1978, 1981) has gone much further than this: he maintains that 'it is a clear fact that there is no primary, basic correlation between P's legal and historical presuppositions and the actual conditions of the post-exilic period' (1981, p. 326)—a statement which evidently includes the narratives as well as the laws of P. A comparison of the laws of P with the 'code' of Ezek. 40-48 has led Hurvitz as well as Haran to conclude that P preceded Ezekiel, and not *vice versa* as had been universally believed. Haran believes that P was composed by a group of Jerusalem priests who were active in the time of Ahaz and Hezekiah, and who influenced Hezekiah's reform. However, P remained in the private custody of this 'semi-esoteric circle' of priests for many years, and was promulgated publicly for the first time by Ezra as narrated in Neh. 8.

If in fact P was not promulgated until the time of Ezra though composed several centuries earlier, Haran's dating of its composition would not upset the usual view that it must represent the latest stage in the composition of the Pentateuch. But in fact there is no general agreement that the law which Ezra took to Jerusalem from Babylonia and read to the people *was* in fact P; and there is also no agreement that, whatever it was, it was a *new* law previously unknown to those who heard it read. The incident of the reading of the 'book of the law of Moses' to the people by Ezra therefore does not prove that P could not have been available for inclusion in the Pentateuch at an earlier date.

Haran's particular theory about the circumstances which produced P is by no means generally accepted. Nevertheless there is a growing recognition that the late date which used to command a virtual consensus of opinion can no longer be taken for granted. Moreover it is not only the date, but also the scope and content, of P which are now being questioned. Even its unity, and hence its very existence—whether as a 'document' or as a comprehensive and consistent redaction of the Pentateuch—have also now become matters for doubt. In this connection the contribution of Rendtorff is particularly significant.

For Rendtorff, P is neither a unified source nor a single consistent and comprehensive redaction of the Pentateuch. Apart from the laws, with which he does not deal in detail but which are clearly for him distinct in origin from what is usually called the 'narrative' material of P, he finds it possible to attribute very little to a 'priestly editing'; and what he does find is of a disparate nature: it consists mainly of a very few passages which, though in narrative dress, are not true narratives but rather theological statements, together with a number of chronological notices which themselves do not form a single consistent series but are the work of more than one hand. Like Haran, Rendtorff is not prepared to accept the general consensus of scholars that this material must be exilic or post-exilic: no criteria, he believes, have yet been produced for an absolute dating of any of the stages of the composition of the Pentateuch (1977, p. 171). However,—although his meaning is not absolutely clear on this point—he does appear to continue to hold the traditional view that the 'priestly' passages were *added subsequently* to the 'first', Deuteronomic, Pentateuch.

The reasons for this continued late dating of P do not, however, appear compelling, and Rendtorff has not given detailed reasons for it. In the few 'theological' passages which he assigns to the priestly material there are, admittedly, certain particular theological emphases; but in view of the wide range of 'theologies' found together in the Pentateuch there appears to be insufficient reason to suppose that these, and only these, are subsequent in date to the rest of the work.

c. *The author of the Pentateuch.* In short, both Van Seters and Rendtorff, and others who argue that the Pentateuch is basically a single literary work—whether its author is called 'late J' or Deuteronomist, and whether or not its composition was preceded by a long period of gradual development of the material—have failed to carry their views to their logical conclusion. There appears to be no reason why (allowing for the possibility of a few additions) the *first* edition of the Pentateuch as a comprehensive work should not also have been the *final* edition, a work composed by a single historian. In all Pentateuchal study up to the present time it has been assumed that it is possible to detect the activity of successive redactors or editors. Yet the variety of conclusions which have been reached by scholars from the time of Wellhausen onwards, of which the results obtained by such scholars as Van Seters are but the latest examples, arouses the suspicion that the methods employed are extremely subjective. The analogy with Herodotus suggests that insufficient allowance has been made for deliberate variations of style and compositional method on the part of a single author.

The recent application of the techniques of modern literary criticism to the study of the Old Testament has served to emphasize the literary qualities of the Pentateuch understood as a single composition. The appreciation of the Bible as literature dates back a very long way; but until quite recently biblical scholars seemed to be unaware of the possibility that the techniques developed by the literary critics for understanding and appraising literary works might be profitably applied to it. Among the first to appreciate this were Alonso Schökel (in publications from 1960 onwards) and Muilenburg (from 1953). In 1969 the latter proposed a 'new' method of Old Testament study which he called 'rhetorical criticism', and so stimulated a whole generation of younger scholars to engage in the attempt to understand the nature of Hebrew literary composition by studying its structural patterns and the various devices by which these are achieved.

Since about 1974 numerous studies of this kind have been published, too numerous to mention here. In many cases these authors have made use of the insights and techniques of modern literary criticism, following a variety of approaches to the literature according to their predilection for one critical 'school' or another. The increasing public interest generated by these new approaches has encouraged some professional literary critics to turn their attention to the literature of the biblical books.

To some extent this new movement has been 'atomistic': the vast majority of these studies have confined themselves to relatively short narratives or poems rather than to the larger literary compositions such as the Pentatuech as a whole. However, the new appreciation of the literary qualities of the biblical narratives has now drawn attention to the possibility that the same techniques which were used to create the smaller narrative units might also have been used on a larger scale.

This new development is well illustrated in Alter's *The Art of Biblical Narrative* (1981), the work of a professional literary critic (in the modern sense of the term). Much of this work is devoted to the study of the Pentateuch. Although Alter does not offer a comprehensive interpretation of the meaning or 'message' of the Pentateuch as a whole, he argues convincingly that the same literary activity can be discerned in both the tiniest units and in the way in which they have been combined. For example, while Gen. 1.1–2.4a ('P') and 2.4b–3.24 ('J') are each subtle, finished literary compositions, their juxtaposition in the present text is not part of a clumsy dovetailing by a 'redactor' who felt himself bound to bow to two conflicting traditions and to include both despite their mutual contradictions, but was a deliberate act of 'montage' (a term derived from film-making) by a literary artist who felt the desirability of presenting his readers with a strong contrast which could enhance the meanings and qualities of both—a procedure, it may be noted, which was adopted by Herodotus, who frequently juxtaposed two contradictory accounts of the same episode. This emphasis on the 'rightness' by which Gen. 2 follows Gen. 1 asserts the irrelevance of the view of the documentary critics that Gen. 5.1 is the 'true' continuation of 2.4a because they both belong to P, while the intervening material belongs to J.

A further feature of Alter's approach is his view, based on purely aesthetic considerations, that many of the 'contradictions' which caused the documentary critics to separate one document from another may not have been felt to be contradictions at all, or, if they were, were felt to be of secondary importance to the author's main purpose: 'We may not fully understand what would have been perceived as a real contradiction by an intelligent Hebrew writer of the early Iron Age, so that apparently conflicting versions of the same event set side by side, far from troubling the original audience, may have been sometimes perfectly justified in a kind of logic which we no longer apprehend' (p. 20). In the case of 'contradictions' *within* a narrative, as in Gen. 42, where verses 27-28 appear to conflict with verse 35, he suggests that 'the Hebrew writer was perfectly aware of the contradiction but viewed it as a superficial one' (p. 138).

Alter does not offer a comprehensive interpretation of the Pentateuch as a whole, nor does he directly discuss the question of single authorship. For him it appears to be a question of secondary importance whether the literary artistry which he finds in the

Pentateuch is that of an author or of a redactor. But his view of the major narrative complexes of the Old Testament, including the Pentateuch, as complete and satisfying literary creations carrying a clear and purposeful message is certainly compatible with a theory of single authorship for the Pentateuch, and indeed provides a detailed picture of what such an author might have been seeking to achieve, and of the methods by which he carried out his intentions. As a literary critic, Alter regards these biblical works as examples of the 'literary imagination' which, in all literary compositions, always involves 'some deep intuition of art that finely interweaves, shaping a complex and meaningful whole which is more than the sum of its parts'.

It is of course easier to demonstrate the inadequacies of earlier attempts to understand how such a work as the Pentateuch was composed than to construct a convincing alternative. But the increasing recognition by a growing number of scholars—despite many differences between them—that the Pentateuch as it has come down to us cannot have come into being without the direction of a controlling genius points towards a more realistic approach to this literary work than has previously been achieved. Much, however, remains to be done, and this alternative hypothesis remains tentative.

B. *The Sources*

The hypothesis of a single author for the Pentateuch does not solve the question of his sources. Indeed, the analogy of the Greek historians suggests that the identification of these sources may be an intractable problem. Since in the case of the Pentateuch there is no corroborative evidence on the matter available in external sources, and since the author himself makes few references to his sources of information, only the internal evidence of style, composition and subject-matter comes under consideration. But, as has been suggested above, these can be misleading. The inventiveness of the author has been underestimated.

It is agreed by all critical scholars that the Pentateuch in its final form cannot have been completed before the sixth century BC. Can it be shown that any of the sources used by the author is significantly earlier than that time?

With regard to oral sources, two facts have emerged from the discussion in Part II above which are relevant to this topic: firstly, there is no assured way of distinguishing written from orally based literature; and secondly, even if it were possible to identify oral traditions in the Pentateuchal narratives, none of the techniques which have been devised is capable of demonstrating the *antiquity* of such traditions in relation to the date of the final completion of the Pentateuch. In fact, such evidence about living oral tradition as we possess suggests that the likelihood of the preservation of oral narratives in recognizable form over a long period of time is extremely remote.

Neither of these considerations, needless to say, precludes the possibility that oral traditions of some kind have been used in the composition of the Pentateuch. Indeed, since ancient Israel no doubt possessed such traditions like any other people, this is probable. But we have no certain method by which their antiquity can be discovered.

With regard to written sources, the rejection of the Documentary Hypothesis simply increases the range of possibilities. The Pentateuch may have incorporated already existing works in their entirety without alteration, or, alternatively, earlier written works may have been excerpted, adapted, expanded, summarized, or simply used as source-material in much the same manner as modern historians (and ancient ones) have used them. Indeed, all these methods may have been employed in different parts of the work. These written materials may have been long or short, few or numerous: the only thing which may be regarded as certain is that they were not comprehensive documents like J, E and P combined into a single narrative by a series of redactors.

As to the dates when such written sources might have been composed, no dates subsequent to the events described can be ruled out *a priori*: there was nothing in the circumstances of Israel at any period which would have made it impossible for narratives about past or contemporary events to be composed in writing. The virtual absence from the narrative sections of the Pentateuch of any hint of the identity of the authors of any part of them leaves the question entirely open.

The advocates of theories of a long period of growth of the Pentateuchal narratives have often pointed to the great varieties of style, treatment and underlying purpose or theme to be found in different parts of the work as proof of both composite authorship and complexity of the process of composition. This consideration, if valid, would apply as much to redactional composition (that is, the combination of written sources) as to oral composition. It has been argued on this basis that such complexity could only be the result of a very lengthy process in which one literary (or oral) unit after another was brought into association with others in the interest, at each of these stages, of a new concept, purpose or 'theology', until the final stage was reached, with its own 'theology', though with no attempt at any stage either to produce any kind of stylistic unity for the whole or to eliminate the traces of earlier 'theologies', which have thus been left for the modern investigator to discover. It must, however, be asked whether this is the only, or even the most probable, explanation of the phenomena.

That these differences of both style and theology exist is undoubtedly the case. Within the book of Genesis alone, there are at least four different sections each markedly different in character: the *Urgeschichte* (Gen. 1-11), the history of Abraham, the history of Jacob, and the history of Joseph. The first of these is a history of the origins of the world, the human race and human culture which is in many ways related to the myths of the surrounding nations, yet has its own Israelite flavour. The second and third, the patriarchal stories, are stories about particular named individuals and their immediate families living in partial isolation from their neighbours, in which, although the divine and the miraculous still play a part, the manner of life depicted is the familiar one of every day. Yet even within these patriarchal stories there are differences: the Abraham stories are more episodic and less closely knit than those of Jacob; and within the Jacob stories themselves the main character is depicted in two different ways in clearly defined parts of the story. The story of Joseph has the marks of a single, carefully structured and articulated novel-like work. Even more striking than these differences is the transition from Genesis to Exodus. If the world of the patriarchs is a different 'world' from that of the *Urgeschichte*, this is equally true of Genesis on the one hand and the books which follow it on the other. In the latter the 'sons of Israel' are now a people, not simply a family, and the stories told are presented as the history of a people. Within these books (Exodus, Leviticus, Numbers) there are again different 'worlds'—the world of the sojourn in Egypt and the Exodus, that of the wandering life in the wilderness, and that of the events at Sinai. Moreover, a very large part of these books consists of extensive bodies of law which have been embedded in the narrative text.

One thing is clear: however we conceive of the date, identity and purpose of the final author, redactor or editor of the Pentateuch, his notion of a literary work did not include a concern for such modern literary concepts as consistency of thought or smoothness and unity of style: the Pentateuch in its final form is concrete proof of this. The existence of such varied material cheek by jowl was evidently entirely congruent with his notion of a history.

The fact that the early literature of the Old Testament shows no awareness of the Pentateuchal story as a whole, and that those themes which are attested early (such as the deliverance from Egypt, the crossing of the Sea and Israel's special relationship with Yahweh) are there expressed mainly in terms different from those in which they are expressed in the Pentateuch suggests that there was a rich vein of folklore and of folklore motifs in Israel of which what has survived is no more than a selection. But if the 'little creed' in Deut. 26 is, as is now generally believed, a creation of the Deuteronomists, there is no evidence that any attempt was made before their time to collect together the various scraps of tradition and to form them into a continuous story. It is in the framework of Deuteronomy, the Deuteronomistic History, the late 'historical psalms' (78, 105, 106, 136) and the historical surveys of the books of Ezra and Nehemiah that we first find such a picture of an historical continuum.

If it may be supposed that the author of the Pentateuch was in some sense an historian rather than simply a writer of fiction, it is probable that, like the other historians of his day, he used many folk traditions of this kind current in his time for the composition of his history, just as he clearly must have done with the poems which he occasionally incorporated into his prose work. Some of his sources were probably in written form: this is likely to be true of at least some of the laws, and of some of the longer narrative complexes.

The prose sections of the book of Job may give a clue to the nature of some of the material which came to his hand, and perhaps to the use which he made of it. The prologue and epilogue of Job are generally believed to be a folktale, or at least to be based on one. Opinions differ about the extent to which the author of the poem of Job was responsible for the final form of the prose story. Now it has frequently been observed that Job, as presented in this story, is a 'patriarchal' figure whose character and way of life strongly resemble those of Abraham and his family as depicted in Genesis. Some scholars, indeed, consider that the story is a deliberate imitation of the patriarchal stories of Genesis: a kind of *pastiche*. The fact that it has not been suggested that, on the contrary, it is the Abraham or Jacob stories which are modelled on the Job story reflects a deepseated *a priori* conviction about the antiquity of the patriarchal traditions of Genesis.

In fact there is no reason to believe that Job is modelled on Abraham or Jacob or *vice versa*. Stories about wealthy but righteous pastoralists may well have been in circulation at almost any period in certain regions of the ancient Near East. The Job story, perhaps in an earlier form, may well be representative of the kind of raw material which was available to the author of the Pentateuch. In fact he chose the figure of Abraham rather than that of Job or of some other such figure presumably because it suited his purpose better. He may have been able to make use of an already growing tendency, which seems to have begun with the Exile, to make of this particular typical folktale figure an archetypal person to whom various gifts and promises had been made by God: as God's chosen one and friend (Isa. 41.8); as blessed and endowed with numerous progeny (Isa. 51.2); as inheritor of the land (Ezek. 33.24; cf. Isa. 63.16). These versions of the theme he could then have combined into one, making Abraham one of the key figures for that part of his work which spans the period between the origins of mankind and the sojourn in Egypt. There is no reason to suppose that these folktales or motifs which he used had originated at some remote period. It is only their present position in the Pentateuch which represents the 'patriarchs' as Israel's remote ancestors and so creates that impression. Indeed, as Van Seters pointed out, the references to Ur of the Chaldees in Gen. 11.28; 15.7 as Abraham's original home would seem to point to the sixth century BC as the time of origin of the story of his migration to Palestine.

What use did the author of the Pentateuch make of these folktales and motifs, and to what extent was he dependent on them? The analogy with the early Greek historians would suggest that they may have been no more than the raw materials of his narrative, and that allowance should be made for the possibility that he not only retold them in quite new ways, but invented some of them himself, imitating the genres of the original ones. It is perhaps unlikely that he should have found such quantities of folktales about these figures already to hand.

It is strange that these possibilities should have received so little attention in Pentateuchal scholarship. Fiction is, after all, a major genre in the Old Testament. Much but not all of it consists of stories about persons who had already appeared in some capacity, major or minor, in earlier traditions.

It is well established that a large proportion of the narratives in the Pentateuch are fiction. The most prominent example is the story of Joseph (Gen. 37–50), which constitutes a large part of the book of Genesis. Its length and literary qualities have earned for this narrative the designation 'novella'. Further, as Gunkel already realized, Gen. 24 also exhibits the same characteristics on a smaller scale. Exod. 32, the story of the Golden Calf, is believed by many scholars to be, at least in its present form, a polemical narrative invented for the purpose of condemning the religious policy of Jeroboam I, rather than an ancient Mosaic tradition. Again, Num. 16, the story of the rebellion of Korah, Dathan and Abiram against Moses, is believed to be in some way related to conflicts about qualifications for the priesthood which occurred many centuries after the time of Moses. Other examples could be given: indeed, the whole presentation of Moses in the Pentateuch in its present form may be described as the religious fiction of a later time.

Outside the Pentateuch, at least the prologue and epilogue of Job, the books of Ruth, Jonah, Esther, Dan. 1–6 and large parts of the books of Chronicles are examples of literary fiction. Of these, Ruth, Jonah, Daniel 1–6 and the additional material in Chronicles are attached to figures found elsewhere in the Old Testament; Job and Esther are not. The setting of the Job story, as has already been remarked, resembles those of the patriarchs in Genesis; Ruth has something of the flavour of some of the stories in Judges, and its first words ('In the days when the judges ruled there was a famine in the land. . .') attest a deliberate *pastiche* and an intention to embellish the collection of judge-stories. The special material in Chronicles—for example, the account in 1 Chron. 22–29 of David's preparations for the building and staffing of the temple to be built in Jerusalem— provides a good example of the fictitious expansion and 'embellishment' of older materal. Jonah, Esther and Dan. 1–6 are early examples of the haggadic tendency or midrash which remained one of the most notable literary forms of Jewish literature for many centuries afterwards.

In view of these varied examples of fictional writing in the Old Testament, not least in the Pentateuch itself, the reluctance of scholars to admit the possibility that some of the other Pentateuchal narratives about Abraham, Jacob, Moses and other figures may also be late fiction is surprising. It is presumably the form of the work as a whole, its disjointedness, and the traditional forms in which many of the component stories are couched which account for this. Although parts of the Pentateuch such as the Joseph story were early recognized as being well-constructed literary works of fiction comparable to the books of Ruth, Jonah or Esther, the mainly brief and relatively unconnected stories in other parts looked to Gunkel and his followers like those traditional *Sagen* of European folklore which, it was thought, had been transmitted orally for many generations; and this observation set in motion the whole traditio-historical programme of the search for the history of their development into larger collections. But while the tradition-historians were correct in supposing that folk tradition of a kind underlies some of the material, they underestimated the ability of the literary artist to create his own material when he wished and to couch it in traditional forms, and also failed to notice that it was not only redactors and editors but also ancient historians who in their creative writing employed parataxis, joining units of narrative loosely together without attempting to produce smooth continuous narrative.

The criteria by which the original contributions of the Pentateuchal historian might be distinguished from his sources are difficult, if not impossible, to formulate; and, since virtually nothing can be checked from external sources (in contrast with, for example, the special material of Chronicles or some of the historical statements made by Herodotus), the task is made even more difficult. Historically, the Pentateuch exists in a kind of limbo. Attempts, for example, to find links with various periods in the second millennium BC when Moses and the patriarchs might have lived have proved fruitless.

It is admittedly possible to make some judgments about the use of sources on the basis of common sense. It is, for example, intrinsically improbable that our prose historian should have invented the laws: the composition of such extensive bodies of law lies completely outside the province of the historian. The same is true of the poems in the Pentateuch.

The situation with regard to the narrative sections, however, is quite different. The only tradition which can safely be regarded as ancient is that of the Exodus. Even here it is hardly possible, out of the whole complex of narratives which now enshrine that event in Exod. 1-15, to point to any ancient narrative which has been verbally or substantially preserved and incorporated unchanged into the present text. Like other popular traditions available to the historian, the Exodus has been buried in an enormously complex body of narrative: the deliverance from Egypt and the crossing of the Sea are themes or motifs rather than ancient narratives. It is possible that the brief Song of Miriam (Exod. 15.1), which was evidently taken over as it stood, is the nucleus of the whole pericope. Parts of Gen. 1-11, too, may be fairly closely based on sources available to the historian, but it is impossible to determine how far he has reworked them. But with regard to the patriarchal stories and the stories of Moses' leadership of the people in the wilderness there appears to be no way in which the extent of the historian's own contribution can be measured.

The Pentateuch, then, it may be suggested, is an outstanding but characteristic example of the work of an ancient historian: a history of the origins of the people of Israel, prefaced by an account of the origins of the world. The author may have intended it as a supplement (i.e. a prologue) to the work of the Deuteronomistic Historian, which dealt with the more recent period of the national history. He had at his disposal a mass of material, most of which may have been of quite recent origin and had not necessarily formed part of any ancient Israelite tradition. Following the canons of the historiography of his time, he radically reworked this material, probably with substantial additions of his own invention, making no attempt to produce a smooth narrative free from inconsistencies, contradictions and unevennesses. Judged by the standards of ancient historiography, his work stands out as a literary masterpiece.

BIBLIOGRAPHY

Ahlström, G.W.
1966   'Oral and Written Transmission. Some Considerations', *HTR* 59, pp. 69-81
Albrektson, B.
1967   *History and the Gods. An Essay on the Idea of Historical Events as Divine Manifestations in the Ancient Near East and in Israel*, Coniectanea Biblica, Old Testament Series 1, Lund
Albright, W.F.
1939   'The Israelite Conquest of Canaan in the Light of Archaeology', *BASOR* 74, pp. 11-23
Alonso-Schökel, L.
1960   'Die stilistische Analyse bei den Propheten', *Congress Volume, Oxford 1959*, VTS 7, pp. 154-64
1985   'Of Methods and Models', *Congress Volume, Salamanca 1983*, VTS 36, pp. 3-13
Alt, A.
1929   *Der Gott der Väter*, BWANT 3/12=*Kleine Schriften zur Geschichte des Volkes Israel* 1, Munich, 1959, pp. 1-78 (ET 'The God of the Fathers', *Essays on Old Testament History and Religion*, Oxford, 1966, pp. 3-77)
1934   *Die Ursprünge des israelitischen Rechts*, BVSAW, Phil.-hist. Klasse 86/1=*Kleine Schriften zur Geschichte des Volkes Israel* 1, Munich, 1959, pp. 278-332 (ET *Essays on Old Testament History* and *Religion*, Oxford, 1966, pp. 81-132)
Alter, R.
1981   *The Art of Biblical Narrative*, London
Anderson, B.W.
1972   'Martin Noth's Traditio-Historical Approach in the Context of Twentieth-Century Biblical Research', M. Noth, *A History of Pentateuchal Traditions*, Englewood Cliffs, N.J., pp. xiii-xxxii
1978   'From Analysis to Synthesis: The Interpretation of Genesis 1-11', *JBL* 97, pp. 5-22
Anderson, G.W.
1950   'Some Aspects of the Uppsala School of Old Testament Study', *HTR* 43, pp. 239-56
Baentsch, B.
1903   *Exodus-Leviticus-Numeri*, HK 1/2-4
Barthes, R.
1971   'La lutte avec l'ange: analyse textuelle de Genèse 32:23-33', R. Barthes *et al.*, *Analyse structurale et exégèse biblique. Essais d'interprétation*, Paris and Brussels, pp. 9-25 (ET 'The Struggle with the Angel: Textual Analysis of Genesis 32.23-33', R. Barthes *et al.*, *Structural Analysis and Biblical Exegesis. Interpretational Essays*, Pittsburgh Theological Monograph Series 3, Pittsburgh, 1974, pp. 21-33)
Bentzen, A.
1948   *Introduction to the Old Testament*, 2 vols in 1, Copenhagen
Berlin, A.
1983   *Poetics and Interpretation of Biblical Narrative*, Bible and Literature Series 9, Sheffield

Birkeland, H.
    1938   *Zum hebräischen Traditionswesen: Die Komposition der prophetischen Bücher des Alten Testaments*, ANVAO 2, Hist.-Filos. Kl. 1
Blum, E.
    1984   *Die Komposition der Vätergeschichte*, WMANT 57
Brekelmans, C.
    1966   'Die sogenannten deuteronomischen Elemente in Genesis bis Numeri. Ein Beitrag zur Vorgeschichte des Deuteronomiums', *Volume du Congrès, Genève, 1965*, VTS 15, pp. 90-96
Bright, J.
    1956   *Early Israel in Recent History Writing. A Study in Method*, SBT 19
Brueggemann, W.
    1972   'The Kerygma of the Priestly Writers', *ZAW* 84, pp. 397-414
Budde, K.
    1890   *Die Bücher Richter und Samuel. Ihre Quellen und ihr Aufbau*, Giessen
    1897   *Das Buch der Richter*, KHC 7
    1902   *Die Bücher Samuel*, KHC 8
Campbell, E.F.
    1975   *Ruth. A New Translation with Introduction, Notes and Commentary*, AB 7
Carlson, R.A.
    1964   *David, the Chosen King. A Traditio-Historical Approach to the Second Book of Samuel*, Stockholm
Cassuto, U.
    1961   *The Documentary Hypothesis and the Composition of the Pentateuch*, Jerusalem (ET of the original Hebrew edn, 1941)
    1967   *A Commentary on the Book of Exodus*, London (ET of the original Hebrew edn, 1951)
Cazelles, H.
    1973   *Introduction Critique à l'Ancien Testament*, Paris
Chadwick, H.M. and N.
    1932-40 *The Growth of Literature*, 3 vols, Cambridge
Childs, B.S.
    1974   *Exodus*, OTL
    1979   *Introduction to the Old Testament as Literature*, London
Clements, R.E.
    1972   *Exodus*, CBC
    1979   'Pentateuchal Problems', G.W. Anderson, ed., *Tradition and Interpretation*, Oxford, pp. 96-124
Clines, D.J.A
    1978   *The Theme of the Pentateuch*, JSOT Suppl. Series 10, Sheffield
Coats, G.W.
    1967   'The Traditio-Historical Character of the Reed Sea Motif', *VT* 17, pp. 253-65
    1968   *Rebellion in the Wilderness. The Murmuring Motif in the Wilderness Traditions of the Old Testament*, Nashville
Coats, G.W., ed.
    1985   *Saga, Legend, Tale, Novella, Fable. Narrative Forms in Old Testament Literature*, JSOT Suppl. Series 35, Sheffield
Coggins, R.J.
    1984/5   'The Literary Approach to the Bible', *ET* 96, pp. 9-14

Craghan, J.F.
1977 'The Elohist in Recent Literature', *BTB* 7, pp. 23-35
Cross, F.M., Jr
1966 'The Divine Warrior in Israel's Early Cult', A. Altmann, ed., *Biblical Motifs. Origins and Transformations*, Cambridge, Mass., pp. 11-30
1973 'The Priestly Work', *Canaanite Myth and Hebrew Epic. Essays in the History of the Religion of Israel*, Cambridge, Mass., pp. 293-325
Crüsemann, F.
1981 'Die Eigenständigkeit der Urgeschichte. Ein Beitrag zur Diskussion um den "Jahwisten"', J. Jeremias and L. Perlitt, eds., *Die Botschaft und die Boten. Festschrift für Hans Walter Wolff zum 70. Geburtstag*, Neukirchen, pp. 11-29
Culley, R.C.
1963 'An Approach to the Problem of Oral Tradition', *VT* 13, pp. 113-25
1967 *Oral Formulaic Language in the Biblical Psalms*, Near and Middle East Series 4, Toronto
1976 *Studies in the Structure of Hebrew Narrative*, Semeia Supplements, Philadelphia and Chico, California
Culley, R.C., ed.
1979 *Perspectives on Old Testament Narrative*, Semeia 15, Chico, California
Dahse, J.
1912 *Textkritische Materialen zur Hexateuchfrage* I, Giessen
Davies, G.I.
1983 'The Wilderness Itineraries and the Composition of the Pentateuch', *VT* 33, pp. 1-13
Derrida, J.
1976 *Of Grammatology*, Baltimore
Dietrich, W.
1972 *Prophetie und Geschichte. Eine redaktionsgeschichtliche Untersuchung zum deuteronomistischen Geschichtswerk*, FRLANT 108
Dornsieff, F.
1934-8 'Antikes zum Alten Testament', *ZAW* 52, pp. 57-75; 53, pp. 153-71; 55, pp. 127-36; 56, pp. 64-85
1959 'Der Verfasser des Pentateuchs', *Das Altertum*, Berlin, 5, pp. 205-13
Driver, S.R.
1896 *A Critical and Exegetical Commentary on Deuteronomy*, ICC, 2nd edn.
1904 *The Book of Genesis*, WC
1909 *An Introduction to the Literature of the Old Testament*, 8th edn, Edinburgh
Dundes, A., ed.
1965 *The Study of Folklore*, Englewood Cliffs, N.J.
Eerdmans, B.D.
1908-14 *Alttestamentliche Studien* I-IV, Giessen
Eissfeldt, O.
1922 *Hexateuch-Synopse. Die Erzählung der fünf Bücher Mose und des Buches Josua mit dem Anfange des Richterbuches in ihre vier Quellen zerlegt und in deutscher Übersetzung darboten samt einer in Einleitung und Anmerkungen gegebenen Begründung*, Leipzig
1934 *Einleitung in das Alte Testament unter Einschluss der Apokryphen und Pseudepigraphen. Entstehungsgeschichte des Alten Testaments*, Tübingen (4th edn, 1976; ET *The Old Testament: An Introduction*, Oxford, 1965)
1938 'The Literature of Israel: 3. Modern Criticism', H.W. Robinson, ed.,

Record and Revelation. Essays on the Old Testament by Members of the Society for Old Testament Study, Oxford, pp. 74-109

1950   'Die neueste Phase in der Entwicklung der Pentateuchkritik', *TR* NF 18, pp. 91-112, 179-215, 267-87

1958   *Die Genesis der Genesis. Vom Werdegang des erstes Buches der Bibel*, Tübingen (ET 'Genesis', *IDB* 2, 1962, pp. 366-80)

Elliger, K.
1952   'Sinn und Ursprung der priesterlichen Geschichtserzählung', *ZTK* 49, pp. 121-42

Emerton, J.A.
1982   'The Origin of the Promises to the Patriarchs in the Older Sources of the Book of Genesis', *VT* 32, pp. 14-32

Engnell, I.
1960   'Methodological Aspects of Old Testament Study', *Congress Volume, Oxford, 1959*, VTS 7, pp. 13-30

1969   *A Rigid Scrutiny*, Nashville = *Critical Essays on the Old Testament*, London, 1970 (ET of articles in *Svensk Bibliskt Uppslagsverk*, Stockholm, 1962, 2nd edn)

Fackre, G.
1983   'Narrative Theology. An Overview', *Interpretation* 37, pp. 340-52

Fehling, D.
1971   *Die Quellenangaben bei Herodot: Studien zur Erzählkunst Herodots*, Untersuchungen zur antiken Literatur und Geschichte 9, Berlin

Finnegan, R.
1970   *Oral Literature in Africa*, Oxford Library of African Literature, Oxford

Fohrer, G.
1955   'Zum Text von Jes. xli 8-13', *VT* 5, pp. 239-49

1964   *Überlieferung und Geschichte des Exodus. Eine Analyse von Ex. 1-15*, BZAW 91

1965   *Einleitung in das Alte Testament*, Heidelberg (ET *Introduction to the Old Testament*, Nashville, 1968)

Fohrer, G. et al.
1973   *Exegese des Alten Testaments. Einführung in die Methodik*, Heidelberg

Fretheim, T.E.
1968   'The Priestly Document: Anti-Temple?', *VT* 18, pp. 313-29

Friedman, R.E.
1981   *The Exile and Biblical Narrative: The Formation of the Deuteronomistic and Priestly Works*, Harvard Semitic Monographs 22, Chico, California.

Fritz, K. von
1967   *Die griechische Geschichtsschreibung*, vol. 1: *Von den Anfängen bis Thukydides*, Berlin

Fritz, V.
1970   *Israel in der Wüste. Traditionsgeschichtliche Untersuchung der Wüstenüberlieferung des Jahwisten*, Marburger Theologische Studien 7, Marburg

Fuss, W.
1972   *Die deuteronomistische Pentateuchredaktion in Exodus 3-17*, BZAW 126

Galling, K.
1928   *Die Erwählungstraditionen Israels*, BZAW 48

Gibson, J.C.L.
1978   *Canaanite Myths and Legends*, Edinburgh

Godley, A.D., ed.
1920   *Herodotus*, 4 vols., Loeb Classical Library, London

Gottwald, N.K.
1979   *The Tribes of Yahweh. A Sociology of the Religion of Liberated Israel 1250-1050 B.C.E.*, Maryknoll, New York (also London, 1980)
Gray, G.B.
1903   *A Critical and Exegetical Commentary on Numbers*, ICC
Greenberg, M.
1984   'The Design and Themes of Ezekiel's Program of Restoration', *Interpretation* 38, pp. 181-208
Gressmann, H.
1913   *Mose und seine Zeit. Ein Kommentar zu den Mose-Sagen*, FRLANT NF 1
Gunkel, H.
1901a   *Genesis übersetzt und erklärt*, HK 1/1 (3rd edn 1910; see also *The Legends of Genesis*)
1901b   *The Legends of Genesis. The Biblical Saga and History*, Introduction by W.F. Albright (ET of the first part of the above. Reprinted New York, 1964)
1906   'Die Grundprobleme der israelitischen Literargeschichte', *Deutsche Literaturzeitung* 27, cols. 1797-1800, 1861-66 (ET 'Fundamental Problems of Hebrew Literary History', *What Remains of the Old Testament and Other Essays*, London, 1928, pp. 57-68)
1917   *Das Märchen im Alten Testament*, Tübingen
Gunn, D.M.
1976   'On Oral Tradition: A Response to John Van Seters', *Semeia* 5, Missoula, pp. 155-63
1978   *The Story of King David. Genre and Interpretation*, JSOT Suppl. Series 6, Sheffield
1982   'The "Hardening of Pharaoh's Heart": Plot, Character and Theology in Exodus 1-14', D.J.A. Clines, D.M. Gunn and A.J. Hauser, ed., *Art and Meaning: Rhetoric in Biblical Literature*, JSOT Suppl. Series 19, Sheffield, pp. 72-96
Haran, M.
1978   *Temples and Temple-Service in Ancient Israel. An Inquiry into the Character of Cult Phenomena and the Historical Setting of the Priestly School*, Oxford
1981   'Behind the Scenes of History: Determining the Date of the Priestly Source', *JBL* 100, pp. 321-33
Hartman, G.H.
1980   *Criticism in the Wilderness*, New York
Hayes, J.H. and Miller, J.M., ed.
1977   *Israelite and Judaean History*, OTL
Hempel, J.
1930   *Die althebräische Literatur und ihr hellenistisch-jüdisches Nachleben*, Potsdam (reprinted Berlin, 1968)
Henry, M.-L.
1960   *Jahwist und Priesterschrift: zwei Glaubenszeugnisse des Alten Testaments*, Arbeiten zur Theologie 3, Stuttgart
Herrmann, S.
1968   'Mose', *EvT* 28, pp. 301-28
Hoftijzer, J.
1956   *Die Verheissungen an die drei Erzväter*, Leiden

Hölscher, G.
1923	'Das Buch der Könige, seine Quellen und seine Redaktion', *Gunkel-Eucharisterion* I, FRLANT 36/1, pp. 158-213
1942	*Die Anfänge der hebräischen Geschichtsschreibung*, Heidelberg
1952	*Geschichtsschreibung in Israel. Untersuchungen zum Jahvisten und Elohisten*, Lund
Holzinger, H.
1893	*Einleitung in den Hexateuch*, Freiburg i. B. and Leipzig
1900	*Exodus*, KHC 2
Hurvitz, A.
1982	*A Linguistic Study of the Relationship between the Priestly Source and the Book of Ezekiel*, Cahiers de la *Revue Biblique* 20, Paris
Hyatt, J.P.
1971	*Exodus*, NCB
Jacoby, F.
1949	*Atthis. The Local Chronicles of Ancient Athens*, Oxford
1957	*Die Fragmente der griechischen Historiker*, 2nd edn, 2 vols, Leiden (1st edn Berlin, 1922)
Jaroš, K.
1974	*Die Stellung des Elohisten zur kanaanitischen Religion*, OBO 4
Jobling, D.
1978	*The Sense of Biblical Narrative. Three Structural Analyses in the Old Testament*, JSOT Suppl. Series 7, Sheffield
Jolles, A.
1930	*Einfache Formen: Legende/Sage/Mythe/Rätsel/Kasus/Memorabile/Märchen/Witz*, Tübingen (reprinted 1958)
Kaiser, O.
1969	*Einleitung in das Alte Testament. Eine Einführung in ihre Ergebnisse und Probleme*, Gütersloh (ET [revised] *Introduction to the Old Testament. A Presentation of its Results and Problems*, Oxford, 1975)
Kikawada, I.M. and Quinn, A.
1985	*Before Abraham Was. The Unity of Genesis 1-11*, Nashville
Kilian, R.
1966	*Die vorpriesterlichen Abrahams-Überlieferungen*, BBB 24
Kirk, G.S.
1962	*The Songs of Homer*, Cambridge
1975	'The Iliad and Odyssey as Traditional Oral Poems', *CAH*[3], vol. 2, part 2, Cambridge, pp. 821-28
Klein, H.
1977	'Ort und Zeit des Elohisten', *EvT* 37, pp. 247-60
Klein, R.W.
1981	'The Message of P', J. Jeremias and L. Perlitt, eds., *Die Botschaft und die Boten. Festschrift für Hans Walter Wolff*, Neukirchen, pp. 57-66
Knight, D.A.
1973	*Rediscovering the Traditions of Israel. The Development of the Traditio-Historical Research of the Old Testament, with Special Consideration of Scandinavian Contributions*, SBL Dissertation Series 9, Missoula
Koch, K.
1967	*Was ist Formgeschichte? Neue Wege der Bibelexegese*, 2nd edn, Neukirchen (ET *The Growth of the Biblical Tradition. The Form-Critical Method*, London and New York, 1969)

Kraus, H.-J.
  1952   'Der gegenwärtige Stand der Forschung am Alten Testament', *Die Freiheit des Evangeliums und die Ordnung der Gesellschaft*, BEvT 15, pp. 103-32
  1956   'Zur Geschichte des Überlieferungsbegriffs in der alttestamentlichen Wissenschaft', *EvT* 16, pp. 371-87
  1969   *Geschichte der historisch-kritischen Erforschung des Alten Testaments*, 2nd edn, Neukirchen
Kutscher, E.Y.
  1982   *A History of the Hebrew Language*, Jerusalem and Leiden
Laing, S.
  1964   *Heimskringla: Sagas of the Norse Kings*, Everyman's Library 847, London
Larsson, G.
  1983   'The Chronology of the Pentateuch: A Comparison of the MT and LXX', *JBL* 102, pp. 401-409
Lemche, N.P.
  1980   'The Chronology in the Story of the Flood', *JSOT* 18, pp. 52-62
Licht, J.
  1978   *Storytelling in the Bible*, Jerusalem
Loewenstamm, S.E.
  1965   *The Tradition of the Exodus and its Development*, Jerusalem (Hebrew)
Lohfink, N.
  1967   *Die Landverheissung als Eid. Eine Studie zu Gn 15*, SBS 28
Long, B.O.
  1976   'Recent Field Studies in Oral Literature and their Bearing on OT Criticism', *VT* 26, pp. 187-98
Lord, A.B.
  1960   *The Singer of Tales*, Harvard Studies in Comparative Literature 24, Cambridge, Mass.
Lüthi, M.
  1961   *Volksmärchen und Volkssage. Zwei Grundformen erzählender Dichtung*, Berne and Munich (2nd edn 1966)
McCarthy, D.
  1965   'Moses's Dealings with Pharaoh: Ex 7:8–10:27', *CBQ* 27, pp. 336-47
McEvenue, S.E.
  1971   *The Narrative Style of the Priestly Writer*, Analecta Biblica 50, Rome
McFadyen, J.E.
  1925   'The Present Position of Old Testament Criticism', A.S. Peake, ed., *The People and the Book*, Oxford, pp. 183-219
McKane, W.
  1979   *Studies in the Patriarchal Narratives*, Edinburgh
McNeile, A.H.
  1917   *The Book of Exodus*, WC, 2nd edn
McTurk, R.W.
  1981   '"Cynewulf and Cyneheard" and the Icelandic Sagas', *Leeds Studies in English*, NS 12, pp. 81-127
Martin, W.J.
  1955   *Stylistic Criteria and the Analysis of the Pentateuch*, London
Mayes, A.D.H.
  1983   *The Story of Israel between Settlement and Exile. A Redactional Study of the Deuteronomistic History*, London

The Making of the Pentateuch

Mendenhall, G.E.
  1962   'The Hebrew Conquest of Palestine', *BA* 25, pp. 66-87 = E.F. Campbell,
          Jr and D.N. Freedman, ed., *The Biblical Archaeologist Reader* 3, New
          York, pp. 100-20
Meyer, E.
  1906   *Die Israeliten und ihre Nachbarstämme*, Halle (reprinted Darmstadt,
          1967)
Michaeli, F.
  1974   *Le livre de l'Exode*, CAT 11
Millard, A.R.
  1972   'The Practice of Writing in Ancient Israel', *BA* 35, pp. 98-111
Miscall, P.D.
  1983   *The Workings of Old Testament Narrative*, Semeia Studies, Philadelphia
          and Chico, California
Moberly, R.W.L.
  1983   *At the Mountain of God. Story and Theology in Exodus 32-34*, JSOT
          Suppl. Series, 22, Sheffield
Morgenstern, J.
  1927   'The Oldest Document of the Hexateuch', *HUCA* 4, pp. 1-138
Mowinckel, S.
  1930   'Der Ursprung der Bil'amsage', *ZAW* 48, pp. 233-71
  1946   *Prophecy and Tradition: The Prophetic Books in the Light of the Growth
          and History of the Tradition*, ANVAO 2, Hist.-filos. Kl. 3
  1951   'Die vermeintliche "Passahlegende" Ex. 1-15 in Bezug auf die Frage:
          Literarkritik und Traditionskritik', *StTh* 5, pp. 66-88
  1964a   *Erwägungen zur Pentateuch Quellenfrage*, Trondheim
  1964b   *Tetrateuch-Pentateuch-Hexateuch. Die Berichte über die Landnahme in
          den drei israelitischen Geschichtswerken*, BZAW 90
Muilenburg, J.
  1953   'A Study in Hebrew Rhetoric: Repetition and Style', *Congress Volume,
          Copenhagen, 1953*, VTS 1, pp. 97-111
  1969   'Form Criticism and Beyond', *JBL* 88, pp. 1-18
Myres, J.L.
  1953   *Herodotus: Father of History*, Oxford
Niedner, F.
  1920-30 *Altnordische Dichtung und Prosa*, 24 vols, Jena
Nielsen, E.
  1954   *Oral Tradition. A Modern Problem in Old Testament Introduction*, SBT 11
          (a translation of articles published in *Dansk Teologisk Tidsskrift*, 1950 and
          1952)
  1955   *Schechem. A Traditio-Historical Investigation*, Copenhagen
  1965   *Die zehn Gebote. Eine traditionsgeschichtliche Skizze*, Copenhagen (ET
          *The Ten Commandments in New Perspective. A Traditio-Historical
          Approach*, SBT, 2nd Series 7, 1968)
  1984   'The Traditio-historical Study of the Pentateuch since 1945, with Special
          Emphasis on Scandinavia', K. Jeppesen and B. Otzen, eds., *The
          Productions of Time. Tradition History in Old Testament Scholarship*,
          Sheffield
North, C.R.
  1946   *The Old Testament Interpretation of History*, London
  1949/50 'Living Issues in Biblical Scholarship: The Place of Oral Tradition in the
          Growth of the Old Testament', *ET* 61, pp. 292-96

Bibliography 251

1951 'Pentateuchal Criticism', H.H. Rowley, ed., *The Old Testament and Modern Study*, Oxford, pp. 48-83

Noth, M.
1940 *Die Gesetze im Pentateuch. Ihre Voraussetzungen und ihr Sinn*, Halle=*Gesammelte Studien zum Alten Testament*, TBAT 6, 1957, pp. 9-141 (*ET* 'The Laws in the Pentateuch: Their Assumptions and Meaning', *The Laws in the Pentateuch and Other Studies*, Edinburgh and London, 1966, pp. 1-107)
1943 *Überlieferungsgeschichtliche Studien*, Schriften der Königsberger Gelehrten Gesellschaft, Geisteswissenschaftliche Klasse 18, pp. 43-266, reprinted Tübingen, 1957 (ET of pp. 1-110: *The Deuteronomistic History*, JSOT Suppl. Series 15, Sheffield, 1981)
1948 *Überlieferungsgeschichte des Pentateuch*, Stuttgart (ET *A History of Pentateuchal Traditions*, Englewood Cliffs, N.J., 1972)
1959 *Das zweite Buch Mose, Exodus*, ATD 5 (ET *Exodus. A Commentary*, OTL, 1962)
1960 'Der Beitrag der Archäologie zur Geschichte Israels', VTS 7, pp. 262-82=*Aufsätze zur biblischen Landes- und Altertumskunde*, Neukirchen, 1971, pp. 34-51

Nyberg, H.S.
1935 *Studien zum Hoseabuche. Zugleich ein Beitrag zur Klärung des Problems der alttestamentlichen Textkritik*, UUÅ 1935:6

Ohler, A.
1972 *Gattungen im AT. Ein biblisches Arbeitsbuch*, vol. 1, Düsseldorf (ET *Studying the Old Testament: From Tradition to Canon*, Edinburgh, 1985)

Olrik, A.
1908 'Episke love i folkedigtningen', *Danske Studier*, pp. 69-89
1909 'Epische Gesetze der Volksdichtung', *ZDA* 51, pp. 1-12 (ET 'Epic Laws of Folk Narrative', A. Dundes, ed., *The Study of Folklore*, Berkeley, California, 1965, pp. 129-41)
1921 *Nogle grundsaetninger for sagnforskning*, Danske folkeminder 23, Copenhagen

Osswald, E.
1962 *Das Bild des Mose in der kritischen alttestamentlichen Wissenschaft seit Julius Wellhausen*, Theologische Arbeiten 18, Berlin

Otto, E.
1977 'Stehen wir vor einem Umbruch in der Pentateuchkritik?', W.H. Schmidt, ed., *Verkündigung und Forschung*, BEvT 22, pp. 82-97

Parry, M.
1932 'Studies in the Epic Technique of Oral Verse Making II. "The Homeric Language" as the Language of Oral Poetry', *Harvard Studies in Classical Philology* 43, pp. 1-50=Parry, A., ed., *The Making of Homeric Verse. The Collected Papers of Milman Parry*, Oxford, 1971, pp. 325-64
1971 *The Making of Homeric Verse. The Collected Papers of Milman Parry*, with an introduction by A. Parry, Oxford

Patte, D., ed.
1980 *Genesis 2 and 3. Kaleidoscopic Structural Readings*, Semeia 18, SBL

Pearson, L.
1939 *Early Ionian Historians*, Oxford
1942 *The Local Historians of Attica*, Philological Monographs published by the American Philological Association, 11, Philadelphia

Pedersen, J.
1926   *Israel I-II*, London and Copenhagen (translated from the Danish original of 1920. Reprinted 1946)
1931   'Die Auffassung vom Alten Testament', *ZAW* 49, pp. 161-81
1934   'Passahfest und Passahlegende', *ZAW* 52, pp. 161-75
1940   *Israel III-IV*, London and Copenhagen (translated from the Danish original of 1934; reprinted 1947)
Perlitt, L.
1965   *Vatke und Wellhausen. Geschichtsphilosophische Voraussetzungen und historiographische Motive für die Darstellung der Religion und Geschichte Israels durch Wilhelm Vatke und Julius Wellhausen*, BZAW 94
1969   *Bundestheologie im Alten Testament*, WMANT 36
Petsch, R.
1932   'Die Lehre von den "Einfachen Formen"', *Deutsche Vierteljahrsschrift für Literaturwissenschaft und Geistesgeschichte* 10, pp. 335-69
Pfeiffer, R.H.
1930   'A Non-Israelitic Source of the Book of Genesis', *ZAW* 48, pp. 66-73
1941   *Introduction to the Old Testament*, New York (reprinted 1948)
Ploeg, J. van der
1947   'Le rôle de la tradition orale dans la transmission du texte de l'Ancien Testament', *RB* 54, pp. 5-41
Plöger, J.G.
1967   *Literarkritische, formgeschichtliche und stilistische Untersuchungen zum Deuteronomium*, BBB 26
Procksch, O.
1906   *Das nordhebräische Sagenbuch. Die Elohimquelle*, Leipzig
Propp, V.
1968   *Morphology of the Folktale*, 2nd edn, Austin, Texas (translated from the Russian edition of 1928)
Rad, G. von
1934a   *Die Priesterschrift im Hexateuch literarisch untersucht und theologisch gewertet*, BWANT 65
1934b   'Die Theologie der Priesterschrift', *Die Priesterschrift im Hexateuch*, BWANT 65, pp. 166-89 = *Gesammelte Studien zum Alten Testament* II, TBAT 48, 1973, pp. 165-88
1938   *Das formgeschichtliche Problem des Hexateuch*, BWANT 26 = *Gesammelte Studien zum Alten Testament*, TBAT 8, 1958, pp. 9-86 (ET 'The Form-Critical Problem of the Hexateuch', *The Problem of the Hexateuch and Other Essays*, Edinburgh and London, 1966, pp. 1-78)
1944   'Der Anfang der Geschichtsschreibung im alten Israel', *Archiv für Kulturgeschichte* 32, pp. 1-42 = *Gesammelte Studien zum Alten Testament*, TBAT 8, 1958, pp. 148-88 (ET 'The Beginnings of Historical Writing in Ancient Israel', *The Problem of the Hexateuch and Other Essays*, Edinburgh and London, 1966, pp. 166-204)
1953   'Josephsgeschichte und ältere Chokma', *Congress Volume, Copenhagen, 1953*, VTS 1, pp. 120-27 = *Gesammelte Studien zum Alten Testament*, TBAT 8, 1958, pp. 272-80 (ET 'The Joseph Narrative and Ancient Wisdom', *The Problem of the Hexateuch and Other Essays*, Edinburgh and London, 1966, pp. 292-300)
1956   *Das erste Buch Mose, Genesis*, ATD 2-4 (9th edn 1972; ET *Genesis*, OTL, 1972)

1971 'Beobachtungen an der Moseerzählung Exodus 1–14', *EvT* 31, pp. 579-88 = *Gesammelte Studien zum Alten Testament* II, TBAT 48, 1973, pp. 189-98

Rast, W.E.
1972 *Tradition History and the Old Testament*, Guides to Biblical Scholarship, Old Testament Series, Philadelphia

Redford, D.B.
1970 *A Study of the Biblical Story of Joseph (Genesis 37–50)*, VTS 20

Rendtorff, R.
1967 'Literarkritik und Traditionsgeschichte', *EvT* 27, pp. 138-53
1969 'Traditio-Historical Method and the Documentary Hypothesis', *Proceedings of the Fifth World Congress of Jewish Studies*, I, Jerusalem, pp. 5-11
1975a 'Der "Jahwist" als Theologe? Zum Dilemma der Pentateuchkritik', *Congress Volume, Edinburgh 1974*, VTS 28, pp. 158-66 (ET 'The "Yahwist" as Theologian? The Dilemma of Pentateuchal Criticism', *JSOT* 3, 1977, pp. 2-10—with responses by R.N. Whybray, J. Van Seters, N.E. Wagner, G.E. Coats and H.H. Schmid, and a reply by Rendtorff)
1975b 'Mose als Religionsstifter? Ein Beitrag zur Diskussion über die Anfänge der israelitischen Religion', *Gesammelte Studien zum Alten Testament*, TBAT 57, pp. 152-71
1977 *Das überlieferungsgeschichtliche Problem des Pentateuch*, BZAW 147
1982 'Jakob in Bethel. Beobachtungen zum Aufbau und zur Quellenfrage in Gen 28, 10-22', *ZAW* 94, pp. 511-23
1983 *Das Alte Testament. Eine Einführung*, Neukirchen

Richter, W.
1971 *Exegese als Literaturwissenschaft. Entwurf einer alttestamentlichen Literaturtheorie und Methodologie*, Göttingen

Ringgren, H.
1949 'Oral and Written Transmission in the Old Testament. Some Observations', *StTh* 3, pp. 34-59
1966 'Literarkritik, Formgeschichte, Überlieferungsgeschichte. Erwägungen zur Methodenfrage der alttestamentlichen Exegese', *TLZ* 91, cols. 641-50

Robinson, T.H.
1925 'The Methods of Higher Criticism', A.S. Peake, ed., *The People and the Book*, Oxford, pp. 151-82

Rose, M.
1975 *Der Ausschliesslichkeitsanspruch Jahwes*, BWANT 106
1981 *Deuteronomist und Jahwist. Untersuchungen zu den Berührungspunkten beider Literarwerke*, ATANT 67

Rudolph, W.
1938 *Der "Elohist" von Exodus bis Josua*, BZAW 68

Rylaarsdam, J.C.
1952 *The Book of Exodus*, IB I, pp. 833-1099

Saebø, M.
1981 'Priestertheologie und Priesterschrift. Zur Eigenart der priesterlichen Schicht im Pentateuch', *Congress Volume, Vienna, 1980*, VTS 32, pp. 357-74

Sandmel, S.
1961 'The Haggada Within Scripture', *JBL* 80, pp. 105-22

Schmid, H.H.
1976	*Der sogenannte Jahwist*, Zurich
1981	'Auf der Suche nach neuen Perspektiven für die Pentateuchforschung',
	Congress Volume, Vienna, 1980, VTS 32, pp. 375-94
Schmidt, L.
1963	*Die Volkserzählung. Märchen, Sage, Legende, Schwank*, Berlin
Schmidt, W.H.
1974-7	*Exodus*, BKAT 2/1,2
1979	*Einführung in das Alte Testament*, Berlin
1981	'Ein Theologe in salomonischer Zeit?—Plädoyer für Jahwisten', *BZ* NS
	25, pp. 82-102 (ET 'A Theologian of the Solomonic Era? A Plea for the
	Yahwist', T. Ishida, ed., *Studies in the Period of David and Solomon*,
	Tokyo, 1982, pp. 55-73)
1983	*Exodus, Sinai und Mose. Erwägungen zu Ex 1-19 und 24*, Erträge der
	Forschung 191, Darmstadt
Schmitt, H.-C.
1980	*Die nichtpriesterliche Josephsgeschichte*, BZAW 154
1985	'Die Hintergründe der "neuesten Pentateuchkritik" und der literarische
	Befund der Josephsgeschichte Gen 37-50', *ZAW* 97, pp. 161-79
Schrey, H.-H.
1951	'Die alttestamentliche Forschung der sogenannten Uppsala-Schule', *TZ*
	7, pp. 321-41
Schulte, H.
1972	*Die Entstehung der Geschichtsschreibung im alten Israel*, BZAW 128
Schüpphaus, J.
1975	'Volk Gottes und Gesetz beim Elohisten', *TZ* 31, pp. 193-210
Scullion, J.J.
1984	'*Märchen, Sage, Legende*: Towards a Clarification of Some Literary
	Terms Used by Old Testament Scholars', *VT* 34, pp. 321-36
Segal, M.H.
1967	*The Pentateuch. Its Composition and its Authorship and Other Biblical
	Studies*, Jerusalem
Silberman, L.H.
1983	'Listening to the Text', *JBL* 102, pp. 3-26
Simpson, C.A.
1948	*The Early Traditions of Israel. A Critical Analysis of the Pre-Deuteronomic
	Narrative of the Hexateuch*, Oxford
1952	'The Growth of the Hexateuch', *IB* I, pp. 185-200
Simpson, D.C.
1924	*Pentateuchal Criticism*, Oxford
Skinner, J.
1910	*A Critical and Exegetical Commentary on Genesis*, ICC (2nd edn 1930)
1914	*The Divine Names in Genesis*, London
Smend, R.[1]
1912	*Die Erzählung des Hexateuch auf ihre Quellen untersucht*, Berlin
Smend, R.[2]
1978	*Die Entstehung des Alten Testaments*, Stuttgart
Soggin, J.A.
1976	*Introduction to the Old Testament*, OTL (translated from *Introduzione
	all'Antico Testamento*, 2nd edn, Brescia, 1974)
1981	*Judges. A Commentary*, OTL (translated from the original Italian)

Sokolov, Y.M.
  1950   *Russian Folklore*, New York
Steingrimsson, S.Ö.
  1979   *Vom Zeichen zur Geschichte. Eine literar- und formkritische Untersuchung von Ex. 6,28–11,10*, Coniectanea Biblica, OT Series 14, Lund
Tengström, S.
  1976   *Die Hexateucherzählung. Eine literaturgeschichtliche Studie*, Coniectanea Biblica, OT Series 7, Lund
Thompson, S.
  1955-8   *Motif-Index of Folk Literature*, revised edn, 6 vols, Copenhagen
Thompson, T.L.
  1974   *The Historicity of the Patriarchal Narratives*, BZAW 133
Turville-Petre, G.
  1953   *Origins of Icelandic Literature*, Oxford
Van Seters, J.
  1972   'Confessional Reformulation in the Exilic Period', *VT* 22, pp. 448-59
  1975   *Abraham in History and Tradition*, New Haven
  1983a   *In Search of History. Historiography in the Ancient World and the Origins of Biblical History*, New Haven and London
  1983b   'The Place of the Yahwist in the History of Passover and Massot', *ZAW* 95, pp. 167-82
Vater, A.M.
  1982   '"A Plague on Both Our Houses": Form- and Rhetorical-Critical Observations on Exodus 7–11', D.J.A. Clines, D.M. Gunn and A.J. Hauser, ed., *Art and Meaning: Rhetoric in Biblical Literature*, JSOT Suppl. Series 19, Sheffield, pp. 62-71
de Vaux, R.
  1953   'Réflexions sur l'état actuel de la critique du Pentateuque. A propos du second centenaire d'Astruc', *Congress Volume, Copenhagen, 1953*, VTS 1, pp. 182-98 = *Bible et Orient*, Paris, 1967, pp. 41-57
  1971, 1973   *Histoire ancienne d'Israël*, EB, 2 vols (ET *The Early History of Israel*, 2 vols, London, 1978)
Veijola, T.
  1984   'Remarks of an Outsider Concerning Scandinavian Tradition History with Emphasis on the Davidic Traditions', K. Jeppesen and B. Otzen, ed., *The Productions of Time. Tradition History in Old Testament Scholarship*, Sheffield, pp. 29-51
Volz, P. and Rudolph, W.
  1933   *Der Elohist als Erzähler. Ein Irrweg der Pentateuchkritik?*, BZAW 63
Vorländer, H.
  1978   *Die Entstehungszeit des jehowistischen Geschichtswerkes*, Europäische Hochschulschriften 23/109, Frankfurt
Wagner, N.E.
  1967   'Pentateuchal Criticism: No Clear Future', *Canadian Journal of Theology* 13, pp. 225-32
  1972   'Abraham and David?', J.W. Wevers and D.B. Redford, ed., *Studies on the Ancient Palestinian World Presented to Professor F.V. Winnett. . .*, Toronto Semitic Texts and Studies, Toronto, pp. 117-40
Watson, G.W.E.
  1984   *Classical Hebrew Poetry. A Guide to its Techniques*, JSOT Suppl. Series 26, Sheffield

Weimar, P.
    1977   *Untersuchungen zur Redaktionsgeschichte des Pentateuch*, BZAW 146
Weippert, M.
    1967   *Die Landnahme der israelitischen Stämme in der neuesten wissenschaftlichen Diskussion. Ein kritischer Bericht*, FRLANT 92 (ET *The Settlement of the Israelite Tribes in Palestine*, SBT 2nd Series, 21)
Weiser, A.
    1957   *Einleitung in das Alte Testament*, 4th edn, Göttingen (ET *Introduction to the Old Testament*, London, 1961)
Wellhausen, J.
    1883   *Prolegomena zur Geschichte Israels*, 2nd edn, Berlin (1st edn 1878 entitled *Geschichte Israels I*; 2nd edn 1883; 3rd edn 1899, reprinted 1927, 1972, 1981. ET (of 2nd edn) *Prolegomena to the History of Israel*, Edinburgh, 1885, reprinted 1957)
    1899   *Die Composition des Hexateuchs und der historischen Bücher des Alten Testaments*, 3rd edn, Berlin (reprinted as 4th edn, Berlin, 1963. First edn in article form in *Jahrbuch für deutsche Theologie*, 21-23 and in Bleek's *Einleitung*, 1876-8)
Wenham, G.J.
    1978   'The Coherence of the Flood Narrative', *VT* 28, pp. 336-48
Westermann, C.
    1964   'Arten der Erzählung in der Genesis', *Forschung am alten Testament*, TBAT 24, pp. 9-91 = *Die Verheissungen an die Väter*, FRLANT 116, 1976, pp. 9-91
    1974   *Genesis I. Genesis 1-11*, BKAT 1/1
    1976   'Die Verheissungen an die Väter', *Die Verheissungen an die Väter. Studien zur Vätergeschichte*, FRLANT 116, pp. 92-150
    1981   *Genesis II. Genesis 12-36*, BKAT 1/2
    1982   *Genesis III. Genesis 37-50*, BKAT 1/3
Whybray, R.N.
    1968   'The Joseph Story and Pentateuchal Criticism', *VT* 18, pp. 522-28
Widengren, G.
    1948   *Literary and Psychological Aspects of the Hebrew Prophets*, UUÅ 1948:10
Wilder, A.N.
    1983   'Story and Story-World', *Interpretation* 37, pp. 353-64
Willis, J.T.
    1970   'I. Engnell's Contributions to Old Testament Scholarship', *TZ* 26, pp. 385-94
Wilson, R.R.
    1984   *Sociological Approaches to the Old Testament*, Guides to Biblical Scholarship: Old Testament Series, Philadelphia
Winnett, F.V.
    1949   *The Mosaic Tradition*, Toronto
    1965   'Re-examining the Foundations', *JBL* 84, pp. 1-19
Wolff, H.W.
    1964   'Das Kerygma des Jahwisten', *EvT* 24, pp. 73-98 = *Gesammelte Studien zum Alten Testament* 2, TBAT 22, 1973, pp. 345-73 (ET 'The Kerygma of the Yahwist', *Interpretation* 20, 1966, pp. 131-58)
    1969   'Zur Thematik der elohistischen Fragmente im Pentateuch', *EvT* 27, pp. 59-72 (ET 'The Elohistic Fragments in the Pentateuch', *Interpretation* 26, 1972, pp. 158-73)

Wright, G.E.
   1958   'Archeology and Old Testament Studies', *JBL* 77, pp. 39-51
Zenger, E.
   1980   'Wo steht die Pentateuchforschung heute?', *BZ* 24, pp. 101-16
Zimmerli, W.
   1960   'Sinaibund und Abrahambund', *TZ* 16, pp. 268-80

INDEXES

INDEX OF BIBLICAL REFERENCES

INDEX OF AUTHORS

JOURNAL FOR THE STUDY OF THE OLD TESTAMENT
Supplement Series